Philosophy of Lyric Voice

Bloomsbury Studies in Philosophy and Poetry

Series Editors: Rick Anthony Furtak, Colorado College, USA and James D. Reid, Metropolitan State University of Denver, USA

Editorial Board:

Daniel Brown, University of Southampton, UK
Kristen Case, University of Maine Farmington, USA
Hannah Vandegrift Eldridge, University of Wisconsin–Madison, USA
Cassandra Falke, University of Tromsø, Norway
Luke Fischer, University of Sydney, Australia
John Gibson, University of Louisville, USA
James Haile III, University of Rhode Island, USA
Kevin Hart, University of Virginia, USA
Eileen John, University of Warwick, UK
Troy Jollimore, California State University, USA
David Kleinberg-Levin, Northwestern University, USA
John Koethe, University of Wisconsin–Milwaukee, USA
John T. Lysaker, Emory University, USA
Karmen MacKendrick, Le Moyne College, USA
Rukmini Bhaya Nair, Indian Institute of Technology, India
Kamiyo Ogawa, Sophia University, Japan
Kaz Oishi, University of Tokyo, Japan
Yi-Ping Ong, Johns Hopkins University, USA
Anna Christina Soy Ribeiro, Texas Tech University, USA
Karen Simecek, University of Warwick, UK
Ruth Rebecca Tietjen, Tilburg University, Netherlands
Íngrid Vendrell Ferran, Philipps University Marburg, Germany

Bloomsbury Studies in Philosophy and Poetry explores ancient, modern, and contemporary texts in ways that are sensitive to philosophical themes and problems that can be fruitfully addressed through poetic modes of writing, and focused on questions of style, the relations between form and content, and the conduciveness of literary modes of expression to philosophical inquiry. With a keen interest in the intertwining of poetry and philosophy in all forms, the series will cover the philosophical register of poetry, the poetics of philosophical writing, and the literary strategies of philosophers.

The series provides a home for work on figures across geographical landscapes, with contributions that employ a wide range of methods across academic disciplines, and without regard for divisions within philosophy, between analytic and continental, for example, that have outworn their usefulness. Featuring single-authored works and edited collections, curated by an international editorial board, the series aims to redefine how we read and discuss philosophy and poetry today.

Titles in the series:

Everyday Poetics, by Brett Bourbon
Thought and Poetry, by John Koethe
A Poetic Philosophy of Language, by Philip Mills
Maurice Blanchot on Poetry and Narrative, by Kevin Hart

Forthcoming titles:

Heidegger and Poetry in The Digital Age, by Rachel Coventry
Philosophical Fragments and the Poetry of Thinking, by Luke Fischer
Skepticism and Impersonality in Modern Poetry, by Joshua Adams

Philosophy of Lyric Voice

The Cognitive Value of Page and Performance Poetry

Karen Simecek

BLOOMSBURY ACADEMIC
LONDON • NEW YORK • OXFORD • NEW DELHI • SYDNEY

BLOOMSBURY ACADEMIC

Bloomsbury Publishing Plc, 50 Bedford Square, London, WC1B 3DP, UK
Bloomsbury Publishing Inc, 1385 Broadway, New York, NY 10018, USA
Bloomsbury Publishing Ireland, 29 Earlsfort Terrace, Dublin 2, D02 AY28, Ireland

BLOOMSBURY, BLOOMSBURY ACADEMIC and the Diana logo are trademarks of
Bloomsbury Publishing Plc

First published in Great Britain 2024
This paperback edition published 2025

Copyright © Karen Simecek, 2024

Karen Simecek has asserted her right under the Copyright, Designs and Patents Act, 1988,
to be identified as Author of this work.

For legal purposes the Acknowledgements on p. viii constitute an extension of this
copyright page.

Series design by Ben Anslow
Cover image: Color Study: Squares with Concentric Circles (1913), Wassily Kandinsky
(© steeve-x-art / Alamy Stock Photo)

All rights reserved. No part of this publication may be: i) reproduced or transmitted in
any form, electronic or mechanical, including photocopying, recording or by means of
any information storage or retrieval system without prior permission in writing from the
publishers; or ii) used or reproduced in any way for the training, development or operation
of artificial intelligence (AI) technologies, including generative AI technologies. The rights
holders expressly reserve this publication from the text and data mining exception as per
Article 4(3) of the Digital Single Market Directive (EU) 2019/790.

Bloomsbury Publishing Inc does not have any control over, or responsibility for, any third-
party websites referred to or in this book. All internet addresses given in this book were
correct at the time of going to press. The author and publisher regret any inconvenience
caused if addresses have changed or sites have ceased to exist, but can accept no
responsibility for any such changes.

A catalogue record for this book is available from the British Library.

A catalog record for this book is available from the Library of Congress.

ISBN: HB: 978-1-3502-4052-0
PB: 978-1-3502-4056-8
ePDF: 978-1-3502-4053-7
eBook: 978-1-3502-4054-4

Series: Bloomsbury Studies in Philosophy and Poetry

Typeset by Deanta Global Publishing Services, Chennai, India

For product safety related questions contact productsafety@bloomsbury.com.

To find out more about our authors and books visit www.bloomsbury.com
and sign up for our newsletters.

Contents

Acknowledgements	viii
Introduction	1
1 Philosophy of lyric voice	25
2 The lyric I: Reading voices, hearing voices	55
3 A sense of us: Individual and collective voices	83
4 Embodied voices	113
5 Poetic cognitivism	141
Notes	169
Bibliography	180
Index	192

Acknowledgements

A very special thanks to my brilliant colleagues Eileen John and Kirk Surgener, who kindly read an entire draft of this book and whose comments have transformed its arguments. I am utterly grateful for their careful and insightful comments and couldn't have wished for more thorough, critical and constructive readers. We had lots of fun discussing the ideas in the book, and I hope I haven't put them off reading more poetry.

Thank you also to John Gibson, Rafe McGregor, Chris Earley, Eliza Ives, Hannah Kim, Tom Crowther and Ian Dunbar, who read parts of this book and gave me invaluable feedback. I am also thankful for audiences at the CRPLA, University of Warwick (2018), London Aesthetics Forum (2021), Dubrovnik Philosophy of Art Conference (2021), the Fact, Fiction and Narration conference, University of Rijeka (2021), and the Work in Progress seminar, University of Liverpool (2022) for useful questions and discussion that helped me think more deeply about the issues I raise in this book.

I am very grateful to the University of Warwick for providing funding to support the development of this book project. I am also grateful to my poet friends – Will Harris, Anita Pati and John Bernard – who not only write wonderful poetry but have helped me to better understand poetry. I want to also thank my former poetry tutor Chris Jones, who inspired my love of poetry.

Finally, I wish to thank Lucy Atkinson, my husband and my daughter, Jasmine, for each helping me believe that I could do this.

Introduction

Introduction

Since romanticism, lyric poetry has been a source of fascination for both literary critics and philosophers who have sought to understand its expressive powers, its particular use of language and the way in which the lyric connects so deeply with its readers and audiences. In his preface to *The Theory of the Lyric*, Jonathan Culler speaks of 'lyrics' strange way of addressing time, winds, urns, trees, or the dead and asking them to do something or to stop doing what they are doing... poets call on a universe they hope will prove responsive, and their demands often prove seductive' (2015, p. vii). Culler's comment captures the odd way in which poetry is able to speak to others – both animate and inanimate; it is not fictional but an actual invocation of address. Others have noted the difficulty of saying what any one poem means, thereby enlivening a long-lasting debate on poetry's resistance to paraphrase.[1] As Peter Lamarque puts it, how does lyric poetry manage to 'compress language in a way that resists initial easy comprehension'? (2015, p. 18). Poetry also appears to present a challenging case to well-worn theories in the philosophy of language. For instance, John Gibson (2016a) speaks of the puzzle of how poetry has communicative power despite not following the rules of ordinary language. Poetry is also celebrated for being exemplary in its articulation of thought.[2] For instance, Robert Von Hallberg describes how poetry 'often reveals forms of thinking and feeling of which one had little idea, and of which one eventually achieves only an indefinite idea' (2008, p. 228). The claim is that poetry helps us think and feel what we couldn't have done otherwise.

My own fascination with lyric poetry stems from its quality of presentness, that is, how the words of a lyric, whether read off the page or heard in performance, unfold in the here and now and seem to connect directly with readers and audiences. As Susan Stewart notes, 'the sound of poetry is heard in the way that a promise is heard. A promise is an action made in speech... something that "happens," that "occurs," as an event and can be continually called on, called to mind, in the unfolding present' (2002, p. 104). Likewise, Bridget Vincent speaks about the presentness of poetry and how lyric poetry 'shifts in mode of address from the conventions of storytelling to conversational immediacy' (2013, p. 62). Through its present quality, lyric poetry is characterized by a *use* of language that is not fictional world-creating but real-world utterance-making and therefore marks a significant difference in form from works of narrative fiction.[3]

Consider the following extract from Audre Lorde's 'A Litany for Survival' (1978):

> when we are alone we are afraid
> love will never return
> and when we speak we are afraid
> our words will not be heard
> nor welcomed
> but when we are silent
> we are still afraid[4]

Reading these words off the page, we not only read the words but look at their form on the page, noticing visual connections that support a semantic relationship. The literary critic might spend time analysing the poem's metre and poetic structure (for instance, the repetition of 'when we' and 'afraid') to uncover what is contained within the text. The possibility and value of such analysis supports the view that a poem is to be treated straightforwardly as a (visual and semantic) text. But to treat the poem in this manner, as an object or mere word-text, is to miss a large part of what the poem can do. In the case of Lorde's poem, to 'hear' these words as spoken or to speak them is to defy silence. In other words, it is only by attending to the poem's presentness, that is, to see the poem as a happening, that we can see it in terms of its action-making powers. To borrow the words of Stanley Cavell, we must attend to the 'here and now, as if everything of significance is happening at this moment, while each thing that happens turns a leaf of time' (1969/2002, pp. 321–2), and in doing so words are transformed from being mere aesthetic objects to being able to perform an action. What we are left with is the question 'what is the poem doing?' rather than 'what does the poem mean?'.

Understanding the lyric poem in terms of action raises the further question 'what is the relationship between the poet – poem – audience/reader?' In order for the poem to be successful in performing an action, it must do so in the reception of the work. This question highlights the importance of bringing to the fore the dynamics of space in reading poetry and seeing poetry in performance as deeply connected to poetry on the page. Rather than focusing on issues of ontology, text and related issues of the possibility of paraphrase and the nature of metaphor, my approach reorients us towards issues about engagement with poetry: What role does embodiment (of performer or reader and audience) play in meaning-making? Can poetry instigate action, not just through the performativity of utterances but through the performativity of utterances as addressed and heard?

My aim in this book is to do three key things: First, to offer an understanding of the nature and value of poetry that includes both page poetry, that is, poetry that is primarily engaged with on the page and poetry in performance to include poetry readings and performance poetry, where poetry is written with the intention of it being performed (in some cases, this is with little theatricality and involves a performer simply reading the poem aloud, but in other cases, the poem is performed in a more bodily way, e.g., Jasmine Gardosi's 'Rollercoaster' [2021], where the poem is not merely the words spoken but the words together with the act of riding a rollercoaster). In discussions of poetry, philosophers almost exclusively take page poetry as the point of reference.[5] By considering page poetry alongside performed poetry, a new way of understanding poetry emerges that shows many of the old assumptions about the use of language in poetry to be overstated. Second, I will develop an understanding of poetry as social through the concepts of voice and relationality. And finally, I argue for the cognitivist claim that engaging with poetry is important for understanding relationships: both positive – such as love, togetherness and community – and negative – such as loneliness and loss that requires a social understanding of how people (do/don't) relate to one another and the significance of relationship. This understanding goes beyond conceptual grasp to appreciating what such relationships mean in our own lives and why they matter to us.

A neglect of poetry

To date, discussions of the cognitive value of art have focused predominately on works of film and literature, and rely on appeals to narrative, character and fiction in explaining how works contribute knowledge through the aesthetics of the work. This has generated much fruitful discussion in the field. However, such an approach does not readily apply to works of lyric poetry. Although poetry may sometimes use narrative structure, present a character or engage the reader imaginatively, this is not common to all poetry and is not central to how it functions as a work of poetry. This calls for investigation into the nature and value of a major art form.

In response, one of my central aims in the book is to present an argument for the cognitive value of lyric poetry. In order to defend such a view, one must address two central questions: What do we learn from engaging with works of poetry? How do we learn from engaging with works of poetry? The first question helps to identify the kinds of knowledge or understanding that can be gained from a work of art and literature. Second, for the cognitivist thesis to be saying anything non-trivial, it must be the case that the cognitive value is somehow tied to the aesthetic value of the work. In other words, the work is only able to make an epistemic contribution in virtue of being a work of art or as Cynthia Freeland puts it 'The cognitive activity they stimulate is part and parcel of their functioning as artworks' (Freeland 1997, p. 19). Therefore, the explanatory burden for the cognitivist is to show what is it about the aesthetics of the work that give rise to, enable or facilitate the production or transmission of knowledge or understanding.

Simply put, cognitivism is the conjunction of two claims: an epistemic one (that we can gain understanding or knowledge from art, that it is non-trivial; in other words, it genuinely arises from the work and is not reduced to mere facts about the work) and an aesthetic claim (that the cognitive value is tied to the aesthetic value of the work; its cognitive value increases its aesthetic value).[6] Therefore, the cognitivist needs 'to support a connection between the capacity of art to provide knowledge having to do with what makes it art and the success or failure of an artwork having to do with its capacity to provide knowledge' (Thomson-Jones 2005, p. 376). The reason for this requirement is due to the distinction between instrumental and intrinsic value. If something has instrumental value, we do not value the thing itself but the effects produced. For example, paracetamol has the instrumental value of pain relief. I don't value the little white pill itself and would cease to value it if it didn't bring about pain relief. Also, there are many other things that bring about pain relief just as effectively (e.g. an ice-pack or ibuprofen). Here is the problem: If we value works for what we can learn from them, then we are valuing them instrumentally. If instrumentally valuable, then there could be something that helps us learn p better than the work. Therefore, the cognitive value of art is not tied to its value as a work of art.

Poetry hasn't been completely neglected from the cognitivism debate[7] but the discussion to date sets the bar very high in terms of poetry's possible epistemic contribution. As a consequence of the so-called ancient quarrel, those who have sought to investigate the cognitive value of poetry have found themselves defending epistemic gains as philosophical. Additionally, there are interesting cases such as Lucretius' *De Rerum Natura* and Alexander Pope's *Essay on Man*, which are treated as both works of poetry and works of philosophy (but note that is not the same as treating them as philosophical in virtue of their being works of poetry). Peter Lamarque argues that if poetry is to offer truth, then it must meet logical standards of philosophy. This analysis provides grounds for Lamarque to reject the possibility of poetry as contributing knowledge:

> The relation between a poem and its themes is not the same as the relation of a philosophical work and its conclusions. We might be misled by talking of 'support' in both cases. A philosophical work supports its conclusions, and a poem supports its themes but they do so in different ways. . . . In philosophy a conclusion is derived through principles of reasoning. Logic not rhetoric dictates whether the conclusion has adequate support. (Lamarque 2009, p. 45)

Yet in discussions of the cognitive value of literature there is no similar demand for knowledge gained to meet the epistemic standards of philosophy (perhaps with the exception of *The Cognitive Value of Philosophical Fiction* (2013) by Jukka Mikkonen, who argues for a theory of philosophy *through* literature). What such discussions of literature reveal is that neither epistemic contributions nor epistemic standards need be singular; we can allow for a wider variety of epistemic gains that go beyond the limitation of philosophical knowledge to include the pragmatic and experiential, for instance, considering something from another point of view. This raises the question: Why insist on the standards appropriate for reasoned argument in poetry when we can accept literature as making other kinds of epistemic contributions?

In his essay 'What Makes a Poem Philosophical?', John Gibson argues that we should reject the idea of poetry as being in the service of or contributing to philosophical projects and instead view poetic works as sharing concerns with the philosopher. He argues that what they share is 'a kind of common cultural property that belongs to neither the poet nor the philosopher, as a shared sense of worries, wonders, anxieties, and puzzles' (2018, p. 15). What both the poet and philosopher bring to these aspects of human life is simply 'another way of working through the same cultural material' (2018, p. 16) with differing results. Both philosophy and poetry are distinctly but equally valuable in what they offer us in terms of understanding human life. Neither have the tools or resources to offer knowledge of every aspect of human experience and value. Together, they offer us richer insights into worldliness.

Even accepting Gibson's argument that poetry ought not to be assessed *as* philosophical (i.e. according to standards of logic and reason), that does not mean that there's nothing to be gained by bringing the philosophical and the poetic together. Gibson's argument merely offers a warning that one cannot be assessed according to the standards of the other. But seeking knowledge and understanding of aspects of human experience and worldliness will involve connecting the poetic and the philosophical. For instance, Tzachi Zamir argues that what Milton's *Paradise Lost* offers the philosopher is awareness of the limitations of philosophical epistemology:

> while philosophy cannot harness *Paradise Lost* to its objectives, by engaging with the poem, philosophy accesses a valuable perception regarding its own possible limits relative to its own ends . . . philosophy attains this perception partly by adopting the poem's own modelling of the proper relationship to knowledge: by permitting itself *to host* the poem. To allow a meaningful challenge to resonate is sometimes more rewarding than merely answering it. (Zamir 2015, p. 229)

From Zamir's example, it's clear that when talking of poetry and philosophy as offering equally valuable insights into matters of human experience and value does not mean necessarily bringing two ways of thinking about a subject together in harmony. And where we find dissonance, that does not mean that we ought to choose between poetry and philosophy as one having the right answer over the other but finding a way of allowing the tension between the two to produce further insight.[8]

For instance, although I may seek understanding of an everyday concept such as love by engaging with philosophical texts such as Harry Frankfurt's

The Reasons of Love, that does not render the project philosophical but offers one way of understanding *love*, which is necessarily incomplete. To read a poem, such as Alice Oswald's 'Wedding' is simply to take a different route to understanding *love*,[9] one which brings together thought and interpersonal feeling. Here's an extract from the poem:

> From time to time our love is like a sail
> and when the sail begins to alternate
> from tack to tack, it's like a swallowtail[10]

Appreciating how love shows up in life, that is, as a particular kind of connection that can withstand and flow with change, and that has a particular felt quality of fittingness, provides important insight into why love is something we value that cannot be captured by analytic thought. It seems that without being able to show and illuminate it, a philosophical analysis of love will have to assume what and how we value love. What engaging with poetry has to offer is enrichment of our understanding of our interpersonal relationships that reflect aspects of shared experience and shared life that goes beyond definitional understanding to a richer appreciation of the meaning and relevance of a concept to experience. To illustrate, we can borrow the following example from Stephen Turner 'When a mother tells her 13-year-old daughter that she does not know what "love" is, she is not making a comment about semantics; she is pointing to the nonlinguistic experiential conditions that are bound up with the understanding of the term that the daughter does not share' (Turner 2019, p. 254). Understanding *love* isn't just a matter of definitional or conceptual grasp but requires a deeper appreciation and acknowledgement of why we value these kinds of relationships can only come from certain sorts of experiences. Such experiences can be achieved through engagement with poetry.

As Adrian Moore argues:

> Much of our understanding of the world, and our position in it, is informed by how it appears from such points of involvement. . . . Our understanding of death, for example, is not purely biological. It is conditioned by our own mortality, our own point of involvement with death. Each of us is affected by the deaths of others, and each understands death from that perspective. (Moore 1997, p. 3)

A concept such as death is interpersonal in the sense that it isn't reducible to absence, or the quality of no longer being present but as connected to loss (that brings into relation one who is present with one who is now absent). As Moore comments, our understanding of death cannot be separated from how we experience the death of others, and how our relationships with others are irreversibly changed. Furthermore, as John Gibson argues:

> genuine understanding is never value neutral, [it] is never merely conceptual, at least not when it concerns human reality. To count as possessing full understanding of something, we must reveal not only that we have the relevant concepts and representational capacities. We must also show that we are alive to those patterns of value, significance, and meaning that are woven into the aspects of the world we otherwise merely know. (2009, p. 14)

Given this background to the debate, my focus in this book is on a particular cognitive achievement that is connected to an appreciation of certain kinds of relationships such as love, loss, loneliness, togetherness, belonging and community. What poetry can help us to do is recognize and acknowledge the ways in which we can relate to one another and why this is of value. For instance, in the case of love (or beloved), one must appreciate particular kinds of positive connection between two people (or a disconnection in the case of unrequited love). In the case of community, one must gain awareness of what connects or bonds a group of people (where the relationship that defines inclusion and exclusion transforms to a community from a mere group). Furthermore, I will argue that poetry also helps cultivate the intellectual virtue of humility by encouraging one to have to negotiate one's own ways of understanding with that on offer in the poem. Such intellectual humility is essential for being able to bring different perspectives together in some form of equilibrium, which includes the poetic and the philosophical.

From lyric on the page to lyric on the stage

As Anna Christina Ribeiro (2015a) notes, poetry emerged as an oral art form and has close links with the tradition of storytelling. It is therefore surprising that consideration of poetry in performance has been largely overlooked in philosophical writing on poetry. Performance poetry is not merely oral poetry, although there is a relationship between the two. Oral poetry is community owned that may then be documented in the written form by any member of the community, often used for transmission of knowledge and sharing stories. Oral poetry may be memorized and performed by any member of the community and so memorization forms a key part of the success of works in the oral tradition. Performance poetry, on the other hand, is most often performed by the poet themselves and is taken to reflect aspects of the self of the poet-performer and is often experimental in form.

Regardless of this difference between oral poetry and performance poetry, we can see performance as having held a central place in the evolution of poetry as an art form, and it is only in the theoretical reflections has this dimension of poetry been obscured. One of the goals of this book is to bring into focus the performance of poetry alongside page poetry. I do not want to argue that one is more valuable than the other; instead, I wish to highlight the distinctive contribution engaging with poetry in both forms affords: reflective, affectively charged thinking that enhances our understanding of ourselves and our relationship to others. In considering these two modes of poetry, I will argue that this demands a reconceptualization of poetry as an art form.

For a large number of contemporary poets (post-2000), reading aloud and performing their work to others is a key part of their practice. What characterizes works of this period is a shift in terms of expectations of authors. No longer are poets (or novelists) allowed to be anonymous authors of their works. Instead, they are required to present their work to the public in the shape of live readings, videos and interviews. Contemporary poetry therefore collapses the distinction between poetry for the stage and poetry on the page. That's not to say that poems are not written with the intention of being either performed or being read off the page (as primarily works of performance or works of written text). Performance poetry is often also published on the page (for instance, Burning Eye and Outspoken Press, who specialize in publishing collections of performance poems on the page). Likewise, page poetry may be performed at poetry readings, therefore blurring any strong distinction between performance and page poetry. Although the poet may have clear intentions about the primary mode of engagement with their work, their poems will have a second life in performance or on the page. Understanding the blurring boundaries between poetry in performance and poetry on the page is to appreciate poetry in the context of its function in contemporary culture and the needs it serves individuals and communities that may be distinct from the needs of those in antiquity.

In her writing about performance poetry, Julia Novak argues that the performance must be analysed in terms of the interrelation of the 'audio text' (the words heard) and 'body text' (aspects of the body and physical performance used in the delivery of the words, including vocal and bodily gestures): the embodied word shapes the meaning-making potential of the words spoken and heard. Although often performed based on a written text, the author is wholly responsible for that text and for interpreting how it is to be performed live. Consequently, the work consists of the relationship between body text and audio text; to consider one aspect without the other is to fail to engage properly with the work. However, when looking at many works of performance poetry, what becomes clear is that the work goes beyond mere body text and audio text to also include some role for the audience. As spoken word poet Pete Bearder puts it, in performance poetry there is 'A heightened recognition of the audience's role in the reception, ritual, and community of performance' (Bearder 2020, p. 82). In the next chapter, through the elaboration of this cultural analysis of the value of poetry, I focus on two important concepts: voice and perspective. I argue that this framework applies not only to poetry in performance but also to page poetry and hearing recordings of poetry. In each case, the embodied voice is central to how we understand the meaning-making potential of the poem.

We can find support for my view of page poetry as related to performance in Jonathan Culler's account of the lyric. He argues that an important dimension of page poetry is the vocal since many works of poetry are structured around a patterning of sound, where aurality, even if merely imagined, is central to the experience of the work. For Culler there are two extremes of the lyric poem, one which is grounded in *opsis* and one which is grounded in *melos*. He provides the following distinction: '*opsis*: the poem **is** a visual construction or the poem **produces/represents** images . . . *melos*: the poem **is** sound patterning (voicing) or the poem **produces/represents** voices' (p. 256). Poetry grounded in *opsis*, such as certain works of concrete poetry or blackout poetry, has more in common with the visual arts and must be analysed in terms of space on the page, typography and visual connection between words on the page. Poetry grounded in *melos* has more in common with performance and must be analysed in terms of temporality (duration, rhythm, movement), musicality (timbre, tone, rhyme, patterning), and the relationship between the poet and poem and reader (as it unfolds in the event of listening or reading). There is, of course, much in-between with poems that draw on both *opsis* and *melos*. On my view, all lyric poetry involves some degree of *melos* (however minimal). As noted by Robert Von Hallberg:

> Poetry and music collaborate deeply and darkly. Sounds warrant what poets say by giving words palpable form: one hears the orders, senses achievement, and extends credence. Musicality underwrites the authority of a proposition (Pope's 'Whatever is, is right'), or of an observation (Eliot's 'I had not thought death had undone so many'), but the collaboration of sound and sense goes further. (2008, p. 228)

By bringing together page poetry and performed poetry, we can shift from viewing the poem as an object (as merely grounded in *opsis*) to view the poem as event (always with some degree of *melos*):

> The poem must be thought of as an event in time. It is not an object or an ideal entity. A poem happens during a coming together ... of a reader and a text. The reader brings to the text his past experience and present personality. Under the magnetism of the ordered symbols of the text, he marshals his resources and crystallises out from the stuff of memory, thought, and feeling a new order, a new experience, which he sees as the poem. This becomes part of the ongoing stream of his life experience, to be reflected on from any angle important to him as a human being. (Rosenblatt 1978, p. 12)

The present quality of lyric poetry marks an important distinction between visual poetry and sound poetry; the latter uses language as a kind of action in creating relationships and connections between the sounds of words, their meaning, images, voices and between the poet, poem and reader/audience, whereas the former is atemporal in the sense that it exists outside of that relationship between poet and spectator. Conceiving of the poem as event, Culler argues that lyric poetry is 'iterative and iterable performance of an event in the lyric present, in the special "now," or lyric articulation. . . . Fiction is about what happened next; lyric is about what happens now' (Culler 2015, p. 226). For Culler, one of the central distinctions between lyric poetry and fiction is its temporal status; fiction is descriptive (of action), whereas poetry is performative; in other words, each reading of the work is a happening (regardless of whether it describes any action itself). As Culler puts it, 'Nothing need happen in the poem because the poem is to be itself the happening' (Culler 2015, p. 226). Poetry as *melos* therefore shifts the parameters of analysis where attempts to understand the poem in terms of word meaning is deeply inadequate and misses the experiential dimension of the meaning-making activity of the unfolding poem. The temporal experience of the poem, although unfolding in time, is shaped through the (attempted) establishing of connection and development of relationship: 'If one major effect of lyric address is the replacement of a narrative temporality with temporality of the poetic event, this contributes to what is perhaps its most important effect, the evocation of poetic power' (p. 229).[11]

However, it is important to acknowledge that emphasizing poetry as related to sound and musicality can exclude Deaf Poetics, and consequently there is a need to extend Culler's analysis.[12] DeafBlind poet, John Lee Clark (2005) writes 'Sound is only one of many vehicles through which poetry can travel from feeling and thought to expression and understanding. In other words, sound is mere medium, not source' (n/p). Clark notes that his own poetry performed in sign-language is motivated by connection and touch, through temporality and event, through the relationship between words, voices and bodies. Understanding the lyric poem in terms of sound helps to open up understanding of the lyric as an event, as something that happens between a poet and their audiences but it doesn't need to be reducible to the heard voice. As Clark notes, sound is merely one way in which we can understand poem as event; bodily movement and touch are further ways such understanding can be achieved.

To include poetry that does not rely on sound may appear to conflict with common assumptions about the significance of musicality in one's experience of lyric poetry. However, extending our understanding of poetry to include Deaf Poetics need not diminish poetry's connection to musicality since movement is able to take on the quality of dance in the same manner that the words of a lyric poem can be experienced as 'musical'. What is important in both cases is the aesthetic attention to language that the poem draws attention to whether that is through the sound of words or the feeling of movement. What's happening in both cases of spoken poetry and signed poetry is aestheticization of language, that is, drawing aesthetic attention to the use of language. In both cases, the aesthetic enhancement of language elevates the act of communication from the everyday to an awareness of the structures of meaning that brings word meaning together with affect. Non-signing audiences of Clark's poems may lack access to the semantic content of the poem, but they are still presented with *melos*. What is still available in their experience of the poem is the temporal event, that is, of patterns of movement unfolding in time. Although I will discuss notions such as voice, hearing and seeing, what I intend to capture is both the heard and the unheard: embodied voice as poetry that makes use of the temporal experience of language in expression, communication and forging connections with others.

Acknowledgement of Deaf Poetics further heightens the importance of bringing together page poetry with poetry in performance where the written text is not treated as superior to performing but as equal to it:

> [The work of Deaf poets] is a collective subversion of the sound – or, to them, unsound – theory of poetry. Breaking the most ground are the Deaf poets who do not write. After all, writing is not native to Deaf culture as is signing. They make poetry out of handfuls of air, their lexicon cinematic and giving rise to a new poetics. Others work with both written and signed languages, with a full range of pidgin and experimental work on and off the page, opening boundaries between languages. (Clark 2005, n/p)

Clark's own work in braille also helps to reimagine page poetry as something that is not necessarily analysable in terms of the visual but uses qualities in common with the performance in bringing the poem to life through touch and connecting physically with the reader. Where Culler emphasizes a tension between the visual and the sonic, the inclusion of Deaf Poetics suggests that what is taken as core to lyric poetry is the temporally now and the possibility of connection between utterance and audience as opposed to the work as object.

Poetry as relational

Lyric poetry is often characterized in terms of being a vehicle for personal expression. Take for instance M. H. Abrams, who writes 'A work of art is essentially the internal made external, resulting from a creative process operating under the impulse of feeling, and embodying a combined product of the poet's perceptions, thoughts and feelings. The primary source and subject matter of a poem therefore, are the actions and attributes of the poet's own mind' (1977, p. 22). A traditional way of understanding lyric poetry is in terms of the expression of the thoughts and feelings of the poet or some persona (constructed through the use of first person in the poem). As Robert Stecker comments, 'Lyric poetry tends to consist, in large part, in the "articulation" of the intentional aspects of an emotional state—the beliefs, desires, perceptions, and so on that are partly constitutive of or accompany such a state' (2001, p. 86). Understanding lyric poetry in this way casts it as a form of testimony and the reader/audience are therefore to take up the role of witness: the poet offers an account of what it is to feel and/or think in a particular way in relation to the subject of the poem (which may or may not relate to how the poet themselves experience that subject). The reader/audience is then thought to gain access to that way of experiencing the subject of the poem. For instance, in his discussion of the cognitive value of poetry, M. W. Rowe comments that what we might gain from reading poetry is 'knowledge of what some experience is like, and it is internally related to pleasure because the writer can only prompt us to have an experience, the experience itself must be the spontaneous product of our own imaginations' (Rowe 1996, p. 3). For Rowe, the poem helps the reader recreate in imagination an experience that enables them to come to know what it is like (i.e. shared with the poet or persona).

However, in Chapter 2, I argue that we need not understand personal expression in terms of the content of the poem but instead in terms of how the poem is structured and the action performed by the work as a whole. Only the latter takes seriously the present quality of the poem, that is, trying to understand what the poem is doing rather than merely what is said or communicated. Reflecting on his own poetic practice, Will Harris writes:

> I'm arranging the world around a point of view. These thoughts, without meaning to, trace out the radial lines of my experience. I might quote other writers, echo different voices, splinter my text, avoid saying 'I' (using 'you', 'we', concrete images only), but something coheres. That expectation of coherence changes what I see. In the chaos of the stars, the plume of milk in my coffee, a unifying shape emerges. A reflection. An implicated 'I'. (Harris 2019, n/p)

Through the effort to make sense of experience, the poet constructs a perspective, a point of view, a way of seeing, thinking and feeling about experience as an offering to the reader or audience to see coherence in a messy and chaotic world. Lyric poems are inherently perspectival; they are unified works in the way they bring words, images, thoughts and feelings together to express a sense of value. Rather than being the expressions of thoughts and feelings of a particular subject, lyric poetry expresses a perspective that actively captures *a way* of seeing and feeling.

Following Harris' thought, I argue that the presence of the first person in lyric poetry is not where we should locate expression. Although at first glance, a poem seems to be offering the expression of some I (and that it is up to the reader or performer to decide on who the I refers), this view is quickly complicated when we take the work as a whole and ask of the poem what is expressed. Of course, we can find countless examples of works by hobby poets where their aim is simply to find ways of expressing themselves directly in the poem. However, my analysis is not seeking to reflect all poetry, good and bad, but is normative. My claim is that a mark of success in poetry is to go beyond mere outpouring of thought and feeling to revealing something about the use of language in such attempts to express. To make plain, consider examples of poems that are about a failure to express such as Phil Wilcox's 'Infect the World with Doves' (2020), in which the image of the dove is used to express the celebration of love for another but as the poem progresses the image becomes corrupted, inflated and even grotesque, thereby failing to meet the poem's demand to express one's love for another ('the raindrops are dead doves / your arms are doves / I'm going to replace all the bandages in all the hospitals with your dove arms'[13]).

The use of the first person in lyric poetry doesn't necessarily represent an expressive subject but is part of the focus of the poem itself. In other words, poetry demands an attention to the *use* of language, which includes the use of the first person. The speaking of an I and/or you performs a relational gesture; it not only calls on the reader/audience for connection but encourages a reflection on that connection and our use of a shared language. As poet Edward Hirsch observes, 'I understand the relationship between the poet, the poem, and the reader not as a static entity but as a dynamic unfolding. An emerging sacramental event. A relation between an I and a You. A relational process' (2006, n/p). Through this analysis, I will make clear how we ought to separate our understanding of voice in poetry from the lyric I. The voice of the poem (by which I mean the way in which a perspective is expressed) is distinct from the use of the first person. Reading and hearing voices triggers reflection that is essential in understanding aspects of human life, such as loneliness, loss, togetherness and separation. Interpersonalilty cannot be adequately understood without an experience of relationality to others, that is, being alive to the human values that are reflected in our need for and use of such interpersonal concepts, whether that's positive in the case of togetherness or negative in the case of loneliness. What relationality provides is an opportunity to expand and refine one's perspective.

Poetry as social

It is perhaps natural to think of performance poetry in terms of being a social event. It is something that unfolds in a (performance) space and over time but necessarily involves a social dimension between performer/poet and audience. As Pete Bearder writes, 'Intrinsically social, spoken word is threaded with a culture of human contact, a sociality that can be said to make up an ethos of the movement as a social form' (Bearder 2020, p. 81). What this suggests is that something important is missing from Culler's *melos/opsis* analysis of lyric poetry. In the case of the poem in performance it seems that not only ought we understand the poem in terms of event (not object) and aesthetics of sound (as opposed to mere word meaning) but the social dynamics of the audience and performer are also important in how the poem constructs meaning and the actions it performs.

However, it is less clear on the surface why we should also think of page poetry as inherently social as well. Part of the answer lies in the use of words that come with both a private and public meaning; the use of words connects people, the speaker to the listener (at least, when communication is successful). Whether spoken or on the page, words still have that power to connect. In Chapter 3, I argue that understanding performance poetry and page poetry as experiments in communication and as other-directed forms of expression (that are relational) brings the social to the heart of how poetry functions, what shapes the writing process and as practice of reception.

Through their use of language, poems invoke public networks, those conceptual associations that are agreed upon by the community of language users, which we depend on in order to communicate with one another. Neil Cooper argues that 'in acquiring the capacity and the disposition to use shared concepts, we thereby learn to take up an impersonal standpoint. In this way the individual can escape the prison of his own peculiar perspective' (Cooper 2000, p. 390). However, that is not quite right. It is not that we learn to take up an impersonal view but to appreciate our shared or interpersonal view characterized by our relationship to others through the development and use of a shared understanding. In reading, we submit our perspective to an encounter with others (that are on offer in the poem), which requires us to negotiate with these other perspectives, thereby moving us towards a shared perspective.

Given this picture of the role of the reader and audience, I present a complex view of poetry as social. Not only can the poem take the social as its subject matter but it can represent and enact community through collaborative writing practices, performing together and blending voices. Poetry can be about sociation; for instance, in Chapter 3, I will discuss poems that attempt to reveal important insights into the nature of community and what it is to relate to others as members of such a community, in particular, attempting to capture a 'sense of us'. I will also demonstrate how it can show us *forms* of sociation through the bringing together of different voices, whether in the writing of the poem (bringing together individual voices to create a shared, blended or polyphonic voice) or in the performance of the work (where splintered voices are brought into relation). Finally, I will discuss how poetry can provide the foundations for sociation itself through the use of common language and presenting a potential to develop shared perspectives.

Lyric poetry offers a space for connection, that is, a connection to language, to the world in which we live and to one another. In writing, reading and listening to poetry we come into contact with others through our use of common language, that is, a language we draw on and borrow every day to commune with others. Coming into contact with others is not a matter of imagining other lives and feeling a connection through sympathetic or empathetic response but bringing about an actual, real-world, connection or relationship between people through the poem. Poetry invokes real-world uses of language as uttered by people: words embodied. Poetry helps to bring us together through relationships of common experience and difference.

Poetry as bodily

The identity poem is a common feature in performance poetry circles in which the poet-performer writes and performs pieces that make reference to some aspect of their identity. Take for instance, Elizabeth Acevedo's 'Hair' (2015). In her performance, she supports the connection between the words spoken and her body by touching her own hair and pulling it out to the sides to reveal its qualities to the audience as she speaks the words 'My mother tells me to fix my hair / and by fix she means straighten / she means whiten / but how do you fix this shipwrecked history of hair?'. The gestures towards her body that place the words spoken in an embodied context serves to ground the whole poem as connected to her identity:

> They say Dominicans can do the best hair.
> I mean they wash, set, flatten the spring in any lock
> but what they mean is we're the best at swallowing amnesia,
> in a cup of morisoñando, die dreaming because we'd rather do that than live in
>   this reality, caught between orange juice and milk,
> between reflections of the sun and whiteness.[14]

Focused on Slam poetry competitions, in particular, where performers must be the author of their work, Susan Somers-Willett observes that in the live performance of poetry

> The author's physical presence ensures that certain aspects of his or her identity are rendered visible as they are performed in and through the body, particularly race and gender but extending to class, sexuality, and even regionality. Embodied aspects of identity provide lenses through which an audience receives a poem, sometimes causing a dramatic shift in the poem's meaning and effect. (2012, pp. 69–70)

This understanding of the significance of the body also extends to cases where a work is performed by someone else since their body, perceived identity, gestures, accent and so on affects not only the reception of the words but what actions those words can perform in that space.

However, there is a question about whether the relevance of the body is something unique to Slam poetry or whether it extends to all poetry in performance (including readings of poems by their authors) and to poetry on the page. In Chapter 1, I argue that considering the ways in which performance poetry is related to page poetry reveals the significance of voice in poetry and the ways in which we engage with that poetic voice. In Chapter 2, I appeal to the idea of voice as distinct from the lyric I, in which the voice of the poem provides a centring (unifying and bringing a sense of coherence to other voices the poem might express or to a shifting, unstable use of first person). Chapter 4 extends this discussion to consider to what extent poetry should be engaged with as embodied; that is, what contribution does the body of the poet and performer make to our engagement with the work?

The idea of the death of the author in the world of performance poetry is shown to be outdated. As Julia Novak writes:

> live poetry is characterised by the direct encounter and physical co-presence of the poet with a live audience. The poet will predominantly perform his/her own poetry and is thus cast in the double role of 'poet-performer.' The story and images of the poem are conveyed through the spoken word rather than through theatrical ostension, as focus is placed on the oral verbalisation of the poetic text. (Novak 2011, p. 68)

The body raises expectations in the audience of identity and authenticity, and awareness that the poet is addressing them (directly or indirectly): 'Even if poets do not openly address their audience they will generally face them in performance and thus recite their poetry directly to the audience and acknowledge their presence' (Novak 2011, p. 58).

In Chapter 4, I turn to the moral and political significance of how we perform and read poetry through a development of the notion of embodied voice. Whereas Chapter 3 seeks to present a positive account of the ways in which poetry can forge connection and enhance a sense of shareability, this chapter is concerned with finding its limits, where what is brought into focus is where there is difference, disconnection and the individual. In Chapter 4, I raise questions around the significance of the body in both poetry in performance, where the body is present and performed as part of the poem, and also in reading certain works of page poetry, where the context provided by knowledge of the author and their project is relevant to engaging with and understanding the work. This is at odds with the New Critic's project of casting out consideration of the author from engagement with the work. In direct challenge to New Criticism and other approaches to lyric poetry that seek to treat the work as separate from the poet, I argue that in order to ensure that the work is properly appreciated in terms of its moral and political contribution, we must engage with the poem as embodied. That's not to say that the author (or body) is always relevant to our engagement with a work of poetry but more that we are only in a position to judge its relevance once we have considered the poem in that context.

Perspective and the virtue of humility

One of the main claims underpinning my view of lyric poetry as performative is that the voice of the poem is expressive of a perspective. In other words, the voice provides a centring in the poem that captures a particular organization of connections and disconnections, associations and disassociations, and resonance and dissonance. Trying to understand a work of poetry and appreciate its perspectival structure puts pressure on our own way of processing information and engaging with the world, that is, our own perspectives.[15] To fully grasp the perspective the poem offers would involve having to set aside one's own perspective, that is, 'our peculiar and local ways of apprehending things' (Williams 2000, p. 482). However, one's perspective is not neutral but configures a sense of value and import that one will find difficult to see otherwise. It is not a flat structure but hierarchical with certain beliefs, commitments, values and so on held more centrally or firmly than others.[16]

It is this difference in how one's perspective configures significance that results in two different people having very different responses to the same stimulus (even if they held the same beliefs relevant to that stimulus). Camp writes that '[a perspective] organizes [our thoughts on a topic] by imposing a complex structure of relative prominence on them, so that some features stick out in our minds while others fade into the background, and by making some features especially central to explaining others. A perspective often also imposes certain evaluative attitudes and emotional valences on its constituent features' (Camp 2009, p. 111). As an illustration, Camp cites the duck-rabbit illusion; depending on where you place your focus, you will either see a duck or a rabbit. Two people can attend to the same image and see something very different.

For a more complex example, consider the difference between a biologist and an artist studying a small butterfly. They are both looking at the same thing and so have the same access to visual information and consequently may share a whole host of similar beliefs (e.g. it has orange-coloured wings with brown spots, two antennae and a long body). However, in observing the butterfly their attention is governed by how they prioritize the perceptual information, which is shaped by their first-person perspective. The biologist sees more significance in the structure of the butterfly's body and so focuses more on its anatomy, noticing the three parts of its body, its six legs and size of its wingspan, which then figure in their explanation of how the butterfly moves. The artist on the other hand sees more significance in the butterfly's behaviour and so focuses more on how it lands on a wall, gently moving its wings, noticing its delicacy and grace. Both have access to the same visual information but attend to and process that information very differently depending on what they take to be of significance.

The elements of one's perspective is in part informed by use of public language; therefore, as members of the same linguistic community there is some commonality in our concept of *Butterfly*. However, the richness of meaning and how concepts relate to one another are idiosyncratic. Having a perspective is more to do with the way one's concepts, beliefs, commitments and so on are related to one another and the affective aspects of thought rather than the content; it is a map that helps one to process and navigate one's pre-existing concepts, beliefs, commitments and so on alongside new information. Camp writes that 'having a perspective is a matter of cognitive action rather than cognitive content: it involves actually noticing, explaining, and responding to situations in a certain way, and not just representing situations as "to be interpreted" in that way. In slogan form, perspectives are tools for thought, not thoughts in themselves' (Camp 2017, p. 79). What we can see from the example of the biologist and the artist is that having a perspective is not in itself interesting or informative, since perspectives are everywhere. What is of interest is what informs that perspective, that is, the way our beliefs, values and commitments connect in a complex network. Although Camp seeks to separate the content of thought from its architecture, it is precisely how the content is configured within that framework that matters. Poetry helps to engage us with the relationship between content and the architecture. In other words, how beliefs and concepts relate to one another is more or less fixed in place by that framework.

In this book, I argue that poetry can play a significant role in developing an understanding of interpersonal relationships while also providing opportunities for one to reflect on the limits of one's own perspective, in other words, the limits in one's ability to encounter the world with a different set of values, commitments and concerns in play. It is only in coming to know those limits that one is in a position to extend or alter their perspective. The final chapter will therefore address directly the cognitive value of poetry and make the case for lyric poetry's role in cultivating the intellectual virtue of humility and revealing the limits of perspective. Intellectual humility is important for moving us away from seeking to fully understand or grasp another's perspective to adopting the more modest project of identifying where there are possible connections between one's own perspective and another (including that expressed by the poem) with attention paid to where the two seem to come apart.

Lyric poetry as connected to the arts

Finally, I want to address a question I have often been asked: Why lyric poetry? My answer is that a focus on lyric poetry enables a different kind of analysis from other forms of literary work, in particular, the novel. It stands apart for the way in which it does not rely on narrative for structure (although may contain narratives), has a quality of presentness (as opposed to creating fictions) and is inherently perspectival (they are unified works in the way they bring words, images, thoughts and feelings together to express a sense of value). Lyric poetry is motivated by expression, communication and connection to language, the world in which we live and to one another. A focus on lyric poetry therefore has the potential to reveal new insights into the value of art and literature that goes beyond the traditional dichotomies and frameworks. Furthermore, lyric poetry's use of language has the potential to show us more about the ways in which we use language, how we communicate and the limitations of ordinary expression.

From the discussions presented throughout, it will become clear that lyric poetry shares much in common with other art forms, including rap, hip hop and musical lyrics more generally (we might even want to go as far as saying that in some cases, where the music is playing a mere supporting role, it *is* poetry). Through my analysis of poetry as performative, it will become clear the ways in which lyric poetry, both on the stage and on the page, has connections with theatre (although, importantly, there are stark differences between typical works of theatre and their performances which are fictional-world creating) and performance art. Much of what I have to say in this book is not intended to be restricted to lyric poetry but may apply to many other works of art and art forms. My project here is simply to take lyric poetry as the focus (both on the page and on the stage) and see what insights it has to offer. Everything I claim is a claim about lyric poetry but that doesn't need to entail that it only applies to lyric poetry. What I hope is that the insights on offer here might spark not only an invigoration of interest in lyric poetry, in particular contemporary lyric poetry, but also new ways of thinking about art more generally that takes seriously the power of art to show us connection and disconnection and encourage a sharing and negotiating of perspectives.

Philosophy of lyric voice

Uniqueness of voice

Poet Edward Hirsch writes,

> Poetry is a voicing, a calling forth. . . . The words are waiting to be vocalized. The greatest poets have always recognized the oral dimensions of their medium. . . . Writing is not speech. It is graphic inscription, it is visual emblem, it is a chain of signs on the page. Nonetheless: 'I made it out of a mouthful of air,' W.B. Yeats boasted in an early poem. As, indeed, he did. As every poet does. (2006, n/p)

Poetry is deeply connected to the voice both in terms of the attention poets pay to the sounding and speaking of words in writing their poems and in how we engage with poetry on the page and on the stage. In writing and performance, poets exploit uniqueness of voice; their own unique voice informs their style, the natural rhythms of their speech inform the rhythms of their poems and their physical breath shapes the length of lines and stanzas. This is also true of other forms of writing in which we are encouraged to 'find one's voice' in order to be better able to express ourselves. However, the claim I make about voice in poetry is that the voice of the poem, which is informed by the poet's own uniqueness of (literal) voice, is not merely useful in terms of being able to express one's thoughts and feelings (i.e. a conduit for expression) but is itself expressive of perspective. The distinction here is between what one might say (or not say) that is indicative of a perspective and the quality of voice itself as a centring of a perspective. The confusion between these two ways of thinking about voice and perspective emerges because a reader or audience must first attend to what is said (through the voice) in order to be in a position to recognize the uniqueness of voice (i.e. the framework/architecture that informs what is said).

Despite the centrality of the concept of voice, there has been surprisingly little philosophical analysis of this important aspect of human communication. Although there have been some attempts to offer a phenomenology of voice (see Dolar 2006; Idhe 2007; Lagaay 2011), voice has been largely overlooked in analytic philosophy of language. Discussions of the nature of language do not, on the whole, consider what role 'vocalizing' plays in meaning, thought and communication but instead focus on public language without reference to the voices that are needed to sound that language. Even more surprising when we look to work in the philosophy of literature where discussions have focused on character, narrative, narrator, metaphor and even expressiveness all with the omission of voice. Yet in literary criticism, voice is central to the analysis of texts and there is a long history of critical practice of interpreting lyric poems as (over)hearing the voice of another.[1] It is important for any reader of literature to be able to distinguish the many voices of the narrator and characters within it, as well as identify the points of view of each and be able to appreciate what and how the work 'expresses'. Although one might think the concept of voice in literature is distinct from the ordinary concept of voice, the two are connected; in both contexts, voice shapes the reception of language. We cannot hear words spoken without hearing them as voiced. We cannot read the words of a work of literature without attending to the point of view from which those words are constructed and presented. Voice provides meaningful context to the words uttered. Consequently, hearing and experiencing words as voiced brings the affective to bear on the cognitive.

In addressing this neglect of voice in the philosophy of literature and language, it is my aim in this chapter to address the following questions: What is the significance of the embodied voice? What is lost if voice is ignored? How are voice and thought connected? What does consideration of voice help us understand/appreciate about poetry?

Voice in everyday communication

It is a curious feature of the human voice that we have the capacity to distinguish and recognize so many different voices. Not only am I able to distinguish several voices from one another but I can also recognize a long-lost friend from the sound of their voice alone. Voice is unique to each individual (each has its own individual and recognizable 'voiceprint') in virtue of the difference in physiology between people but also in virtue of differences in use of grammar, syntax and lexicon (not only one's vocabulary but their choice of words): 'The typical freedom with which human beings combine words is never a sufficient index of the uniqueness of the one who speaks. The voice, however, is always different from all other voices, even if the words are the same' (Cavarero 2005, p. 3). There are some excellent impressionists who are able to recreate another's voice; it can seem as if they have conjured another person into the room (Rob Brydon and Steve Coogan, for instance, who have a wide repertoire, including famous actors such as Roger Moore, Michael Caine, and Mick Jagger[2]). However, in each case it is illusory. Listening carefully, what the impressionist has captured are the pattern, inflection and intonation of speech of another together with imitation of physical gestures. Another's voice is brought to life *through* their voice (their own voice is still audible) and, crucially, is still centred in the impressionist's body (the voice isn't experienced as disembodied).[3]

When we hear an utterance, we hear it as having a location in space and time in the sense that some set of words was spoken or voiced by a particular person at a particular time (and for a particular duration). Joel Krueger comments that all auditory experiences, which includes experience of voice, are locational: 'They represent both what is happening (e.g. children playing outside) as well as how what is happening stands in relation to oneself (e.g. slightly behind me and to the left)' (Krueger 2011, p. 65). Alice Lagaay argues that voice is both temporal and transcendent: 'the voice resonates beyond its physical transience; as "phantasmagoric" voice it transcends the body, becoming in a certain sense atemporal' (2011, p. 64). There are therefore two parts to vocal expression: (1) it emanates at a particular time from a particular body (or speaker in the case of the artificial voice) that has a spatial location and provides context of intentionality, and (2) the sounds produced enter the space of the room and resonate in the ears and memories of the listeners (this is the sense in which Lagaay thinks it transcends the body and becomes atemporal). Similarly, in his essay 'The Ethics of Voice', Steven Connor writes: 'The voice's capacity to act at a distance, to influence a world outside and beyond itself, comes about, not only as a result of its emanative power, but also from the fact that, unlike seeing, feeling, smelling and tasting, the exercise of the voice results in the production of something separate from the body' (1999, p. 222). The voice comes from within yet has the capacity to 'touch' others as sound travels through space to ears and is interpreted in the minds of others.

Uniqueness of voice is not merely a matter of individuality of the aesthetics of voice but, as Cavarero argues, it also relates to the ontological; that is, each voice signifies an individual entity:

> In the uniqueness that makes itself heard as voice, there is an embodied existent, or rather a 'being there' in its radical finitude, here and now. The sphere of the vocal implies the ontological plane and anchors it to the existence of singular beings who invoke one another contextually . . . the voice manifests the *unique being* of each human being, and his or her spontaneous self-communication according to the rhythms of a sonorous relation. (Cavarero 2005, p. 173)

The individual voice locates and centres expression but is also inherently relational as one embodied voice communicates with another: vocal expression is aimed at others and calls for a response from the other. Therefore, implicit in the act of vocal expression is the acknowledgement of others. A similar point is made by Idhe: 'In the voice of embodied significance lies the *what of* the saying, the *who* of the saying, and the *I* to whom something is said and who may also speak in the saying. In the voice is harboured the full richness of human signification' (Idhe 2007, p. 168). A newborn baby's cry is an example of pre-linguistic vocal expression that calls to others for attention; using one's voice is a way of asserting oneself in the world among others. A toddler who is at the beginning of learning to talk can use their voice for social engagement, taking it in turns with their pre-linguistic babble to speak and listen. What a toddler picks up on is the patterns of speech and the interpersonal dimension of communication before they can understand and use words intentionally.

Uniqueness of voice does not entail that one's voice has the same character throughout one's life. Many things can change the texture and timbre of voice – from the development of the vocal cords to influence of regional accent and dialect. Some also undergo 'voice training', whereby they learn to minimize or exaggerate certain features of their natural voice (in some cases temporarily in the portrayal of a character, or speaking another language that calls for a shift in speech patterns, and in others to hide some feature of one's identity[4]). But in all cases, uniqueness of *that* voice remains; what changes is the repertoire, and limits of one's voice and vocal expression. In other words, your voice still picks out you whether or not you speak with a New York accent, converse in Japanese or in the manner of someone from the home counties in England.

The voice doesn't just indicate uniqueness of being but draws attention to one's humanness; in other words, hearing a voice invokes the human. In *De Anima* Aristotle writes, 'Voice (*phōnē*) is a kind of sound characteristic of what has soul in it; nothing that is without soul utters voice, it being only by a metaphor that we speak of the voice of the flute or the lyre' (2.8.420b). Even where technology has progressed to recreate the human voice, this is experienced as uncanny in that we 'hear' humanness that is not centred in a human body (it is disembodied). Aristotle highlights the importance of the body in voicing words – it is the breath that enables voice:

> Voice then is the impact of the inbreathed air against the 'windpipe,' and the agent that produces the impact is the soul resident in these parts of the body. Not every sound, as we said, made by an animal is voice (even with the tongue we may merely make a sound which is not voice, or without the tongue as in coughing); what produces the impact must have soul in it and must be accompanied by an act of imagination, for voice is a sound *with a meaning*, and is not *merely* the result of any impact of the breath as in coughing. . . . This is confirmed by our inability to speak when we are breathing either out or in – we can only do so by holding our breath. (Aristotle 2.8.420b-421a)

As noted by Aristotle, there are many sounds one makes that do not count as vocal expression. Some sounds we make are not intended to be communicative. Take for instance a cough or sneeze, where it is an involuntary reaction to symptoms of a cold or allergy. In such cases, we would not consider that an instance of vocal expression. However, sometimes a cough can be used to express one's disbelief or desire for another to stop talking. In which case, the cough *is* expressive. Alice Lagaay writes, 'what distinguishes voice from noise is its intrinsic relation to the possibility of silence. For, insofar as silence can be considered as a mode of vocal expression, voice cannot be defined in clear opposition to silence (nor vice-versa)' (2011, p. 65). The example of the sneeze is one in which not sneezing is not an option; one is not able to choose between sounding and silence. Of course, silence itself can be expressive but only if one is deliberately with-holding their voice. One also makes use of silence within speech, that is, using silence to punctuate the sounding of voice.

It is in this sense that silence should be seen as a part of vocal expression. One's voice interacts with the silence of the space that it projects into. That's not to say that the space needs to be silent but that one's relationship to the space is silent or not.

It is the relationship to silence that voice gives expectation of meaning/intentionality. Voice is required to speak or sound language, and importantly voice is prior to (or foundational) to language. As Dolar argues:

> The voice is something which points toward meaning, it is as if there is an arrow in it which raises the expectation of meaning, the voice is an opening toward meaning. . . . [The voice] is a sound which appears to be endowed in itself with the will to 'say something,' with an inner intentionality. We can make various other sounds with the intention of signifying something, but there the intention is external to those sounds themselves, or they function as a stand-in, a metaphoric substitute for the voice. (Dolar 2006, pp. 14–15)

Even in cases where someone talks nonsense, there is still an expectation that their use of voice is meaningful; it's just in such cases that this expectation is not met (this can lead to frustration or amusement on part of the listener). Furthermore, there are noises one can make that are not linguistic, for instance, a hum or a groan that can be expressive by indicating agreement or discomfort. In both cases, the non-linguistic noises are still intentional and directed at others.

The function of voice is expression, address and call for response (of some sort).[5] Due to uniqueness of voice and the thought that the words one chooses to speak are related in some way to one's thoughts, there's a sense in which the voice signals the presence of the subjective self (the inner world expressed outwards). One does not merely express but expresses to be heard by another. It's in this sense that voice entails address. However, that does not mean that one must always be addressing someone in particular but that they are addressing anyone who can respond (whether or not they are in a position to actually respond. For instance, it seems plausible to describe someone as using their voice for self-expression in a situation where they take another in the room to be able to hear them even if it is the case that the other person is precluded from hearing perhaps due to hearing impairment or some peculiar feature of the acoustics of the room). But what about someone who talks to themselves? Are they expressing themselves to an imagined other?

Cecilia Sjöholm writes:

> We may hear our own voice, as in an echo. Sometimes, thoughts appear, as voices in a cave. They strike us, as from the outside. We hear them, as if they are aspects of what Chion calls *acousmètre*, the invisible point that we can only hear but not see, and yet it is structuring our perception and our apprehension of space. When we hear our own thoughts, we experience ourselves somehow as naturally double, as beings capable of reflecting in the world internally and silently, in our own minds. When the voices appear as foreign, as the voices of angels or devils, or simply as belonging to other people, this is a sign of psychosis, or, as in Descartes's doubt, is as if we are in a dream. (Sjöholm 2018, p. 79)

In attending to one's own voice, people often play the role of both the voice expressing and the voice responding and thereby take on a dual role. This is made possible due to the phenomenological separation of voice experienced internally, as emanating from the body and as being given to the space external to the body (and therefore being in a position to be heard through the speaker's ear). In other cases, this could be thought of as anticipating reception (for instance, one might practice saying something alone that later they will deliver to some audience).

Voice is shaped through interaction with others; we learn to use our voices with others. Accent and dialect emerge through repeated interaction with others who belong to a community and share a way of speaking. 'Mirroring' and 'contagion' are terms often used in relation to emotion but they also apply to the voice. For instance, my friend leans over and whispers in my ear, and my response is to whisper back mirroring her texture of voice, even before knowing what she will tell me. Likewise, if someone speaks with a happy, joyful tone, it will likely be met by the same tone in response. There are also situations in which when one spends a lot of time with another, a shared vocabulary emerges and shared pronunciation of words. This conception of voice as social is echoed by Dolar in his analysis of voice: 'We are social beings by the voice and through the voice, it seems that the voice stands at the axis of our social bonds, and that voices are the very texture of the social, as well as the intimate kernel of subjectivity' (Dolar 2006, p. 14). Not only is one's voice used to communicate with others but the voice becomes a representation itself of one's social bonds and becomes an important part of one's identity.

Speaking is not merely thinking out loud. For instance, we talk of misspeaking (when one says something they didn't intend) but we don't talk of misthinking. The difference between speaking and thinking is down to the distinction between the public and the private. My thoughts can be mistaken but I cannot misthink since they are not open to interpretation only refinement and rejection. On the other hand, when speaking, we are speaking to others and this relational aspect opens up the possibility of being misunderstood, or interpreted in a way that was unintended. What such a distinction reveals, Cavarero argues, is that 'thought is as solitary as speech is relational. . . . There is a dependence on others that passes through a plural connection of mouths and ears' (2005, p. 175).[6] Contra to Aristotle's view that voice manifests thought, Cavarero argues, 'speaking is not at all a thinking that expresses itself out loud, nor is it merely vocalized thought, nor is it an acoustic substitute for thinking. The phenomenology of speaking possesses an autonomous status in which the relationality of mouths and ears comes to the fore' (2005, p. 175). According to Cavarero, thought is of a very different character to speaking and so it is a mistake to simply declare vocal expression to be the articulation or voicing of thought. That there is *some* relationship between thought and vocal expression is uncontroversial, but what she is doing here is drawing our attention to the way inner thoughts are experienced and function differently to outer vocalization. In part, this is due to the fact that in vocalization, what is said takes on a necessarily communal and relational dimension that affects the content of that vocalization. One's thinking thoughts are only ever for oneself and form connections internally. Vocalization seeks to share meaning with others and is shaped by the relationality of communication. But it is also due to the uniqueness of voice in that more than what is thought is expressed in that vocalization; that is, the individual and idiosyncratic voice is affective and thereby shapes how the meaning of words is received in virtue of the context provided by the body who speaks them. From this analysis, we can see voice and vocal expression as centring meaning in the body of the individual speaker that brings affect to bear on cognition in the expression of meaning as the result of uniqueness, humanness, intentionality, spatial and temporal location and relationality to others.

Although we must treat vocal expression as distinct from the experience of thinking (and also as separate from the notion of 'inner speech'),[7] that does not mean that there is no relationship between the two. Identifying this relationship is the topic of the next section.

Vocal expression as expressing perspective

Expression is a central human activity and reflects a deep need we have as social beings.[8] For example, in saying aloud, 'I am thirsty', my expression is made with the intention that someone else will hear and help meet my need for a drink. We make use of public language to express ourselves and commune with others, at least as best we can but we often do not rely on words alone to do this but draw on features of voice (such as those outlined in the previous section) that enable one to go beyond word meaning to add attitudinal, affective and emotional information. For instance, there are numerous ways I can utter the sentence 'You have a new job' to express surprise, joy, exasperation, approval, disapproval and so on depending on where I place stress as well as intonation and the facial gestures that accompany the utterance.

One way in which we use the term 'expression' suggests a direct connection between thought and language: the utterance 'I need a drink' means *I am thirsty*, where the utterance is taken to reliably correspond to a particular mental state. Of course, this is part of what's going on in one's use of words; that is, one is making an utterance that they hope connects with a publicly and culturally shared meaning. It is largely uncontroversial to say that we are able to express, at the very least, an approximation of some thought and that voice and body plays a key part in how this is achieved but here I want to motivate the idea that we are able to express our individual perspectives in virtue of features of the embodied voice. Not only can the voice and body express one's perspective but encountering another's act of self-expression can in turn shape one's own thinking.

Mitchell Green in his book *Self-Expression* argues that 'In expressing ourselves we manifest some part of our point of view' (Green 2007, p. 1). As I approach my one-year-old daughter, her outstretched arms express her desire for me to pick her up. In doing so, her gesture manifests not only her desire but also her relationship to me (as her parent but also in terms of her being down on the ground and away from me). Not all acts of self-expression are voluntary; for instance, her giggles on being tickled express her delight but she does not giggle with the intention to express delight (contrast this with the case of the involuntary cough or sneeze where the noise made is not expressive of a mental state). According to Green, what can be expressed by the self must be an introspectable state. I do not take this to mean that it must be the case that one has already gained awareness of such a state prior to expression, only that it is the kind of thing that could be made explicit by introspection. In his account of self-expression, Green proposes a version of the *extended senses* model of communication, according to which 'our primary aim in communicating with one another is to widen each other's perceptual reach' (Green 2007, p. 10). Self-expression manifests aspects of one's perspective, which is made available to others through perceptible features of expression. In communicating with one another through self-expression, we aim to share knowledge of one's beliefs, commitments, feelings and experiences (whether we are successful or not in doing so).

Embedded in vocal expression is one's spatio-temporal position: the voice emanates from a particular moment and place (the speaker's body). On hearing another speak, I am attendant to their place in the room as it relates to me e.g. whether that is close by, the other side of the room, with nothing filling the space between us or as separated. But vocal expression can convey other dimensions of one's perspective, for instance through the content of what is said (what one chooses to say), the words they choose to say it, the intonation as expressive of attitude and emotional valence. All aspects of vocal expression help to express one's perspective, that is, what one prioritizes and cares about, connections one makes in thought, experience but also reflect the identity of the speaker whether confident, unconfident and the history of their body (as indication of experience and place).

According to Green, how one expresses one's perspective is through signals and showing. My daughter's rubbing of her eyes is a signal of her tiredness and desire for sleep, in other words, eye rubbing *indicates* tiredness but is not constitutive of tiredness.[9] Signalling is indirect whereas showing is direct; I might declare 'That's so funny' to signal or indicate that I have found something amusing or I might laugh aloud which directly shows or displays my having found something amusing. Green specifies three types of showing: showing that (presenting something as fact e.g. I have the belief that I feel sad by uttering the sentence 'I feel sad'),[10] showing something (making something perceptually available to others e.g. my mental state of sadness through the act of crying) and showing how something is experienced (bringing to life an experience for another e.g. 'how it feels to experience sadness' represented through artistic expression, that is, creating an object or event to bring about the same response or experience in another). In each case we can succeed or fail to show our mental states, that is, beliefs, commitments, feelings/emotions and experiences.

We can analyse vocal expression as consisting in two parts: the words used to signal meaning and the way in which those words are used has the capacity to show something about the speaker in terms of their commitment to a belief, sincerity, attitude, emotion and experience (although some aspects of voice might also be classed as signals rather than showing). In her discussion of Green's view, Dorit Bar-On writes, 'we may take ourselves to be *witnessing* how things are with the expresser. We often speak of *seeing* someone's anger, *hearing* the nervousness in someone's uneven voice, *feeling* the tension in someone's body, and so on' (2010, p. 219), it is in this sense that one's self-expression makes perceptible one's beliefs, commitments, feelings and experiences. Witnessing vocal expression makes available information relevant to the perspective of the speaker for the one hearing and attending to their self-expression through voice. The meaning of the act of vocal expression goes beyond the word meaning of the utterance to include affective aspects of the embodied voice such as the tensing of the body or the nervousness in the voice.

However, as Green points out, 'Not all self-expression makes what is within literally perceptible. An assertion expresses, and thus shows, a belief if it is sincere, but beliefs are not the sorts of things that can be perceived. Rather, a sincere assertion shows a belief by showing *that* we believe the content asserted, thereby enabling others to be aware of it' (Green 2007, p. 25). Of course, this raises an issue of sincerity, as Green notes, since we do not always express what we actually think.[11] According to Green, self-expression can be defined as follows:

> Where A is an agent and B a cognitive, affective, or experiential state of a sort to which A can have introspective access, A expresses her B if and only if A is in state B, and some action or behavior of A's both shows and signals her B. (Green 2007, p. 43)

Building on Green's account, I want to make some further claims about how thought and embodied voice are related. Thought is experienced as resonant or dissonant (due to my perceiving our perspectives to overlap or conflict). There are two sides to this: On the one hand, experiencing hearing one express certain thoughts and attitudes through one's own voice may be experienced as fitting or not (for instance, one might feel their words as belonging to them, as fitting with their natural rhythms of speech or they may experience them as difficult to articulate, that is, as in tension with their natural patterns of speech). But also, hearing the expression of another can be received as resonant or dissonant: what I mean by this is when someone says something that feels to you to get something right (or not) about what you are both looking at. But another dimension of resonant and dissonant is in the form of witnessing another's act of self-expression that seems fitting to oneself (where this is not as strong as identification; it is the recognition of *something* shared).

For instance, another's self-expression of nervousness on walking across a bridge (shown through their grasping at the rails, the sound of their voice, things they are saying etc.) may resonate with my own nervousness if I too perceive the situation to be precarious (I perceive we are having a similar emotional/affective response to the same thing but crucially I am not claiming to feel as they do). Alternatively, I may see no danger whatsoever and so see their expression of nervousness as unfounded, which jars with my own feeling of confidence. The idea of resonance and dissonance here is affective, in other words, it only concerns how I perceive the other and what they are expressing, it doesn't bear on their sincerity (they might be pretending to be nervous). This generates a feedback loop between thought and expression. Thinkers are often not settled on what they think about something or in their response to a situation. A thinker may have an initial reaction to something but one's reaction is dynamic, unfolding over time and can shift both in terms of intensity and valence (my nervousness might increase/decrease or I might reassess the situation as not dangerous after all) and one's reaction/response is open to the responses of those around them who either reinforce or disrupt one's response. What we can take from such an example is that one's experience is not in isolation to those around and that we respond to the expression of others. One's experience of another's expression as resonant or dissonant in turn shapes one's own experience further.

Becoming aware of one's own self-expression can add in additional information relevant to one's thinking. For example, one may repeatedly try to express through words how they feel to another (perhaps in trying to explain why they reacted a particular way), and it is only when they have tried several different formulations of articulation that they find the one that seems to capture how they feel that in turn explains their reaction, thereby shifting one's understanding of themselves.

Voice in poetry: Witnessing and co-creating expression

Lyric poetry is often characterized as the expression of the personal. Here I want to take up the idea from Green that self-expression (through one's voice, that is, one's vocal expression) manifests one's point of view and affords the opportunity to encounter other perspectives. However, voice as it figures in poetry is not just one thing: we must separate our encounter with voice in performance of (witnessing self-expression), reading of (co-creating expression) and listening to (partial witnessing of self-expression) poetry since the means of self-expression are different in each case.

Several critics have commented on the relationship between voice and poetry. For instance, Anne Stevenson defines lyric poetry as the poetry of the voice and the ear. Through her analysis she draws a distinction between two ways of understanding the poet's voice:

> There is the physical voice, an *articulation*, either vocal or mental – a pattern of long or short, stressed or unstressed syllables as they come to mind in the course of writing a poem. Then there is a sense in which the phrase 'the poet's voice' is used metaphorically to refer to an individual's speech idiom or characteristic mode of expression. (2017, p. 24)

For Stevenson, the poet is concerned with words as voiced; soundings come prior to meanings. The first understanding most closely matches how I have been thinking about voice – one's vocalization of speech, which shapes how one uses language and reflects how they think. As Francis Berry comments 'since poetry is of active language, which is vocal sound, the poet's sensation of language is a specifically intimate, passional, nervous and somatic (or bodily) one' (1962, p. 5). In writing poetry, the poet attends to their own use of language as vocalized. The second understanding captures voice in the poem itself, which bears a relation to but is not identical to the voice of the poet; the poet's voice grounds the voice of the poem.

The difference between poetry on the page and poetry in performance is one's relationship to voice in the work. In the case of page poetry, voice is decoupled from the poet and offered to the reader (in the case of someone reading their own poetry, the words on the page are experienced as 'othered' or external to the poet and therefore re-experienced as a reader). Such decoupling cannot happen in the live performance; to hear a poem is to hear it already voiced with the body in context.[12] To listen to a recording of a poem read aloud is to only have partial access to the embodied voice.

Voice in performance: witnessing self-expression

Of the three modes of poetic delivery, the performance of poetry (to include performing works of page poetry as well as works of performance poetry) will be closest to the way Green characterizes self-expression. To see a performance of a poem is in some sense to be witnessing the performer's act of self-expression, that is, voice as expressive of a perspective.

The nature of the live performance brings to the fore not only word meaning but affective aspects of the body of the performer that contribute to the performer's ability to express more than mere word meaning. As Julia Novak comments, 'The physical co-presence of poet and audience in a live poetry performance allows for a range of other sense perceptions (facial expression, body communication, audience interaction etc.) that considerably impact on the impression the audience has of the performance and thus on the meaning-making process' (Novak 2011, p. 55). The poem in performance consists of the interplay of the audio text (the words heard), the body text (aspects of body used in the delivery of the work, including vocal and bodily gestures) and the relationship to the audience. Although this is also true of acting, the difference in the case of the performance of a poem is that the body and action serve to draw greater attention to the words spoken. In the case of acting, words, body and action are given equal weighting in one's experience and interpretation (and in some cases, body and action may be taken to be more central).

To illustrate, consider 'The Last Poet Standing: A Poem for Young People' by Joelle Taylor (2012), which concerns how our cities fail young people through deprivation, neglect, exposing them to the violence of street crime and gang culture as a consequence of class. In her performance, Joelle Taylor recreates the sound of a flick knife. She holds her thumb up to represent the knife and draws attention to its presence, thereby recreating the feeling of a knife being unexpectedly pulled out in the middle of a fight.

> Our thin children have dug themselves in to their own fragile skin
> and hide behind sandbags, colours, postcodes and lies
> and cheap pound shop pride
> and a knife.

always a knife –

that reflects the hand that holds it;

the blade reflects the hand that holds it.

When you see your face

can you remember your name?[13]

Her performance isn't overly emotional but it is expressive of emotional attitude towards the subject matter. For instance, she expresses exasperation through facial expressions and bodily gestures (e.g. the way she throws her arms down). Through the patterning of words, Taylor builds intensity: a fast pace followed by a break to build tension that draws attention and sense of significance to particular lines. Significance is also expressed through her gestures as she points to the stage, the audience and gestures to her own body (e.g. the tensing of the arm as she says 'these umbilical streets'). The role of the breath is also important to her performance: what is said on the outbreath expresses meaning and intentionality. The breathing itself is audible and you can hear her need for breath in delivering these lines, which signals her effort in speaking. Her performance is a call to attention and call for response, not only in the direct command of 'shut up and speak' as she points to the audience but throughout as she voices what she takes to be of significance not only to her but between herself and the audience. Simply put, she's asking to be heard.

The physical vocalization situates the poem in the present and centres in the body of the poet-performer. In Taylor's performance, she draws attention to a matter of urgency: the things she is pointing to are happening now, while she speaks. The repetition and building of phrases out of the same words ('and a knife / always a knife / that reflects the hand that holds it / the blade reflects the hand that holds it' alongside the repetition of 'your name') expresses the connection between knife crime, gang culture and lost childhood (the presence of the knife leads the one addressed to be holding the knife). The linking in sound, the rhythmic gestures of the body and sense of unfolding expresses the inevitability that leads one thing to another.

The meaning of the work is grounded in the body; the words make reference to the self, to the individual perspective, as an act of self-expression. The fact of her saying these words at this time, in this place, brings into play questions of sincerity (does she endorse the views she expresses?), authenticity (does she have knowledge of what she is speaking about?) and what's being asked of me in response (is her expression purposeful?). If we were to discover that she is being insincere, or inauthentic or pointlessly speaking, this would devalue the piece. This is partly due to the nature of poetry. As Culler argues, poetry engages in discourse about value in the actual world; it concerns what we care about, and that we take as significant and important, which transcends any fictional or aesthetic construct (2015, p. 115). But it is also due to the expectations we have of acts of self-expression. As Green argues, we expect acts of self-expression to be sincere, for them to correspond to beliefs, feeling and experiences of the individual. Where a fictional construct is used in self-expression, it has the function of expressing one's actual beliefs, feelings and experiences metaphorically. The poet is creating an event or happening that is itself subject to interpretation (what does the poem express?). The construction of a persona in a poem (such as having the voice of the poem be that of an inanimate object) is still constructed by the poet and therefore expressive of the poet's perspective in virtue of their choice to invoke such a persona. The persona is used to express an idea and represents, albeit indirectly, the poet's perspective. Through the vocalizing of the words of the poem a direct connection is drawn to the body, thereby signalling the poem as self-expression.

Of course, the performance of poetry is not spontaneous self-expression but a mix of delivery of a construct of expression (the poetic work) and the delivery itself (the performance), which will express aspects of self of the performer at that particular moment in time. The text of the poem (whether or not actually written down, we can take to be the words of the poem) depends on the body of the performer in the live performance space to give voice to the work and create the work as event. As poet Pete Bearder writes, 'In live poetry, the body is the material, the media through which the poetry is published. In entering it, poetry becomes a product of that body; from its muscles, gut, and cardiovascular rhythms, through to its larynx, eyes, and facial expressions' (Bearder 2020, p. 190).

As discussed in the previous section, voice is expressive of perspective; it emanates from a location in space and time. In addition, the history of the body is manifest in the inflections of voice. The audience cannot separate the body of the performer from the performance: 'We cannot disentangle the poem from the fact of him standing on stage, making an intensely private picture visible' (Bearder 2020, p. 76). The embodied voice can be viewed as expressive of the context, history and identity of the person performing and thereby takes on a duality in terms of what is expressed. Not only does the poet-performer create an event that may show the audience how they think and feel about something, how something felt or was experienced but brings to the fore a context for that showing of thinking, feeling and experience that reveals aspects of their perspective on such feeling and experience. Presenting aspects of the self that reflect one's identity exaggerates the sense of one projecting their perspective into the performance space.

Take the significance of the accent of the voice of the performer. Every voice is accented (perhaps computer-generated voices are the most neutral, but even then, they are shaped by the technology involved in transmitting the sound, that is, the limitations of the speaker). Accent represents the history of the voice both in terms of the physiology of the body but also a history of social interactions that have shaped the patterns of speech, formation and articulation of words as discussed above. As poet and critic Charles Bernstein comments, 'While [the page poem] permits the poet to elide (if not disguise) accent, performance is an open wound of accentual difference from which no poet escapes. This is not the accent of stress but accents of distressed language, words scarred by their social origins and aspirations' (Bernstein 2011, p. 127). Consequently, the poet performing their work performs more than the written word but contributes affectively a context of their body, their social origins (accent can reference both place and class), and attempts to modify one's voice (that may express one's aspirations or difficulties in speech). For example, British spoken word poet Kae Tempest (2013) performs their poem 'Renegade' in their Southeast London accent that makes connections with the words of the poem, and the words themselves are stretched and contracted as a consequence of the patterns of delivery:

> But you can recognize me because I'm you, mate
> It's never too late to see deeper than the surface.
> Trust me, there's so much more to it.
> There's a world beyond this one
> That creeps in when your wits have gone soft
> And all your edges start shifting
> I mean it
> A world that is breathing
> Heaving its shoulders and weeping
> Bleeding through open wounds
> That's why I'm grieving.
> Down on my knees and I am feeling everything that I'm feeling[14]

Rhythm and intonation are also important features of the delivery of the poem in performance that are also contingent on the voice of the performer and their expression of self on the stage: 'Rhythm and pitch/intonation are not something inherent in the alphabetic script of the poem, but are extended, modified, improvised, invented, or enacted in performance' (Bernstein 2011, p. 126). In some cases, the rhythm of the poem is created by the poet-performer's accent and pronunciation of words.

Bernstein goes on to argue, 'Performance allows the poet to refocus attention to dynamics hidden within the scripted poem, refocusing emphasis and overlaying immanent rhythms. The performance opens up the potential for shifting frames, and the shift of frame is itself perceived as a performative gesture' (Bernstein 2011, p. 127). Placing emphasis, weighting words and connecting words in the way they are sounded not only expresses the poet's natural patterns of sounds but expresses aspects of their perspective, that is, the architecture of one's way of thinking and feeling that shapes what is expressed as thought and felt. The aesthetics of their delivery signals significance (where attention is drawn), connections of thoughts and shows their attitudes, judgements and feelings in the shaping of patterns of speech. Furthermore, the timbre, such as the sharpness or smoothness of the voice, alongside pitch and intensity (loudness) also contribute to how the words of the poem are expressed. These qualities might change during the reading of the poem rather than being constant.

Raymond Antrobus, a British poet who has a hearing impairment, performs his poems with exaggerated hand gestures (acting out the meaning of the words) that physically make present difficulties experienced due to deafness. In interviews and directly referenced in his poetry, he speaks about having undergone speech therapy, which has shaped the way in which he reads his work. Take for instance his poem 'The First Day I Wore Hearing Aids' (2014), where he stresses strong consonant sounds and places syllables carefully:

> I can still hear
> Miss Williams taking register.
> every present syllable in
>
>   Ray-mo-nd-Ant-ro-bus
>
> was a silent prayer for absence.[15]

The voice in performance of the poet-performer invokes intentionality not only in the sense of speaking deliberately and purposefully but also in terms of authorial intention: it is an act of self-expression that belongs to the poet-performer. This shapes the relationship with the audience and what they can and should do in hearing the poem performed. In the performance space, we become aware of what we can't do with words. The audience must pay attention to the embodiment of the words and consequently, the perspective of the performer. This acts as a constraint on interpretation but is precisely what provides the audience with an encounter with another's perspective. What enables the projection of the performer's perspective into the performance space is the live feedback between performance and audience, and the attention the performance space demands of the words spoken by the performer.

The audience are witnesses of the poet-performer's act of self-expression. As discussed, Green argues that we communicate with one another with the aim of extending the perceptual reach of others; in other words, we aim at sharing our own perspective. We can apply this to the performance context: the poet-performer aims at bringing the words, ideas, attitudes and images into the performance space to share their perspective with the audience. Witness is neutral with respect of address (which I will discuss in more detail in the next chapter): I can bear witness to being the one addressed or overhearing another being addressed. However, that does not mean the role of the audience is passive. Bearing witness to self-expression demands appropriate attention (i.e. being attentive to the words, their delivery and the speaker who speaks them) and response. The relationship between poet-performer and audience is ethical in this respect. As a witness of self-expression, the audience ought not remain passive but are required to attend to the speaker and respond appropriately (silence counts here as a possible response).

The role of voice in performance is not a mere display of voice but has the potential to shape the voices of those listening, even if only in one's emotional register. On hearing a poem on a difficult subject, the character of voice (at least judged to be appropriate) will reflect that in the space immediately after the performance tempering the voices of the audience as they begin to fill the silence post-performance (in some cases, leaving the audience feeling unable to speak temporarily). The poet-performer's voice in its demand for attention and call for response can also shape thinking and consequently expression of self of the audience in the way the audience is invited to vocalize their own response (for instance, Toby Campion's performance of 'Notes From The Sexual Health Clinic Waiting Room', in which he invites the audience to 'awkwardly cough' between the poems that form the sequence) that heightens their awareness of their relationship to others but also in enabling the audience to become aware of words embodied, as a relationship between audio text, body text and performance space.

Voice in reading: Co-creation of voice and meaning

Let's now turn to how voice manifests in reading poetry. Here I argue that the embodied voice, as I have been thinking of it, is still an important concept in reading poetry despite the lack of physical presence of a performer distinct from the reader. The body still plays an important role in meaning-making. However, given the words on the page are given as uncoupled from the body, they are left for the reader to take up and embody through their inner voice in the case of silent reading or to be read aloud. It is interesting to note that there are many recordings of people reading aloud page poetry, yet rarely will a work of performance poetry be performed by someone other than the poet (I do discuss one such case in Chapter 4).

When reading a work of poetry, I am deliberately attending to the words on the page and imagining how the words sound. There's a sense in which this is the voluntary exercise of my inner voice. As Peter Kivy argues:

> even when reading poetry silently to yourself became widespread, poetry remained and remains a literary form in which the sound of language is an integral part, as it is not, in the case of the novel, to anywhere near the degree to which it is in poetic texts. What this means is that even when you read a poem silently to yourself, you must, in your reading, 'hear' the sound of the poem in your mind's ear, be very conscious, in other words, of its sound if it were recited . . . a poem must, even when not recited, be 'voiced' . . . in the mind's ear. (Kivy 2006, p. 55)

However, the words themselves are written by another and so I also find myself 'voicing' and 'hearing' words and sentences that I did not choose. This can lead to the unexpected, particularly where the first person is voiced (simultaneously referring to the reader and the poet, and perhaps some other) along with expression of attitude and emotion.

Literary scholar Patricia Parker holds that 'in the absence of contrary indications, we infer a voice even though we know that we are reading words on a page' (1985, p. 16). The suggestion that we infer a voice (as distinct from one's own) presents a curious experience of reading poetry since it is not clear whose voice it is (is it the poet or a persona?).

Anna Christina Ribeiro suggests that who the voice of the poem belongs to shifts during the experience of reading:

> When listening to or reading a poem, we begin by hearing someone else's voice, by attending to what the poetic persona might have to share with us. Without presuming to account for all poetry reading experiences, I submit that, typically, by the end of the poem we have come to identify with that voice. . . . Our experience of lyric poems is therefore peculiarly personal: we either assume the role of the speaker in the poem, or of the one who is spoken to.' (Ribeiro 2009, pp. 69–70)

For Ribeiro, the page poem offers the opportunity to forge an intimate connection (either identification or address) with the voice of the poem. Such connection evolves through the reading process rather than being given from the outset. I will return to the idea of identification in poetry in the next chapter.

New critical approaches to poetry answered the question of who the voice belongs to by appealing to the text as a construct of voice: 'while texts do not absolutely lack speakers, they do not simply have them either; they invent them instead as they go. Texts do not come from speakers, speakers come from texts' (Tucker in Hosek and Parker 1985, p. 243). The advantage of Tucker's view is that it takes seriously the idea that the text on the page provides a frame for a reader that presents the interconnection of words and images through the patterning of the language of the poem. There is something in the written poem as it appears on the page that resists the reader being able to take up as if they were their own words (cf. Ribeiro 2009).

However, what's wrong with these ways of viewing voice in page poetry is that they fail to take into account what readers do with texts in the act of reading. As Robert Pinsky argues, 'The reader is not merely the performer of the poem, but an actual, living medium for the poem . . . In its intimacy and human presence, reading a poem may resemble a live performance' (Pinsky 2002, pp. 61–2). Through my discussion of poetry in this book, I will adopt a reader-response view, and extend to include performance, as a way of capturing the relationship between poet/poem and audience/reader. Reader-response criticism is not just one view but varies in degrees in terms of how much responsibility to the text and freedom of interpretation and engagement these approaches grant the reader (and audience). The fundamental view of any reader-response theory is the commitment to considering the role of the reader/audience and the process (through reading or seeing a performance) in arriving at the meaning of a work of literature.

There are three versions of reader-response theory. The first version (reader-dominant) takes it that meaning is merely in the mind of the reader, and acknowledges that different readers/spectators will have different interpretations (the work is a mere prompt for their own thoughts, feelings and appreciation of significance). On this view there is no objective meaning of a work of literature, allowing multiple interpretations to be equally valid; the work only has meaning when the reader/spectator has arrived at an interpretation of the work. This view emphasizes the subjective nature of reading (or experience of performance), and the possible differences in how readers/spectators will engage with and respond to the work.

The second version of reader-response theory (text-dominant) takes it that the meaning is contained in the words on the page (or body text plus audio text in the case of performance), but the reader must recover this meaning. On this view there are ideal readers who will interpret the work in a similar way since they are jointly attending to the same structures of word meaning, images, representations of feelings and so on to which they respond. Consequently, there is a right way of engaging with the work – the reader/spectator must follow certain conventions to recover the meaning in the work. This view sees the process as more objective, that there is a fixed or expected relationship between the text and the experience this gives rise to. However, that's not to say that the reader/spectator does not contribute to the experience of the work. As Wolgfang Iser writes:

> As a literary text can only produce a response when it is read, it is virtually impossible to describe this response without also analyzing the reading process. Reading . . . sets in motion a whole chain of activities that depend both on the text and on the exercise of certain basic human faculties. Effects and responses are properties neither of the text nor of the reader; the text represents a potential effect that is realized in the reading process. (1978, p. ix)

On such a text-dominant view, the idea is that the relationship between reader/spectator and text is still important because the work requires a reader/spectator to respond. However, the reader/spectator is constrained in their response by the text; in other words, their response must be appropriate to the text. Iser argues, 'The work is more than the text, for the text only takes on life when it is realized, and further-more the realization is by no means independent of the individual disposition of the reader – though this in turn is acted upon by the different patterns of the text' (1972, p. 279). Organizing themes of the poem are given in the text but can only be identified through the experience of reading/performance.

The third version (transactional reader-response[16]) holds that the poem, in its precise form, sets the terms that the reader/spectator must engage with but that there is a subjective element to the poem, in that the actual thoughts and feelings of the reader/audience are required to appreciate the work. Returning to Anne Stevenson, she writes:

> The style or period of a poem ... doesn't matter. Its rhythm does. Its diction does. And so does its imagery. All of these intermingle in varying degrees, according to how a poem 'gets to' its reader. And that means the reader himself (herself) has to put something imaginative into the poem. As poetry moves away from the past, with its pre-set forms, and closer to the present, reading a poem makes more, not fewer demands on you. (2017, p. 85)

The experience of the reader is responsible to the words and form but that does not constitute the meaning of the poem – the reader must work with the reading/listening experience to develop organizing themes to make sense of the complex whole. This view emphasizes the partnership between the reader and the work – that the work closely facilitates a kind of experience for the reader. Louise Rosenblatt argues that a 'literary work exists in the live circuit set up between reader and text: the reader infuses intellectual and emotional meanings into the pattern of verbal symbols, and those symbols channel his thoughts and feelings' (1983, p. 25). There is a kind of negotiation or feedback loop taking place between the reader/audience and the poem. This view gives equal weight to the subjective and objective. On this view the role of the reader does not give rise to infinite valid interpretations because the reader's response must be relevant to the text; that is, their interpretation will need to make sense of as much of the work and their experience as possible in a coherent and consistent way. Also, the stimulus for the experience is the same, so although two people might have different emotional responses to a particular word, phrase or image, they are responding to the same thing and having to understand their response in relation to the use of that word, phrase or image.

In response, I want to make the case for an alternative conception of voice in reading poetry. There's a sense in which the poet's voice is partially present but incomplete, requiring the reader to co-create the voice: what the act of reading the page poem affords is a kind of 'blended' or collaborative voice. Timbre, intonation, pronunciation and embodied sound are the reader's; word choice and patterning (how words are connected by sound) are embedded in the text (what Culler refers to as 'voicing'). The breath and public language are the communal/shared that brings the reader together with the text. The resulting voice will be constrained by features of the poem (the suggested patterning of sound produced by the arrangement of words, the grammar and lexicon) but also one's own voice (intonation, inflection, pronunciation).

However, Culler suggests that in some cases, we may still identify the voice of another in our reading of lyric poetry: 'we encounter lyrics in the form of written texts to which readers give voice. What we "hear" is our own ventriloquizing of ambiguously directed address, though we may, and in some cases certainly do, construe this as overhearing a distinctive poetic voice' (Culler 2015, p. 187). Although this may seem like a problem for my view, Culler's shift from talking of 'giving voice' to the notion of address is in fact a shift in consideration of the voice as articulated by the self, that is, an act of self-expression on part of the reader to consideration of the relationality of voice/s, that is, who is addressed by the voice. The reader in giving voice to the words on the page is implicated by them in the sense that the reader is called upon to resolve issues of expression and address (in making sense of the relationship between their own voicing of the poem and where to locate the act of expression and address). As already mentioned, it is consistent with my view that one can take on the dual role of speaker and addressee, and the feeling of separation here is in virtue of the fact that the speaker's voice is the product of negotiation between reader and text, whereas who is addressed may straightforwardly be the reader. I will return to discuss the issue of address in the next chapter.

Peter Kivy (2006) describes the act of reading a literary text as if it is a performance: one imagines sounding the words and hearing them just in the same manner as one who 'reads' a musical score: 'If, when we read poetry silently to ourselves, we "voice" in our heads . . . we are, in effect, having a performance in our heads: our performance to ourselves' (Kivy 2006, p. 55). Echoing this view, Culler suggests, 'Rather than imagine that lyrics embody voices, we do better to say that they create effects of voicing, of aurality' (2015, p. 35); in other words, he holds that poems offer patterns of sound that 'represent' or 'produce' voices (through the reader's voice). The reader is required to voice the words in order to realize the poem but there are features of the poem that constrain voicing of the poem as indicated by its physical inscription on the page. For instance, much like how on reading a musical score, the performer must pay attention to not only the notes but the space between the notes, the reader of a work of poetry must pay attention to the white space that acts a symbol of silence. As Charles Olson writes in his essay, 'Projective Verse':

> if a contemporary poet leaves a space as long as the phrase before it, he means that space to be held, by the breath, an equal length of time. If he suspends a word or syllable at the end of a line . . . he means [for the] time to pass that it takes for the eye – that hair of time suspended – to pick up the next line. (Olson 1997, p. 245)

Juliana Spahr's *This Connection of Everyone with Lungs* (2005) provides an excellent example of the shared breath between poet and reader, who are united through the poem. The poem starts without the use of a single personal pronoun, just a description of 'the hands', 'the feet':

> There are these things:
>
> cells, the movement of cells and the division of cells
>
> and then the general beating of circulation
>
> and hands, and body, and feet
>
> and skin that surrounds hands, body, feet.
>
> This is a shape,
>
> a shape of blood beating and cells dividing.[17]

There is a deliberate space in between each line, where the reader has a chance to breathe in and out, with awareness of the breath filling this silence. The breathing of the poem is enacted in our own breathing in reading the poem; the breath is controlled to some extent by the line lengths and use of enjambment.[18] This sense of connection or 'relationality' builds towards the first use of a personal pronoun in the poem, which comes nine pages in: 'How connected we are with everyone.' The build-up to this moment leads us to see this as deeply intimate because in reading we have moved from considering our own internal workings and our own rhythms to acknowledging this in relation (as connected) to others. This shapes our understanding of the final part of the poem: 'The space of everyone that has just been inside of everyone mixing inside of everyone with nitrogen and oxygen and water vapor and argon and carbon dioxide and . . . titanium and nickel and minute silicon particles from pulverized glass and concrete' (p. 9).[19] Reading these words, we experience a kind of asphyxiation as the length of this stanza leaves us little space to take a breath, until we reach the final line, 'How lovely and doomed this connection of everyone with lungs', which draws attention to our shared vulnerability.

The reader cannot be a passive witness to the 'voice' of the poem because the words depend on the reader to bring them to life and requires the reader to enact the breathing that is symbolized by the white space on the page. However, there is a difference in voice between the poem in performance and the poem on the page. The performer's voice is an inescapable feature of the work with all its natural inflections. There is a sense in which the poem on the page can shift away from personal, individual, accented voice to present something between selves – as waiting to be taken up by another's (that is, the reader's) voice.

It is important to acknowledge that some poems are better read on the page. As discussed in the introduction, Culler draws a distinction between lyric poems grounded in *opsis*, or visual patterning, and those grounded in *melos*, or sound patterning. Take for example, 'Florist's at Midnight' by Sarah Maguire (2001), which has a strong visual patterning. Each stanza is made up of three-tiered (indented) lines that mirror the tiered shelving of the flowers in the Florist's shop. Something is lost if read aloud without consideration for how the poem takes shape on the page. However, it is equally true that something is lost if one doesn't consider the words as soundings. As much as the visual pattern is important to the poem, so is the feeling of movement between the lines and stanzas. Therefore, even in cases where the poem is more strongly grounded in opsis, it still involves voice but it demands that our voicing of the poem is related to the poem on the page (and is constrained by that visual presentation of words).

The upshot of my view is that in the act of reading, the reader embodies the words of the poem and so there's a sense in which the poem implicates the self and draws on their identity and perspective. What's created by the reader grounding the words of the poem with their embodied voice is an interlocking of perspectives (the reader, the poem and the poet). Such interlocking comes about through negotiation. There is not a *right* way of reading: pauses for breath are suggested but the reader can play with pronunciation, articulation, intonation and tempo, thereby shaping the poem as they read according to the reader's own natural voice. There will be a natural way for the reader to read, and in doing so, the reader will experience a kind of intimacy with the poem. But it is the reader's act of reading and bringing to life the words on the page that creates the event of the poem, an event that is connected to the physical presence of the reader (their body and their location in time and space). It is within this space that the reader will experience either resonance or dissonance between their own voice and perspective and the freedoms and constraints of the text of the poem.

Voice and listening: Partial witness

My analysis of voice in poetry would not be complete without also considering the experience of listening to recordings of poems read aloud, particularly as there are many recordings available through online archives (in many cases, of dead poets) reading their work. Of recorded poetry, Bernstein writes, 'The implied or possible performance becomes a ghost of the textual composition, even if the transcriptive pull is averted, just as a reader can't help but hear an overlay of a previously sampled voice of the poet, a ghostly presence steaming up out of the visual script' (Bernstein 2011, p. 127). Many works of poetry cannot be read off the page without invoking memories of a particular recording. One of the most iconic audio recordings available is Ginsberg's reading of *Howl* in 1956 at Portland's Reed College. After hearing Ginsberg, it's hard to read *Howl* without imagining his voice and imitating his delivery. What such a recording does is disrupt the potential for the reader to occupy the space of the voice in the poem, thereby precluding the sense of co-creation discussed earlier.

The experience of voice in these cases falls somewhere between experience of poetry in performance and on the page for it is heard as an outer voice yet it lacks embodiment: it has been separated from its temporal and spatial location as well as the body from which it emanated. Returning again to Bernstein, he writes: 'one of the fundamental conditions of the grammaphonic voice of the poet is its ghostly presence. Listening to such recordings, we hear a voice, if not of the dead, then one that sounds present but is absent, a voice that we can hear but that cannot hear us' (Bernstein 2011, p. 125). As Bernstein notes here, the audio-recording also disrupts an important dimension of self-expression; the voice is a call to attention and response, and yet in listening to a recording one is not able to respond to the speaker (although one, of course, can respond to hearing a voice). In other words, what's missing here is the relationality between speaker and hearer. It's therefore tempting to see listening to recordings of poetry as inferior to both experiencing poetry in the live performance and reading off the page.

Conclusion

In this chapter, I identified three ways in which the nature of voice in each mode of poetic delivery (performance, reading and listening) relates to the audience/reader. In the case of performance, the audience are witnesses of fully embodied vocal expression; in listening, the audience is only partial witness since some aspects of the body are withheld; in reading, voice is left implicit in the text, requiring the reader to bring to life the voice of the poem while being unable to take it on as if their own (leading to co-creation of voice – the reader 'voices' the poem but aspects of vocal expression are embedded in the text and constrain the reader's voice). From this analysis it's clear that the way in which the audience and reader engage with the voice of the poem is complex. This also suggests an important way in which performed poetry is paradigmatic since in performance, the audience has a pure encounter with the voice of the poem in virtue of the grounding of voice in the body of another. In the case of reading, I argued that some aspects of voice are withheld from the reader, which requires the reader to engage in a kind of co-creation of voice. Such co-creation demands an imperfect negotiation since the reader cannot simply engage with the poem on its own terms but must bring certain resources to that experience in order to attempt to realize the perspective on offer in the poem. Although the reading experience demands more from its reader than an audience of a performance, it is important that the reader still attends to the significance of the embodied voice and the ways in which that connects them to the perspective of the poem; the reader must be self-consciously other-directed in their engagement with the poem.

Understanding voice in lyric poetry is more than identifying the speaker of the work or the author of the words. What we are required to do is attend to the expression of a perspective (which may be distinct, albeit related to the author of the work). Our everyday speaking voices express aspects of ourselves, that is, one's own perspective, such as expressing our beliefs and desires through the words we speak and the manner in which we speak them (for instance, expressing approval or disapproval through intonation of voice) and in expressing something of the way in which we process thought and feeling through our unique lexicon and grammar, as well as reflecting aspects of our own histories and influences. A consequence of this view is that voice and the use of personal pronouns in lyric poetry come apart; the voice of the poem does not necessarily track the lyric I, since the perspective is expressed through the complex whole (the words, images, associations suggested through aesthetic connection such as the rhythm, metre, assonance and consonance) of which the use of personal pronouns is just one small part. In the next chapter, I give more attention to the notion of the lyric I and the use of the first person within a poem as it relates to the reader and audience. Whereas voice in a poem is expressive of a perspective, the use of the first person is not itself necessarily expressive of a self. Instead, the use of the first person functions to draw attention to relationality, that is, to the relationship between I and You, and between self and other.

2

The lyric I

Reading voices, hearing voices

Introduction

Often the notion of voice and the lyric I (the invocation of the first person) are seen as one and the same thing: the subject of the lyric I is taken to be the voice of the work. In this chapter I seek to separate the two. The perspective (or structural network of sounds, associations, images and other connections supported by poetry's appeal to the musicality of language) that brings the poem together as a unified whole represents the voice of the poem rather than the first person necessarily being the representation of a self. I will argue that the lyric I, the addressee and intended listener are not always fixed or static in works of contemporary poetry, whereas the poem may still have a unified voice. I argue that lyric poetry has cognitive value in virtue of the ambiguous and dynamic way these three roles are experienced whether in performance or on the page. One of my key claims is that the lyric I performs a relational gesture that necessarily brings to the fore an appreciation of self-other differentiation; in other words, we are able to appreciate the separation of one's own thoughts, feelings and sense of self from that expressed by another (yet in relation to another).

The voice of the poem expresses relationality through the use of the lyric I but the lyric I need not itself refer to an individual, singular self. In other words, I claim that the lyric I does not offer enough to present us with an expressive subject who thinks and feels particular things, nor is it merely offering thoughts and feelings for the reader/audience to take up. The poem's concern is more to do with connection and communication, and less to do with the self in construction and expression. That's not to say that the voice of the poem and the lyric I cannot overlap; the aim of my account is to provide a model that captures the bare structure of voice and expression in lyric poetry. The use of the first person doesn't ground expression (it doesn't indicate an expressive subject or character); rather, the voice of the poem is expressive (as spoken by someone) and may use the first person as a feature of that expression (which could involve merely drawing explicit attention to or 'thematizing' the relationality of I-you where the I doesn't function to pick out the expressive subject). To make the case that voice and lyric I come apart, it only need be the case that we can sometimes find examples where the use of the I is not expressive of a self but invokes the structural feature of first-person expression. The experience afforded by lyric poetry is therefore not best characterized as the expression of self but as the experience of a relationship.

The poet Will Harris is also interested in poetry's communicative function. Through his poetry, he experiments and interrogates the ways in which we do/don't relate to one another. Take for instance, his poem 'Object' (2017), which explores the relationship between subjects:

> X → Y What have you taken?
> Y → X What you have taken.
>
> X → Y What have I taken?
> Y → X What you have taken from me.
>
> X → Y I have taken nothing from you.
> Y → X Then I have taken nothing.[1]

The poem not only resists take-up of the 'I' and the 'you' by the reader but also resists being reduced to simple address between the poet/poetic persona and an addressee. The poet is not really using these personal pronouns but mentioning them yet is still performing an action. The poem presents a relationship between first person and second person, between a self and other that is represented by the variables or place-holders X and Y and uses this structure to express something about the relationship between the (unknown and unstable) I and you. The poem is ambiguous as to whether the X and Y are singular or represent groups. This ambiguity is important to how the poem works. Commenting on Harris' poem, Sarah Howe writes:

> The poem sketches out a map of social bonds, power relations and lines of influence, which speak to the experience of an individual 'I' puzzling over what is handed down between generations, but also the predicament of nations locked together by their colonial histories. The verb 'take', which resounds through the poem, might suggest plundering by Western imperial powers past and present. (2017, p. 52)

The reader's role is not to resolve that ambiguity but embrace it. Ordinarily ambiguity is seen as a defect in communication and expression that the speaker or listener must resolve in order to be understood. Sometimes, of course, one might be deliberately ambiguous in ordinary conversation, but there's no guarantee that a listener will attend to and appreciate the value of that use of ambiguity and may well respond with frustration. However, in poetry ambiguity is valued as it is and attempts to fully resolve such ambiguity on part of the reader or audience lessens the aesthetic experience of the work and limits what the work can do. In other words, the ambiguity itself is treated as an important feature of the work that the reader/audience is encouraged to pay special attention to and the possibilities it throws up.

In 'Object', it is the mapping out that is expressive of a perspective, a way of viewing the relationships between I and you. To put it another way, it is the revealing of connection and disconnection between the abstracted and ambiguous I and You that is expressive of a perspective. The perspective of the poem is not an outpouring of some 'I' but an attempt to perform some action by using the lyric I.[2] In other words, the indexicals of 'I' and 'You' are not subject to normal indexical shift in the sense that we can simply appeal to the concept of the speaker to track how the personal pronouns refer since the speaker or voice of the poem does not map onto the use of the I. To assume a singular speaker would be to lose the ambiguity at the heart of the poem. What this example reveals is that the poetic use of the first person disrupts ordinary use, rather than serving as pure indexicals (where what they refer to is fixed by the context of who is speaking and when); its meaning becomes sensitive to wider contextual features that go beyond the notions of speaker and self, and in doing so opens up reflective space.[3]

Although one might argue that such a poem is not typical of much contemporary and lyric poetry, what I argue in this chapter is that the structures of relationships such as that laid bare in Harris' poem are at the heart of contemporary lyric poetry. In other words, the use of personal pronouns in poetry expresses relationality (between I and You, connection and disconnection, presence and absence, and public and private). Through the event of self-expression, co-creation of expression (expressing together) and being heard, the experience of the poem is an enactment of a relationship. This is not a simple relationship of poet-poem-listener but a relationship of perspectives or perspectival relationships; in some cases, the relationship between perspectives but in others it is the forging of a shared perspective that comes from the role of voice in the poem, not the lyric I.

The lyric I: Encountering 'I' thoughts and hearing other voices

A popular view since Romanticism is that the lyric I is expressive of a self (or aspects of a self). In other words, the poem expresses the thoughts and emotions of the poet or poetic persona (that is a construct of the use of the first-person pronoun). This is suggested in Wordsworth's (1802) declaration that poetry is 'the overflow of powerful emotions'. More recently, Jenefer Robinson argues that the poet gives 'us his *reflections upon* his emotional experience as well as a sense of what the experience is like. The poem is the result of his cognitive monitoring of the experience' (2005, p. 279). On such a view it doesn't matter whether this is the expression of the poet or some fictional construct; what is important is that there is an expressive subject doing the expressing (the thoughts and feelings expressed by the poem must be someone's, and that someone might be a fictional persona).

In rejection of such expression theories, Kendall Walton argues that the lyric I refers to neither the poet nor a fictional/constructed poetic persona. He motivates this view by comparing works of music and poetry; he argues, both are able to be thought of as expressive without there needing to be an expressive subject. He supports this claim by arguing that poetry is a form of 'thought-writing', which he takes to be analogous to a speech-writer who produces words for another to speak. In outlining his view, Walton quotes R. K. Elliott as follows: 'A poem can be perceived . . . as if it were the speech or thought of another person . . . it is possible for us to make this expression our own' (1972, p. 146; cited by Walton). Likewise, Helen Vendler argues, 'the lyric is a script written for performance by the reader – who, as soon as he enters the lyric, is no longer a reader but rather an utterer, saying the words of the poem *in propria persona*, internally and with proprietary feeling' (Vendler 1995, p. xi). On such a view, there is no need to posit an expressive subject to understand its expressive qualities, much like a speech-writer, the expressive properties of the text are simply made available to others (to readers). The activity of the poet is therefore to make 'available' words, thoughts, attitudes, sentiments, feelings, emotions, and they are only made available because they are presented as not being attached to a particular speaker or persona.

What is central to Walton's view is the idea that a poet doesn't *use* the words of the poem to express but merely *mentions* them. This is an important distinction and I agree that we must engage with the words of the poem as not being strictly expressive in that way. However, where my view differs is that I take the act of mentioning to be expressive; the poet is trying to do or say something by presenting these words in poetic form. Many people borrow lines from poems to express themselves in everyday life or find parts of poems useful in articulating what they are feeling about a particular situation they find themselves in. For Walton, this reveals why we take certain poems to be so expressive: the reader is able to take up the role of the expressive subject. But that misses a great deal of what we can do with the poem and how lyric poetry works. Let's think back to Will Harris' poem 'Object': the value of the poem is not in offering me ways to express thoughts, feelings and so on. To try to treat it that way would miss the kind of analysis Sarah Howe offered of the significance of the ambiguity at the heart of the poem.

As we saw in the previous chapter, Anna Christina Ribeiro also puts forward a version of the identification model of engagement with poetry and argues that '[poetry] shows us what can be thought and felt in ways we may not have thought or felt before, but now discover, or in ways that we may have, and now recognize and find felicitously expressed. Poetry thereby enlarges our own potentialities for thought, feeling, and expression' (2015b, p. 103). What's common to both Walton and Ribeiro is a rejection of the view that what we are concerned with is the voice or speaker of the poem and the idea that poetry does not merely provide a thought or set of thoughts for the reader to entertain but involves the reader engaging in a particular activity of thought and thinking that is enabled by the poem. On this view, the lyric I becomes expressive of the reader's first-person perspective. What's problematic here is that the reader is being asked to contribute too much, which potentially moves us too far away from what the poet is trying to do with their poem. In other words, the reader needs to be sensitive to the perspective expressed by the poem even if they take up lines for their own use in expression. Furthermore, both views take the value of poetry to be in its precision of expression, that is, in offering ways of thinking and feeling that help the reader to articulate how they think and feel. Although we might find such value in poetry, much of what we value in poetry is ambiguous, open-ended and generative. Despite these problems, I do want to build on the idea of the poem offering a script of some sort where we shift from treating the words of the poem as expressive to treating the presentation of those words as expressive. By making such a distinction, I am able to accommodate Walton's criticism of expression accounts of poetry (which seem to be committed to their being either a fictional I or seeing poetry as giving us direct access to the thoughts of the poet) while still being able to view lyric poetry as expressive (what is communicated through the act of mentioning).

Identification models of lyric I: Readerly and plural

As an alternative to rejecting the notion of an expressive subject or equating this with the reader, Hannah Kim and John Gibson (2021) argue that the lyric I is not representative of a singular 'I' – whether that is of a poetic persona or the poet themselves – but instead should be thought of as expressing a multitude. In making their case, they raise the question of what it is for a poem to express: Is it the literal self-expression of the poet or is it the expression of some fictional or constructed poetic persona? In their discussion, they focus on developing Walton's account that the lyric I is to be understood not in terms of self-expression of the poet but in terms of self-expression of the reader (Gibson labels this the 'readerly' model), from which they argue that the lyric I does not act to pick out one person.

As Kim and Gibson highlight, one advantage of the identification model is that it seems to solve the puzzle of how a poem can be a vehicle for thought and feeling when the page poem is not something that can think and feel and doesn't provide enough detail of the poetic speaker to construct a character 'with sufficient subjective life such that we can justify our ascription of psychological and expressive predicates to it' (2021, p. 98). They argue that there needs to be an expressive subject that the act of self-expression belongs to. For example, to say a poem expresses loss of a beloved, there needs to be a subject who experiences such loss to then be in a position to express that loss. The identification model merely posits the reader (or, if we are to include poetry in performance, the performer) as the expressive subject.

Although not mentioned by the proponents of the identification model, another key motivation can be found in the rejection of the shareability thesis of first-person thought.[4] Typically, first-person thoughts are indexical and self-reflexive, where the 'I' refers to the thinker and can capture one's expressions of states of the self; for example, 'I feel sad'.[5] The thinker is therefore privileged with respect to first-person thought: when I think 'I feel sad', I am not thinking the same thought as you when you think 'I feel sad', since when I think that thought, I use my mental capacity for self-reflexivity of thought that makes me (and not you) the subject of the thought. For me to entertain the idea that you are feeling sad, I must alter the structure of the thought from 'I feel sad' to a corresponding you-thought.[6] What this means when applied to the experience of engaging with poetry is that I cannot entertain first-personal thoughts expressed in the poem as belonging to some other without altering the nature of the thought (it either becomes second person in character – a you-thought – or the subject, you, is changed to me). According to the identification model, in bringing the thoughts of the poem to life through me, I must take up and embody the I of the poem. Consequently, the question for the reader is whether the utterance (whether spoken aloud or imagined) is truly reflective of their own thoughts and feelings (i.e. whether it *can* be used as self-expression). In other words, does it articulate something about the reader and therefore enable them to engage in self-expression through the poem?

We might respond that poetry is a special case that enables the *shareability* of first-person thought; we entertain both the first-person and corresponding second-person thought simultaneously. I take Kim and Gibson to be doing just that in their view that the lyric I is able 'to stand for and speak on behalf of the experiences of more than one mere subject, fictional or otherwise' (2021, p. 95). This can be seen as an extension of the identification model in the following way: In reading first-personal expression in poetry, the reader is invited to take up the lyric I as the expressive subject but with acknowledgement that they are not alone in being able to do this.[7] It is therefore through the uptake of the first person that the reader becomes aware that certain aspects of their expression are shareable with others (in other words, the I-thought becomes plural in nature). This is made possible in virtue of the lack of subjective life offered within the poem; in other words, 'the I of lyric poetry is often nothing more than a center of perceptual, cognitive, and affective *attention*: the subject of *an* experience. It is a self effectively reduced to a perspective' (2021, p. 108).

There is a subtle but important difference between Kim and Gibson's view and the standard identification model (such as Ribeiro's). Kim and Gibson make the important point that at least *some* poems require that the reader acknowledge self-other differentiation (through the notion of speaker and addressee). They introduce the example of Langston Hughes' poem 'Dinner Guest: Me', in which they offer an example of a poem where the reader is not free to identify with the lyric I and use the words in an act of self-expression. The limits of perspective-taking in poetry, according to Kim and Gibson, 'are the ones where the flexible transferring of the "I" is unauthorized, inappropriate, or impossible. It is not a matter of differing opinions, desires, and attitudes, nor even cases of imaginative resistance. It is rather that the reader sometimes, in fact often, lacks the requisite authority or experience to stand behind a poem's voice' (2021, p. 102). The value 'is presumably to get them to *acknowledge* the experience of others, not to self-identify with them' (2021, p. 103). This is a criticism of Walton's view since his thought-writing account cannot make sense of those cases in which the reader is precluded from take-up of the lyric I; if there is no expressive subject, then self-other differentiation isn't possible. However, Kim and Gibson's view seems to allow that (in at least some cases) what poetry makes available *is* shareability or non-exclusivity of first-person expression but that there are important cases where such identification is prohibited, that is, where the lyric I may resist exclusivity but is not all inclusive either.

Ultimately, they argue that what we do when we engage with the lyric I is imagine a kind of human experience – not a particular person but something more general that is shared between people (that the reader may or may not be part of): 'The lyric I often "gives voice" to experiences that are manifestly not those of one mere subject. They are often *shared* forms of experience, and the implied subject of the lyric I is thus a creature not of fiction but of culture: it organizes and gives expression to thoughts, desires, anxieties, and feelings of a constellation of selves' (2021, p. 106). If we think back to the shareability thesis, this has the consequence that either there is no one who has had these thoughts to express or we are back to the position that the lyric I is that of the poet but an abstracted form of the poet's identity that enables their thoughts and feelings to be representative of some more general perspective. Kim and Gibson write, 'It represents not just a voiced subject but a poetic speaker who is attempting to *give voice* to forms of experience broader than her own. Our sense of both what the lyric I is speaking about *and* whose experiences it is giving voice to are thus often plural in nature' (2021, p. 107). What we should take from this is that it is still a first-person perspective but something that presents itself as potentially shareable with others (not necessarily as shared). It is still bound to the individual perspective but one that attaches to aspects of the self that are shared with or common to others (such as being a woman, philosopher, British Citizen, human being[8]). The important thing to note is that this does not need to entail that the lyric I is attempting to speak on behalf of others but is an offering to others to connect with it, to share with it but not to reduce it to either mere expression or an individual, personal experience that one can simply co-opt.

Relational model of lyric I

In 'Cultivating Intimacy' (2019b), I discuss the identification model and argue that there are important cases of poetry in which identification with the lyric I is prohibited and importantly so. The value of the work is in part in showing the limits of attempts to take up a perspective. What a work such as *Citizen* (2014) by Claudia Rankine reveals to its reader is that being too ready to identify with the perspective of the poem denies another of their individual experience and perspective. For instance, Rankine's documentation of racial microaggressions in *Citizen* is importantly contextualized as being experienced by someone who experiences the effects of racism but that is not the same as saying that the lyric subject presents some character who centres that experience; in many ways, it is the success of the work that the voices of the poem aren't reducible to construction of some character. Without acknowledgement of such context, one might fail to identify such incidents as racist and fail to appreciate the impact such subtle forms of racism can have on a person in terms of their dignity, confidence and self-esteem. But it is also important that such experience isn't generalized either – when generalized, we can clearly see patterns of behaviour as racist but individual episodes are left ambiguous and so fail to capture the full picture of the damage done to individuals.

A key part of my own argument was to show how the use of the first person is an invitation to identify only to find oneself recognizing what is problematic about doing so. The poem pushes back, complicates and makes difficult the attempts of the reader to take up the position of first-person expression. What it pushes against is the shareability thesis: there's some sense in which we can share thoughts and experience but there's an important sense in which we can't due to limitations in one's access to first-person knowledge. We may jointly attend to something but how we negotiate it, make sense of it and respond to it will be different in virtue of our differing perspectives. What *Citizen* presents is a collection of voices, including the reader's own, that represents such differing perspectives. Awareness of connection and disconnection is important for appreciating the relationality of I and/to you that provides the structural framework for intersecting/colliding voices. Types of experience may be shareable but the experience is shaped by an individual's perspective. The use of the first person in poetry is an *attempt* to reach others through the first-person singular by forging a relationship. It is an *invitation* or a *gesture* to share one's perspective while simultaneously revealing that such sharing is impossible, which triggers awareness not only of separation but of relationality. The lyric I resists ownership but that doesn't mean it cannot forge connections.

Introducing the notion of affect here can help to unpack the shareable and non-shareable in such episodes of sharing (i.e. joint attention). Eve Kosofsky Sedgwick (2003) argues that there are different ways of 'seeking, finding and organising knowledge', and acknowledgement of this entails being open to the unexpected; rather than looking for verification of theory, one must let new ideas emerge, however surprising and difficult they may be. Sedgwick's project was not one of merely noting difference but taking difference as the base assumption, which enabled her to examine the epistemology of the individual self in terms of interpersonal relationships that reveal sameness through difference. For Sedgwick, identity and identification are not fixed categories but enable an openness to connect with others or, as Sedgwick puts it, 'being available to be identified with', which is important in cultivating empathy. Commenting on Sedgwick's work, Fawaz notes, 'It is a description of the very condition for friendship, which requires a bond of trust developed through mutual vulnerability and provides one highly potent basis for long-term associations across difference' (2019, p. 19). It is important to understand the way in which such identification works; it is not through coming to see sameness in others as meaning one is identical to them but recognizing that sameness to some degree requires one 'to negotiate the apparent gaps that distinguish people on the basis of their distinctions and to produce new identities from that negotiation, perhaps ones that are better equipped affectively to engage, think through, and do something productive with the fact of human variation' (2019, p. 20). In other words, identifying with others is not something that can come prior to interaction with them – it is not given in advance based on aspects of the self but is cultivated through the interaction between people, through an openness to share with another. The starting point is the private, personal, disconnected rather than sharing an experience, response, identity; one looks instead for *moments* of sharing, that is, those aspects that bring the you and I into relationship. This need not be cognitive but can be a felt, affective connection. What the relational model holds is that the lyric I performs a relational gesture in bringing the poet, addressee and listener together. This relationality enables moments of interaction to unfold from which sameness and difference, connection and disconnection emerge.

Although my view adequately deals with the rejection of the shareability thesis, it seems I am still exposed to the problem of how to account for who the expressive subject is; that is, 'how can we conceptualize the poetic speaker as endowed with sufficient subjective life such that we can justify our ascription of psychological and expressive predicates to it?' (Kim and Gibson 2021, p. 98). Here I return to the notion of the embodied voice as set out in the previous chapter. We are able to grant expression of the self in everyday situations when we do not have access to other minds. In the case of the poetry performance, the answer is that the expressive power of the poem is grounded in the body of the performer. It is the performer's own body that provides evidence of subjective life. In the case of reading page poetry, the answer is more complex. The expressive subject of the page poem is partial or incomplete (which explains Walton's intuition that in some cases we are presented with mere expression, although I argue it is incompleteness rather than absence). In neither case is the lyric I needed to take on the burden of centring the voice and expression of the poem. Although I agree with Kim and Gibson that what the poem does is offer the bare bones of a perspectival self, on my view, in reading and giving voice to the words on the page (whether reading aloud or imaginatively), I contribute subjectivity. As noted earlier, this is not a simple process of filling in the gaps but a negotiation of perspectives.

In poetry the use of and expression of the first person is not static or stable but shifts throughout the reading of the poem. The use of the first person also behaves differently across works of poetry. We must therefore adopt a pluralist view of the lyric I. As an alternative to the readerly identification model (Walton, Ribeiro) and the plural identification model (Kim and Gibson), what I propose here is a relational model, according to which the lyric I invites first-person uptake but ultimately resists this; one strives for identification but is left having to make sense of difference (in connection and disconnection). It is my claim that the self-other differentiation that Kim and Gibson argue is important to only some works of poetry ought to be taken as central to our experience of lyric poetry in performance and on the page. In doing so, what the use of the first person in lyric poetry does is reveal connections between perspectives – connection despite a background of disconnection. Crucially, it is not the lyric I that provides the perspective but the presentation of a structure or form.

Consider the following poem 'Nigh-No-Place' by Jen Hadfield:

I will meet you at Pity Me Wood.
I will meet you at Up-To-No-Good.

I will meet you at Stank, Shank and Stye.
I will meet you at Blowfly.

I will meet you at Low Spying How.
I will meet you at Salt Pie.

I will meet you at Coppertop.
I will meet you at Scandale Bottom.

I will meet you at Crackpot Moor.
I will meet you at Muker.

I will meet you at Dirty Piece.
I will meet you at Booze, Alberta.

I will meet you at Bloody Vale.
I will meet you at Hunger Hill.

I will bring you to New Invention.
I will bring you to Lucky Seven.

I will bring you from Shivery Man.
I will bring you to The Lion and Lamb.

I will bring you to the North Light.
I will bring you to Quiet-The-Night.

I will bring you to Hush.
I will bring you to Hungry Hushes.

I will bring you to Grace, Alberta.
I will bring you to Nigh-No-Place.

I will meet you at Two O' Clock Creek.
Will you go with me?[9]

'NighNo-Place' is structured by the promises of 'I will meet you' and 'I will bring you' that reveal something about the nature of promise of connection.[10] All of the places named (although perhaps inspired by real-world places) only succeed in referring to particular places if the addressee or listener has shared knowledge with the speaker of the I.[11] In the promise of connection, the separation between the knower and unknower cannot be fulfilled. But it is not simply an issue of whether such places exist (or my knowledge of them). Even if I knew where Scandale Bottom or Hungry Hushes was, they are not places that have significance in my life (or significant for the right kind of reasons as gestured by the poem) and so there is still a failure of connection to place. The poem is a promise of significance of place. It depends on my 'being taken to' for them to have meaning. Equally, the movement in the promise of 'I will bring you' gestures at a move to connect the disconnected while leaving ambiguous who is being addressed. The poem reveals not only something about the nature of naming but the relationship between names, places and perspectives. The final line 'Will you go with me?' reveals how a promise only has purchase if it is a promise to someone and a someone, a you, that reciprocates the gesture; 'I will meet you' and 'you will meet me' – one cannot happen without the other. It is necessarily relational.

None of the alternative models (expression, thought-writing, or identification) can provide an analysis of this poem and its use of the lyric I, for the thought content of the poem isn't enough to enable the reader to do the kind of work that each model takes as central to our engagement with poetry. Merely naming does not express a thought or feeling; it doesn't offer the reader anything interesting to think or feel (as the expressive subject) and neither does it capture a kind of experience, but instead what the poem achieves through the use of the lyric I and the act of naming is to express something through the relational structure of the promise.

Addressing, listening and being heard

Talk of the lyric I and how we should treat this in lyric poetry has the potential to obscure another important dimension to the poetic experience, that is, what it is to listen to and hear the voice in the poem (whether that is of the poet-performer or co-created with the reader). Adopting Sedgwick's mode of openness in approach to texts requires that we do not try to fix the perspective of the poem; we should not try to 'own' it or see it only in relation to oneself (for instance, as speaking to me directly). The idea of the relationality of poetry is a consequence of poetry requiring self-other differentiation. In the case of the performance of poetry, it is the difference between speaker and audience. In the case of page poetry, it is the difference between the words as voiced (as 'sounded' or presented to the mind) and listening to that voice (the reader is involved in both activities). As discussed in the previous chapter, that is not to say that one undergoes a psychotic episode in reading poetry but that one is simultaneously aware of voicing the words of the poem and attending to the voicing of those words in a way one does not usually do when one speaks (it requires attention to the vocalizing of the words; when one speaks, one already knows what one is saying without listening – although, there are cases where what one thinks one says and what one actually says come apart but this just goes to show how inattentive we are to our own vocalizing of speech in everyday life).

The notion of poetic address would not make sense unless we accept some kind of duality in the role of the reader; the giving of voice and listening to voice: 'To some extent, poetry always includes the social realm because poetry's very voice evokes the attentive presence of some other, or its lack: an auditor, significantly absent or present' (Pinsky 2002, p. 30). As argued earlier, this is also reason to reject the identification model of the lyric I. But what is the nature of poetic address? Culler (2015) notes that direct address is rare ('To the reader'), and consequently, this places attentive listening to poetry in a different category to attentive listening in everyday life (I pay attention to others speaking when I think or am made to feel that what is said is relevant to me, either concerns me or is directly addressed to me; in much poetry I am neither directly addressed nor is the poem about me, although I assume it has something of value to say). Although one might argue that due to the nature of poetry in performance that the audience is directly addressed, it's not clear that this is straightforwardly so when we take a closer look. By turning to how the nature of address functions in the performance of poetry, we can see a more complicated picture emerge for both page poetry and poetry in performance.

A distinction emerges here between who or what is addressed in and by the poem and who is the intended listener. A poem may address another person, an inanimate object, an animal or even themselves in an act of self-address but such addressees are rarely intended to be the primary listener of the work. Helen Vendler (2005) argues that poetic address can be understood in terms of 'overhearing'. However, as Culler argues, such analysis suggests that the reader or audience is unintended in the relationship. The poet intends to connect in some way with the audience/reader, whereas overhearing leaves the listener disconnected. Instead, he argues that poetry invokes a triangulation of address: the reader is an intended listener of a relationship of address between the poetic voice and some other. Furthermore, understanding the reader's relationship to the work in terms of overhearing suggests that what one hears is incomplete and the product of inattention. However, the poem is temporally bound (although the poem may invoke meaning beyond what's on the page) and commands the reader's attention; entering into the triangulation of address requires effort on part of the reader. Rather than overhearing, the relationship between reader and poem (and address) might be better captured with the notion of 'witness'. Thinking of the reader and audience as 'bearing witness' suggests they are engaged in an activity that demands a certain kind of responsiveness; in other words, they are brought into a kind of relationship. To illustrate, consider the role of active bystander as a model for the role of witness within a poem. A bystander is merely present but does not act; an *active* bystander, on the other hand, is expected to make value judgements in relation to what is heard; they don't participate in the exchange but are still expected to respond. The difference here can be characterized as the difference between merely hearing and listening.

In providing a general analysis of listening to an object (which includes a speaker), Thomas Crowther argues, 'Listening to O, for example, is not a process that is, necessarily, terminated by hearing O. One generally hears O throughout a period of time during which one listens to it. Similarly, if one watches or looks at O one generally sees O throughout the time that one watches or looks at it' (Crowther 2009, p. 176). What Crowther highlights here is that there is a separation between the activity of hearing and the activity of listening. Although listening entails hearing to have occurred, hearing does not entail that listening takes place. Hearing is a process of absorbing sounds; listening involves attending to the what and where of sound. In poetry, this might be the difference between hearing words spoken and listening to particular words spoken by the performer or by the poetic voice. Hearing is insufficient for relationality because it lacks any reciprocity; it's neutral, passive and inconsequential.

As Crowther points out, the essential difference between mere hearings and listening is to do with 'active attending'. In developing this view, Crowther draws on O'Shaughnessy's (2000) discussion of the notion of 'active attending' in perception: 'The world does not come upon us epistemologically like a clap of thunder, and we most of the time go more than half-way to meet it, actively directing our attention onto whatever outer phenomena happen to interest us' (p. 379). O'Shaughnessy argues that listening is a form of active attending and so invokes the notion of 'Striving-to-listen'/'willing-to-listen':

> given a fixed external auditory object, one might bring to bear upon it various intentional listening-strivings – each with different causal power – and result. This power is in the nature of an attractive power, and its presence is determined by choice. Freely selecting whichever feature interests us, say the timbre of the sound, we overtly open the door to timbre's causal influence upon the attention. And we actively do so. (O'Shaughnessy 2000, p. 397)

Hearing is a passive absorbing of sound, whereas listening involves seeking and attending to sound. Listening cannot happen without the hearer actively contributing to enable the experience of listening: 'In listening one sets oneself up to be causally influenced by particular sounds, and the structure of listening is completed by hearing these sounds' (Crowther 2009, p. 179). The listener is required to maintain attention to what is heard but listening does not bring about the hearing (the former is active, the latter passive); what is required in listening is both perception and attention. Building on Crowther's view, Louise Richardson argues that listening also involves that 'one *agentially* keeps the things that one is monitoring in the foreground of experience' (Richardson

2015, p. 152). Listening therefore involves actively maintaining attention to what is heard and prioritizing, or foregrounding, this in one's experience.

Poetry requires listeners. Not only is the listener intended to hear the poem but the listener must intend to hear it as well. To listen is to meet the demand of what is heard. The relationality of poetry requires the reader/audience to make this kind of effort, to bring themselves into the poetic fold. The poem is where the poetic voice and reader/audience meet, for there is effort required on both sides. The meeting is through listening, not in take-up or identification with the lyric I. Where the sounds as heard and listening come together, a relationship is established between the voice and the reader/audience. The reader's/audience's role is relational, and embedded in the structure of the listening experience is self-other differentiation (in virtue of a different effort being needed to listen to external voices).

Listening to/for loneliness and loss

The notion of self-other differentiation or the 'relationality' of poetry is crucial in understanding the cognitive potential of poetry. My aim in this section is to make the case that in virtue of poetry's potential in revealing relationships between subjects ('I' and 'you'), including poet – poem/addressee – reader/listener, poetry can play an important role in helping one to more fully understand aspects of interpersonal relationships, for instance, loneliness, loss, love and togetherness, that cannot be understood without invoking appreciation of self-other differentiation (even when loss or love are experienced as self-reflexive, there's still a sense in which the self is experienced in a twofold structure, that is, in both a first and second personal way). I will begin by saying more about interpersonal relationships and why such relationships cannot be fully understood without invoking awareness of others. I will then move on to show, through three examples – Claudia Rankine's *Don't Let Me Be Lonely* (2017), Sumita Chakraborty's 'Dear, Beloved' (2019) and Maggie Nelson's *Bluets* (2009) – how the relationality of lyric poetry helps to better understand the value and significance of human relationships. All three are page poems (although I have seen Chakraborty read her poem at the Verve Poetry festival, UK, 2019, and so will also draw on the experience of her poem in performance). Implicit here is that one of the differences in the value of page poetry and poetry in performance is how they deal with relationality. In page poetry, it is predominately the singular relation between I and you; in poetry in performance, it is the plural relations between we, us and a plural you.

There are some aspects of thought that are necessarily intersubjective/interpersonal. Some second-person and first-person plural thought depend on self-expression of others in order to grasp it. My witnessing of another's expression will generate corresponding you-thoughts. Of course, my thought 'you are wearing a disgusting T-shirt' does not depend in any way on another's self-expression and instead involves one's own expression of disgust. However, there are many thoughts that do in fact make reference to another's act of self-expression; for example, 'you found that T-shirt to be disgusting' – for this to go beyond mere assertion, I would need to make reference to your expression of disgust towards the T-shirt. My witnessing and interpreting of your self-expression provides the evidential grounds for my thought about you. Equally, we can give such analysis of 'we'-thoughts[12] of the nature 'we found that disgusting', which refers to a set of people having expressed disgust towards an object of joint attention.

You-thoughts and I-thoughts are not only important for capturing a range of thoughts about other people but are important for our grasp of some concepts that concern the interpersonal (concepts that necessitate self-other differentiation). Take for instance, the concept of loneliness. One of the key aspects of grasping the concept of loneliness is to contrast it with solitude. Being alone is not sufficient to make this distinction. Instead, what is needed is grasp of a perceived absence of (valuable) connection with others coupled with a desire for connection with others. Solitude lacks the desire. That seems simple enough on the surface – surely such a distinction is available through thinking alone? However, what is missing is the social dimension to this thought, in other words, acknowledgement of the lack: what it means to connect with others, that is, understanding what is of value here in order to recognize and appreciate the lack. We cannot appreciate what an absence of connection means without being able to appreciate what it is to be connected to others (e.g. what the lack is that loneliness refers to). People experience loneliness in all sorts of ways. In some cases, people are lonely despite having lots of social contacts. It is particular kinds of valuable contact and connection that are lacking.

As Gibson argues, 'To count as possessing full understanding of something, we must reveal not only that we have the relevant concepts and representational capacities. We must also show that we are *alive* to those patterns of value, significance, and meaning that are given expression in the aspects of the world that we otherwise merely know' (Gibson 2007, p. 107). Applying Gibson's thought to interpersonal relationships, it is not sufficient to know some definition of the concept. To count as truly understanding what loneliness is involves having the right kind of response, to be alive to recognizing in what respect someone is lonely (what is it that they desire that they lack?). One must be able to grasp the value and significance of certain kinds of relationships. According to Gibson, literature can offer a demonstration of what it is to possess full understanding including what it is to be 'alive to patterns of value, significance, and meaning' through representations of dynamic interactions.

'Understanding, if fully possessed, establishes a type of dramatic relation between a knower and the world. It places us in the world as agents who are responsive to the range of values and experiences that are the mark of human reality' (Gibson 2007, p. 108). The work of literature does not merely present content but also has a response to it, and it is through that response that as readers we are witnesses to acknowledgement. Although Gibson's concern is with what the work of literature does, or what it shows, we can make claims from this about its value for the reader. In witnessing demonstration of what it is to possess full understanding (but equally valuable is to witness a lack of understanding where the work highlights such a lack), a reader has the opportunity to reflect on their own understanding. Consequently, what literature offers is not novel conceptual knowledge but an opportunity to see concepts 'as very precisely shaped human situations. And this contextualization of these concepts, this act of presenting them to us in concrete form, is literature's contribution to understanding, the particular light it has to shine on our world' (Gibson 2007, p. 116).

Connection and Disconnection: 'I am still lonely'

Thomas Dumm characterises loneliness as a deeply social and relational concept: 'Loneliness is deeply entangled in all paths of life because it reveals in sharp profile some of the most important limits of who we are and how we are with each other. It may be said that loneliness is fundamental to the very constitution of our selves' (2008, p. 26). The experience of loneliness is an experience of a separation or disconnection from others, that is, an awareness of the space between us that enables one to move away (or towards) another: 'When the reach of our selves to others becomes so fragmented and confused that we find ourselves arrested, or halted, or otherwise blocked from contact with them and from ourselves, we become lonely' (Dumm 2008, p. 28). An understanding of loneliness involves an appreciation of affective connection and disconnection with awareness of the seeming impossibility of lack of presence of connection. But how do we come to appreciate the affective here? Dumm compares loneliness to the experience of pain, and therefore something we can only know through experience; it is beyond words: 'rather than destroying the world, [loneliness] establishes a barrier between the self and the world, leaving the world intact as a torment to the isolated person' (2008, p. 32).

Recalling Mitchell Green's view of self-expression as discussed in Chapter 1, we can argue that if self-expression (and the reception of self-expression) involves access to another's perspective in some form, thereby extending 'perceptual reach', then communing with others (expressing and witnessing expression) is an important source of information for development of meaning of interpersonal relationships. In witnessing another's self-expression of loneliness (including affect), I am in a position to not only come to know my own loneliness but I come to my own loneliness with the additional information from your act of self-expression of loneliness. What results in the reader is a form of relational expression (in other words, awareness of what connects the reader and the poet through what is expressed).

Claudia Rankine's *Don't Let Me Be Lonely* (2017) not only presents a dynamic relationship between knower and the world in terms of what loneliness means but reveals the lack at the core of loneliness in the relationality established with the reader. Throughout the poem, there's a separation between the first and second person, between the 'me' and 'you', between the self-expression in the poem and my reading of the words. The resulting experience of reading this work is loneliness itself; that wanting to connect with another but ultimately failing by virtue of the fundamental aloneness and individuality that characterizes the human condition.

Define loneliness?

Yes.

It's what we can't do for each other.

> What do we mean to each other?
>
> What does life mean?
>
> Why are we here if not for each other?[13]

Rankine's poem not only is about loneliness but expresses loneliness through the disconnect in response, and the ambiguity in whose voice is speaking (is it a single voice or multiple?).[14] According to Roberts and Krueger (2021) 'loneliness [is] an emotion that essentially concerns absence . . . the experience of loneliness involves the feeling that certain social goods are missing and out of reach, either temporarily or permanently' (p. 2). To experience loneliness in vocal expression would be to fail to solicit a call to attention or response of another. Hearing other voices but failing to be heard oneself can deepen the feeling of loneliness and what it means to be lonely. In this way, we can also see Rankine's poem as *enacting* loneliness since the questions call for a response from another that is not met. And the reader is unable to address the poet through their response to what's written on the page, thereby intensifying the experience of enactment of loneliness – the reader becomes isolated in their desire to respond to the voice of the poem. The reader/audience is actively attending to the words of the poem – they are present yet left isolated. The singular voice offers a response that undermines attempts at connection, thereby reinforcing the sense of isolation and loneliness expressed by the work. Through active listening/striving to listen, the reader/audience is placed in a relationship of disconnect.

> Life is a form of hope?
>
> If you are hopeful.
>
> Maybe hope is the same as breath – part of
> what it means to be human and alive.
>
> Or maybe hoping is the same as waiting.
> It can be futile.
>
> Waiting for what?
>
> For a life to begin.
>
> I am here.
>
> And I am still lonely.[15]

Rankine highlights those things that we share individualistically, such as breathing, waiting and hoping. These are all things I must do individually but you do these things too. Although my breath is not shared with you, we both share in breathing. My waiting and hoping are also mine but we can wait and hope together. But that is still to acknowledge the space between us.

Presence and absence: 'I wish you could know this feeling'

The notion of loss bears some relationship to loneliness in that to appreciate the state of loss is to acknowledge the impossibility to solicit a response from the other. Both loss and loneliness are relational, requiring an appreciation of connection and disconnection between people. Unlike loneliness, which is vague about what is lacking, loss relates to absence or lack of something that was once present but is no longer. Chakraborty's elegy for her sister, 'Dear, Beloved', uses the first person (the lyric I) to express loss through its singularity. The poem presents her 'visio', that is, her dreamscapes, which provide the backdrop to the lyric I and its relationship of unfulfilled address to her sister and other objects of loss.

Writing about 'Dear, beloved', Anthony Vahni Capildeo comments:

> Chakraborty's great lament is a positive assertion, an act of world-building, the reclamation of life – a treatise, among other things, on love and carnal being, addressed to one who cannot know such things. From the outset, the narrator is a creator. She establishes whatever is to come as paradoxically neither present nor future. Whatever ensues must be understood as belonging in conditional time ('It would be winter'), which is also transhistorical time, illuminated by the spotlight movement of an 'aged sunbeam.' (2019, p. 5)

In their commentary, Capildeo points to the tension at the heart of the piece: the voice of the poem uses words to create a world as an offering to her sister that cannot be fulfilled. The strange temporal status of the visio moves back and forth to connect the present to her sister yet the landscapes continue to push forward as winter melts to spring and so on.

> It would be winter, with a thin snow. An aged sunbeam
> would fall on me, then on a nearby summit, until a mass
> of ice would come upon me like a crown of master diamonds
> in shades of gold and pink. The base of the mountains

would be still in darkness. The snow would melt,
making the mountain uglier. The ice would undertake
a journey toward dying. My iliacus, from which orchids bloom,
would learn to take an infant's shape, some premature creature
weaned too soon. My femoral nerve, from which lichen grows
in many shades, would learn to take breaths of its own
and would issue a moan so labored it could have issued
from two women carrying a full-length wooden casket, with dirt
made from a girl inside. The dirt would have been buried
with all of the girl's celestial possessions. Bearing the casket
would demand more muscles than earthbound horses have.
The girl would have been twenty-four. This was my *visio*.
Sometimes I think of it as prophecy. Other times, history.
For years it was akin to some specific land, with a vessel
that would come for me, able to cross land, sea, the spaces
of the universe, able to burrow deep into the ground.[16]

Throughout the descriptions of mountains, horses, sunbeams, snow, fog, plant material from lichen to orchids to prairie grasses draws a landscape of visible and invisible relations – a surface that places things in juxtaposition that are connected beneath the surface. Longing and loss are experienced as the shifting out of view of what was once rooted together. Her visio magnifies the loss not only through the repeated return to the death of her sister but in the overwhelming, all-consuming pull back into the imagined world of the visio. The poem captures the desperation to bring things to mind in the imagination as the only way to feel connected to the object of loss. But it acknowledges the impossibility of imagining this as a sanctuary. Instead, it decays (as memory decays) and infects, for instance, the beauty of snow melting, which could have evoked hope and promise but instead merely leaves 'the mountain uglier'. The passing of time moves one further away from the object of loss.

Hearing Chakraborty perform this poem brought to the fore awareness of the insignificance of the present versus the absent. No matter how many listeners are in the audience, their listening is not enough to meet the need/desire expressed. The relationship of audience to poet-performer reveals the significance of the particular, singular and small as having special value, which is at the core of experience of grief: the small becomes large in its absence. The poem shifts from vast landscapes (including the minutiae that contribute to the landscape) to the intimacy and smallness of the I and you, that is, a very present I (as related to the voice sounding in the theatre space) and absent you (that fails to respond and remains mute).

> ... Sister, I was very young
> when I found out you were cloven-hooved. I did what I could.
> I want to say that you can trust me, that I am listening to you,
> and that you can speak to me and that I will speak to you
> at last. Tell me about the beasts that got you.[17]

One of the ways this poem expresses loss is through the sense of the impossible response in the use of address. The poem expresses for the intended listener as witness of loss, as the one who is in a position to judge the failure of response on part of the addressee. 'I am listening to you' yet the effort and attention involved in listening is futile.

> ... I want to say:
> Sister, I promise. But the definition of *myth* is *noun*,
> the idea that any one creature can ever hear another.[18]

The contrast in the declaration 'I want to say' collapses into the 'myth' of being heard. The failure to be heard by her sister transforms into a failure of anyone hearing another.

Private and public: 'This is how much I miss you'

Maggie Nelson's *Bluets*, a long poem (or sequence of aphorisms), speaks about depression, fixation, love and loss through an exploration of blue. One of the significant things about colour is that it has both a public/objective and private/subjective quality. We have a shared language to talk about colours, yet we can never know how colours are experienced by an individual or how colours show up as significant for some particular person. Nelson's *Bluets* brings this dichotomy of the public/objective/scientific and the private/subjective/affective to the fore.

> I admit that I may have been lonely. I know that loneliness can produce bolts of hot pain ... which ... can begin to simulate, or to provoke ... an apprehension of the divine.[19]

The personal/private revelation in 'I admit that I may have been lonely' is followed by an attempt to connect with common feeling and experience.

The 'I know' places the description of loneliness at a distance; this belongs to the public understanding of loneliness, an understanding that tries to cast loneliness as a positive (through isolation from others, one becomes connected to 'the divine').

> It is easier, of course, to find dignity in one's solitude. Loneliness is solitude with a problem. Can blue solve the problem, or can it at least keep me company within it?[20]

It is not the divine she finds in her loneliness but the experience of connectedness to the colour blue. Part of being lonely is having awareness of one's aloneness. Her connectedness to the physical space, to blue, is a reminder of her existence, which is necessary for recognizing a lack of connection to others.

Throughout *Bluets*, Nelson grapples with the space between her experience and response and how this is interpreted by others:

> Eventually I confess to a friend some details about my weeping. . . .
>
> This is the dysfunction talking. This is the disease talking. This is how much I miss you talking.[21]

The failure or avoidance of addressing those witnessing her depression and aloneness represents a loss of hope at the heart of her experience. Self-other differentiation consumes the personal, intimate revelations of feeling to reduce to unfeeling, public and empty language of love, loss and depression: 'Perhaps it is becoming clearer why I felt no romance when you told me that you carried my last letter with you, everywhere you went . . . unopened . . . I wrote it because I had something to say to you.'[22]

The reader is drawn into the public/shared-private/not-shared dichotomy. The factual language is easily grasped by the reader but lacks meaning and grounding in experience (and affect). The private can only be gestured at. The words 'I had something to say' gesture at the value of self-expression that feels impossible to communicate or share with others, which Nelson presents as being similar to how we might attempt to share in experience and beauty of certain colours: we can publicly appear to be sharing in experience and value of the colour blue, for instance, collecting blue objects and expressing one's aesthetic judgement using shared language, but in the end all we are doing is hoping that some connection between our private, subjective experiences emerges from the relationships between the objects of our attention.

One of the problems with the identification model is it doesn't take seriously the demands of listening. 'Appropriating' (and I use that word provocatively) words of a poem is to fail to take seriously others as having an important voice, as having a perspective worth sharing. We need not embrace actual intentionalism in order to see language as being intentional and expressing a way of thinking, feeling and experiencing the world that is different to our own.

Conclusion

Although Cavell is discussing theatrical performance and the way audiences relate to the characters performed on stage, what he says about presentness is important to understanding the reading and experiencing of voice in poetry. He writes:

> It is in making their present ours, their moments as they occur, that we complete our acknowledgement of them. But this requires making their present *theirs*. And that requires us to face not only the porousness of our knowledge (or, for example, the motives of their actions and the consequences they care about) but the repudiation of our perception altogether. (1969/2002, p. 310)

In making the voice of the poem present, we are able to give it a location and it is only in locating the voice/s in the poetic work that we can be brought into relation. In other words, we are brought to acknowledge self-other differentiation. Commenting on Cavell, Maria Jose Alcarez Leon writes:

> separateness between the spectator and the work and formal autonomy – and what this formal autonomy reveals in terms of the necessities that arise from a particular grammar – are intimately intermingled. Without separateness, the characteristic experience of dramatic necessity will not be possible and, hence, the kind of insight that experiencing these sets of dramatic necessities affords would not be available. (2023, p. 208)

If we fail to appreciate the distinction and separation between my voice (and perspective) and that on offer in the poem, then we fail to experience all that the poem has to offer, and as I will argue in the final chapter, this will mean missing out on important aspects of cognitive value that the poem has to offer.

The idea of relationality is not meant to exclude the lyric I as singular or plural but rather it aims to capture the fundamental or foundational structure of the first-person and second-person pronoun in lyric poetry. In the use of the I and/or you in a poem, the poet is drawing attention to the relationship that is structurally implicit in the use of these pronouns. In reading a work of poetry that uses the first-person pronoun, we experience the words with awareness of the presence of another as distinct from oneself. According to the relational model, rather than focusing on what is shared, we come to appreciate moments of sharing and overlap through interaction, through connection that is forged between the I and you, between the poet and reader and the poetic text.

3

A sense of us

Individual and collective voices

Introduction

In the previous chapter, the focus was on interpersonal relationships that are singular in the sense that they require appreciation of the relationship (or lack of) between one person and another. The focus in this chapter is on interpersonal relationships that are plural in the sense that they require appreciation of how the individual relates to others (i.e. more than one other), take for instance, community, family, togetherness and belonging. The first-person plural ('we' and 'us') is at the core of such interpersonal relationships: at once making reference to a group that is connected in some way, yet still spoken from an individual, first-person perspective. This plural understanding of interpersonality involves recognition of self-other differentiation but within the context of a group, the individual within the collective, the self in relation to the social. Such interpersonal relationships also capture an achievement: it is something that can happen from a coming together of people but is not guaranteed. This point is expressed in Imtiaz Dharker's poem 'This Line, This Thread' (2018). The poem is structured around drawing lines, seeking connections and seeing what results. The poem is an invitation to make connections within the self (from heart to mouth), between people (your neighbour, your face) and then to consider what it is to create something through connection. Here we get the image of the thread:

> loop it to others, weave it to lace.
> Spread it out to see if the holes
> are an imperfection or a kind of grace.[1]

The presentation of the disjunction between imperfection and grace reveals the achievement at the heart of interpersonal relationships, in particular the richness of our communities. In our most treasured relationships, we often have both: grace despite imperfection, grace because of imperfection.

At the heart of understanding plural interpersonal relationships is an appreciation of what it is to relate to others, that is, having a 'sense of us' (e.g. shared identity, joint action, collective intention), which involves relationality, mutuality and cooperation. As John Searle argues, having a sense of us is not merely relating to others but involves some kind of awareness of that relationship to others and may even require mutual awareness. He goes on to add that 'others are agents like yourself, that they have a similar awareness of you as an agent like themselves, and that these awarenesses coalesce into a sense of us as possible or actual collective agents. And these conditions hold even for total strangers' (Searle 2002, p. 104). What's important to highlight here is that a 'sense of us' is prior to the establishment of a community, since this awareness of the possibility of reflection on the actual connection between individuals is necessary for embedding the connections that form the group or community. A sense of us makes possible a community but it does not guarantee it. However, a group having a sense of us only comes about where mutual awareness of those in relationship is brought to the fore.

There is a basic 'sense of us', which is a simple awareness of a gathering of people, and then there is an ethically thicker 'sense of us', which goes beyond merely having an awareness to holding one another to a set of expectations: 'To the degree to which the family really functions as a group (and not as a couple of parents simply dragging their kids along), it is assumed that there is something between the participants in virtue of which each individual is licensed to see the others as having (tacitly) agreed to (or at least accepted) their being a group' (Schmid 2014, p. 12). On this view, a 'sense of us' goes beyond an individual's recognition that others are in relation to them, to also hold that this relationality generates a set of expectations of one another. A sense of us therefore involves both internal conditions (recognizing that the demands of the group are relevant to me) and external conditions (having the relevant features to qualify for membership of a group). This distinction helps to make sense of cases in which one thinks they are part of a community but are not (they take the demands of a group to be relevant to them but they do not meet the external conditions of group membership) and in cases where someone is part of a community but fails to meet the standards of the group (they meet the external conditions but fail to meet the internal conditions of group membership).

Here we might flesh this out by appeal to the notion of a shared perspective. Throughout the previous chapters, I have discussed the individual perspective – a network of beliefs, values, commitments, associations and so on that reflects what I care about and prioritizes information (e.g. through perception) accordingly. For Helm 'sharing an evaluative perspective, at least within a certain domain, where this shared evaluative perspective enables each to have the sort of dynamic, rational influence on the other's life that [the relationship] demands' (2012, p. 34). A shared perspective emerges from the negotiation and interaction of two or more people who both have a stake in that sharing. One way to understand a shared perspective is as a kind of contract or agreement. Scanlon argues:

> The parties whose agreement is in question are assumed not merely to be seeking some kind of advantage but also to be moved by the aim of finding principles that others, similarly motivated, could not reasonably reject. The idea of a shared willingness to modify our private demands in order to find a basis of justification that others also have reason to accept. (Scanlon 1998, p. 5)

However, Scanlon's view is too strong in the idea of *demanding* a contract; community is more fluid. Communities can be more or less strong, and emerge and dissolve gradually rather than sudden collapses in community due to a break in contract. Additionally, there needs to be room for disagreement and holding one another to values we thought were important to the community (in some cases that will lead to one recognizing their transgression, in others it may simply result in a change in the perceived values held). We want to have a sense of how we hold one another to expectations but that need not be contractual. Furthermore, Scanlon's view misses the affective richness of what it is to have a sense of us; it is not merely an agreement of some sort but is supported through a feeling of connectedness. We make all sorts of agreements with others, take for instance my agreement with my mortgage lender. This is a contractual relationship but no 'sense of us' emerges from this. I feel no affection or bond towards my mortgage provider and do not engage in any kind of self-reflection in virtue of this agreement.

Rather than contractual, we can understand a shared perspective in terms of sharing a set of values, concerns and commitments:[2] if two people are said to share a perspective perhaps as parents thinking about their children, then they should be able to view a situation with the same set of concerns and pick out what is of value to both of them with reference to their shared identity, that is, what is good for them as parents. Crucially that does not require me to adopt a new perspective but to attempt to separate aspects of my own perspective as shareable (in the sense of overlap) with another's. I can understand myself both as an individual and as a member of a group, for example, as a parent. In other words, I can distinguish what I care about from what we care about as parents of our child (or at least what I think we *ought* to care about). The former includes the latter, of course, but not vice versa.

On Helm's view, what we share with another is a pattern of emotions and desires that reflect a commitment to the import of certain things as tied to an intersubjective understanding of self that is established by that relationship, which can happen to a greater or lesser extent. Such a pattern takes time to emerge and is shaped through the establishing of a group and ongoing interactions. We can deliberate with one another about values we share to form a shared pattern of emotions and desires. Our shared perspective brings to the fore those things that we *jointly* take to be significant (as a product of our interactions and negotiations; in other words, there is mutual influence), and this is something that need not be fixed but can evolve as the group evolves (over time as well as due to change in membership). So long as each person has a stake in that shared perspective and where mutuality is present, they are a member of the group or community.

The role poetry can play in helping one to better understand such interpersonal relationships is twofold: first, it can *display* connections. It can raise awareness of the different ways in which we can relate to one another as a community; and second, it can show us what it is to *make* connections. Poetry has the potential to show what it is to bring different voices together and create feelings of togetherness, belonging and community through writing and performing poetry. The use of the first-person plural in poetry might be used as a testing ground for a potential community. What we will see in the following examples is an attempt to invoke plurality, togetherness and 'sense of us' that collapses back into the singular 'I'. Building on the arguments in Chapter 2, this presents another example of where the use of first-person pronouns is not fixed or stable but attempts to draw attention to a kind of structure. The first-person plural may express a feeling of connection with others (joint attention and joint action) that is not sufficiently grounded in the formation of a shared perspective, awareness or understanding.

In this chapter, I will sketch the different ways lyric poetry can contribute to an understanding of community: there are some poems about community (content) and those produced through collaboration but there are other ways that poetry contributes to this achievement of community through reception and also by forging connections (enacting community/laying the foundations of community).

Community, sharing and togetherness

Community can be defined simply as a group of people who share something in common whether that is a shared set of concerns, geography, experience, values and/or beliefs. It is clear then that the individual must possess certain features in virtue of which they relate to others, or in other words, the thing that connects them. On one level, one might wonder what more needs to be said about community and why it is that poetry can help facilitate further reflection. The answer lies in the fact that this definition is inadequate to explain why it is that *that* feature connects individuals in a non-superficial way and why such coming together is valuable. Merely sharing something in common is not enough to create a community although the common is necessary for community formation. According to Jean Luc Nancy, the common is a foundational aspect of human experience. He writes, 'The common should be understood at once as the banal – that is, the element of a primordial equality irreducible to any effect of distinction – and, indistinguishably, as shared, in other words, that which only takes place in, through, and as relation' (Nancy 2016, p. 1). If the common is the basis of what connects individuals, there must be something in addition that strengthens the bond between them and elevates those relations in significance.

Sharing is not necessarily the sharing of a particular property (on its own, that would get us to a group or collection not a community); there must also be a particular kind of relationship between those individuals that might manifest in collective action, joint attention or simply mutuality and reciprocity. What transforms a mere group to a community is a sense of care, belonging/acceptance and solidarity with other members of a group (even if only momentary). The grouping is not something external to those individuals and imposed on them (for instance, people attending the same university) but forged by those individuals.

It is important to acknowledge that an individual is never just a member of one community but many (both small and large). For instance, I am a member of a family unit, a geographic place (the village in which I live), a workplace (together with my colleagues in the philosophy department) but also those who are committed to researching the philosophy of art and literature. The first three communities are easy to identify. I simply have to look around and see who else is in my community. However, the community of philosophers working on art and literature is a community I have a stake in, yet its membership may not be fully in view. This still counts as a community since in virtue of my membership I have a disposition to care about the contribution other members of that community make. This may manifest itself in attending talks and reading books by those I do not know personally but who are making a contribution to the field. As the community is dependent on its members having such a disposition, it does not mean that one must be actively contributing to the field – each must share this disposition, and if they were to make a contribution, this would activate the disposition of others. Communities overlap and intersect. I mentioned two communities – my family unit and the village in which I live. The family unit is a part of the village community but separable from it. The notion of community that I am developing here is one that is both active and unstable, or at least, requiring active participation, reciprocity and mutuality to sustain it. The forming of one community may (temporarily) dissolve another.

Momtaza Mehri's poem 'Glory Be to the Gang Gang Gang' (2019) is a celebration of a community of people who have relocated (displaced, migrated) and come together:

> In praise of all that is honest, call upon the acrylic tips
> and make a minaret out of a middle finger, gold-dipped
> and counting. In the name of Filet-O-Fish, pink lemonade,
> the sweat on an upper lip, the backing swell and ache
> of Abdul Basit Abdus Samad on cassette tape, a clean jump shot,
> the fluff of Ashanti's sideburns, the rice left in the pot

the calling cards and long waits, the seasonal burst
of baqalah-bought dates.

Every time they leave and come back
alive.

Birthmarks shaped like border disputes.
Black sand. Shah Rukh's dimples, like bullets
taking our aunts back to those summer nights,
these blessings on blessings on blessings.

Give me the rub of calves,
rappers sampling jazz,
the char of frankincense
and everything else that makes sense
in a world that don't.[3]

The poem makes reference to the value of multicultural communities in which people bring together different aspects of their own cultural heritage to share with others. The poem shifts through references to Somali, Muslim, Bollywood and British (youth) culture that signal the roots of the community as stretching far and wide yet are brought together with a sense of cohesion, specificity and uniqueness that is reflected in individual moments. The poem searches for where the bonds are located, that is, whether these things alone or together make for a sense of belonging. The poem also gestures at (unspoken) trauma of refugee communities, such as references to 'border disputes', comparing Shah Rukh's dimples to bullets and the phrase 'they come back / alive'. Yet these references are suppressed by the celebration of community (as they are blended into the description). Rather than suggesting such trauma is itself suppressed, the poem gestures more towards the value of belonging and togetherness as being unshaken by past trauma (the sense of belonging doesn't arise from sharing traumatic experiences).

The idea of 'community' suggests being more than the sum of its parts (for instance, the common phrase 'stronger together'): 'Every time they leave, they come back / alive.' Relationality is what community brings that's more than the collection of individuals. However, a complexity emerges since community cannot be understood as a singular entity either. Not just because community never has a singular voice (although there might be a collective voice) but also because communities themselves are not stable entities: communities form and dissolve; they intersect and diverge. What is revealed is that community is possible in the absence of a unified voice. To make clear, my issue here is not the ontological status of a community: even if there was an object that was the community, this wouldn't help us understand what makes that a community since communities involve individuals relating to one another. Understanding those relationships goes beyond knowing *that* individuals relate to one another; we must also understand the meaning of those relationships.

Jean Luc Nancy argues that we must recognize that an individual is never separable from others; the foundation of human life is *being-with*. In other words, understanding of human existence is necessarily understanding humans as coexisting. He argues that our existence is defined through relationality, through connection to others. Through his conception of *being-with*, Nancy tries to capture an understanding of community that preserves the idea that groups, collectives and so on are made up of individuals but are not reducible to those individuals:

> It is obvious that *we* exist inseparably from our society, if *one* understands by this neither our organizations nor our institutions, but rather our *sociation*, which is certainly something more and something other than an association (as contract, a convention, a grouping, a collective, or a collection). Sociation is a coexisting condition that is coessential to *us*. (Nancy 2010, p. 103)

Talk of 'we' to grasp our connectedness with one another is inadequate since it doesn't capture the relationality of the individual. Equally, the first person 'I' is only required to differentiate one from others. Community must also therefore respect self-other differentiation; in other words, acknowledgement of how the individual relates to others only comes from a recognition that the community is made of individuals. While reflecting the meaningful connection between people, that is, 'being-in-common', community also depends on the differences between individuals. Nancy's emphasis is on the individual as connected; for him, there is nothing to bring awareness of the individual self if not in relation to others, which necessarily depends on there being connection to others. He writes, being-with 'is always a proximity, not only a brushing against but a reciprocal action, an exchange, a relation of more or less mutual exposure. It is not pure concomitance' (Nancy 2010, p. 104). We are not mere bodies existing alongside one another but we interact, share and exchange. In this sense, for Nancy the notion of 'being with' implies community (not necessarily developed and stable) for it involves relationality, mutuality and reciprocity. However, what he misses is the importance of individuality and difference between people. Relationality only has significance when it is connecting despite difference.

For instance, the community referenced in Mehri's poem are not united by their trauma since each has different experiences and a different story to tell. Instead, where community emerges is through developing significance of certain things and moments together (despite their trauma): by creating meaning together and experiencing a 'being-with' in rituals of drinking pink lemonade and eating McDonalds. These are not things that are private, even though one might attach private meaning to them. They are experienced with a sense of being in common yet valued individually.

Not only can works such as Mehri's help us to better understand the meaning, value and significance of community, poetry raises awareness of how language use itself connects us, which is important in both community formation and community identity. Poetry can achieve a sense of 'being with' through exploiting features of public language from the particular use of words, and playing with grammar and syntax. For example, the final lines of Mehri's poem: 'and everything else that makes sense / in a world that don't'. This use of 'don't' rather than 'doesn't' will resonate with those who also use 'don't' in this manner and therefore produce a sense of connection. The use of the voice makes clear the duality of language to be at once private and public, and in the speaking voice, the private enters into the public and therefore adds to the public atmosphere and connects to those who can hear that voice. As a further, more complex example, consider Caleb Femi's poem 'Community' (2020), in which he uses colloquialisms and slang that connect with working-class areas of south London (such as the North Peckham Estate, where Femi grew up): 'you'ge'me / you can't pass thru my bits / do you know who man is? ... true to say you look like a fed / you a fed /on some obbo shit / so what you doing on my block then?'[4]

Language is the stuff of the common; we share it with others but we also make it our own (with our own private meanings and systems of associations). In using language and its resources, the poet is contributing to the atmosphere of public discourse by extending the use of words and offering alternative uses and meanings. In Mehri's poem, the references to Filet-O fish, pink lemonade and so on are not mere mention of stuff but stuff that has significance to the community she is writing about. Where communication succeeds, there is a sense that the poet succeeds in altering public language since another was able to recognize that use of words in meaning-making. In writing poetry and making that public, the poet is performing an act or an offering that implies a desire to connect with other users of language, not only in successful expression but in affecting public language by establishing connections and associations.

> For a writer, it is language that carries thought, perception and meaning. And it does so through a largely metonymic process, through the discovery and invention of associations and connections. Though it may seem merely technical, the notion of linkage – of forging connections – has in my mind a concomitant political and social dimension. Communities of phrases spark the communities of ideas in which communities of persons live and work. (Hejinian 2000, p. 166)

Lyric poetry raises awareness of the social bonds that are carried in language, of the way associations and connections are shared, which is something obscured in our everyday use as we focus not on the mechanisms of communication but merely on succeeding in communicating.

In his discussion of Nancy, Butchart argues for the centrality of communication and language to the idea of *being-with*: 'To be human is to exist communicatively, a constant task that demands awareness of human coexistence as we are "suspended in language" together' (Butchart 2019, p. 13). Being a user of language ties us together. In speaking, I use the words of others, not as belonging to them but as shared with them.

> the word is not a material thing but rather the eternally mobile, eternally fickle medium of dialogic interaction. It never gravitates toward a single consciousness or a single voice. The life of the word is contained in its transfer from one mouth to another, from one context to another, from one social collective to another, from one generation to another. In this process the word does not forget its own path and cannot completely free itself from the power of those concrete contexts into which it has entered. (Bakhtin 1984/1999, p. 202)

The poet voices words that have been used by people before them and will be used again. Public language is the medium for our own stories, and in this sense one's own story expressed in words cannot be uncoupled from the stories of other language users. However, one's perspective is expressed in the way one uses words, that is, the way lines and sentences are formed to create meaning and bring concepts into relation in the poem. And with each modification of articulation or meaning, there is a potential uptake of their perspective on the linguistic community (even if only one other is affected by this use of language).

Language is a powerful medium for expressing community and through which we can negotiate to form a shared perspective. Language as common enables community formation; communities form by forging linkages, making connections and associations together. Poetry can show us what it is to forge such connections and associations and how a negotiation of perspectives can offer a sense of belonging and a sense of us (the grounds for community).

Self-other differentiation and the (dis)connected voice

In this section, I want to complicate the view of the way in which the first-person plural operates in poetry. Previously, I outlined a positive account whereby a 'sense of us' emerges from the voicing of the poem, thereby gesturing at the relationality at the heart of community. However, use of the first-person plural doesn't always successfully pick out a group but instead gestures for connection that may be left unmet by another/others. In such cases, the 'us' or 'we' simply refers to a lyric I that desires connection; it is a fragile or illusory 'sense of us' that fails to be supported by the mutuality and reciprocity required for togetherness. In voicing the first-person plural, one gestures at the group voice, at a speaking with others, yet this is not always successful in speaking together. What the poetic use of the first-person plural can reveal is a desire for connection that may be left unfulfilled.

'Us' by Zaffar Kunial (2018) explores the meaning of the first-person plural and how the use of 'us' expresses the desire and promise of connection and reveals the ways in which 'us' is a claim to community (even if unfounded):

> If you ask me, *us* takes in *undulations* –
> each wave in the sea, all insides compressed –[5]

Even the phrase 'tell us where yer from', in which 'us' actually means 'me' is an invitation to another to share – not a sharing of a particular property but a sharing through exchange and mutual acknowledgement (in this case, where the other is from) – and such sharing offers opportunity for connection, to transform the me of you and I to an 'us'. But the 'I' can also offer itself up to an 'us' as in the example of supporting a football team; I choose to become a member of an 'us' perhaps only ever glimpsing (e.g. through the collective action of giving a standing ovation) the bigger of which one is a part. But as the first line, 'If you ask me, *us* takes in *undulations*', suggests, 'us' is not a simple concept but expresses shifting relations (connections made – brought together as 'us' – and connections dissolved, tightening and loosening). 'Us' is only ever temporary and requires active connection, which is revealed through the experience of hearing each utterance (and assertion) of 'us'; in other words, with each 'us' there is an attempt to bring a group together but the poem is unable to keep track of one group throughout. The connection gestured by 'us' depends on reciprocity; I cannot make an 'us' alone: 'I'd love to think I could stretch to it – us':

> I hope you get, here, where I'm coming from.
> I hope you're with me on this – between love
>
> and loss – where I'd give myself away, stranded
> as if the universe is a matter of one stress.
> Us. I hope, from here on, I can say it
>
> and though far-fetched, it won't be too far wrong.[6]

The separation of 'love' and 'loss' between the sixth and seventh stanzas quoted here expresses the fragility of 'us'. Throughout the poem, each stanza pivots around 'us'. However, by the sixth stanza, 'us' loses out to the separation of 'I' and 'you', which expresses the idea that because an us involves the actions of others, I cannot guarantee alone that we have succeeded in creating an 'us'. All I can do is hope: 'hope you're with me on this.'

Plural interpersonal relationships such as togetherness, sharing and community require that one appreciates simultaneously self-other differentiation (that the collective is made up of individuals) and relationality (that there is something that brings these individuals together, not merely a something shared but how each relates to one another such as a particular disposition towards one another in virtue of some shared property). For instance, members of a linguistic community use the same words but bring different meaning to those words both in terms of differing connotations or associations and indexicality (the quality of being spoken by *that* person at *that* time), yet it is through use of language that we can deepen relationships between people:

> We humans are social animals . . . a central feature of our lives that is characteristically human is our use of language – to relay information, to teach, to play, to gossip, to coordinate, and ultimately to reinforce our social connections with others. It would be absurd to deny the obvious and fundamentally social nature of humans, even as we acknowledge that individual humans can live, and can live quite well, in isolation from others. (Helm 2017, p. 1)

Conversation (i.e. speaking *with* another) is a basic form of community building; through the act of speaking, listening and acknowledging the other, a common space forms. To hear another is to be brought into relation with that other. In *Poetry and the Fate of the Senses*, Susan Stewart observes, 'When we invoke or call for sound, we bring ourselves, too, into a certain path: we take our place in time. And when we attribute sound to a voice, we wonder what figure will be made, who speaks and from where – when the voice arrives, we learn something, too, about where we stand' (2002, p. 145). Voice is the very thing that enables reciprocity and mutual exposure; hearing another's voice locates me (in space and time) as the one hearing those sounds, but it also locates me in the sense of call to response (as discussed in the previous chapter). How I respond and how I participate either reveals the self to the other/others, and therefore laying the foundation for community, or it fails to acknowledge the other, and therefore prevents connection.

Acknowledgement of a community (either that one is part of the community or excluded from it) is to acknowledge one's individual relationship to others. Not only does one need to be able to recognise the group as a community but also have an appreciation of how they relate or don't relate to that group. Consequently, such acknowledgement involves self-revelation in that attending to how one does or doesn't relate to others reveals something about the self that would otherwise have gone unnoticed (I can only become aware that I relate or don't to others by attending to possible connection and disconnection). To borrow from Cavell, in the case of gaining awareness of being on the outside of a community, 'What is revealed is my separateness from what is happening to them: that I am I, and here. It is only in this perception of them as separate from me that I make them present. That I make them *other*, and face them' (Cavell 2002, pp. 311–12). Although what Cavell has in mind is the experience of seeing a performance of Othello (and of the performers as being 'other'), there is a more general point to be found as well.

Through my acknowledging of the other, what is revealed is my separateness but that awareness of separateness is relational; what is revealed is self-other differentiation that actively brings 'us' into relation. But what this tells us about the first-person plural is that the nature of the relationships it expresses can be more or less expressive of togetherness. Awareness of relationality brought through self-other differentiation is a form of minimal relationship of 'us'. Cavell goes on to say, 'The only essential difference between them and me is that they are there and I am not. And to empty ourselves of all other difference can be confirmed in the presence of an audience, of the community, because every difference established between us, other than separateness, is established by the community' (2002, p. 312).

Take, for example, Degna Stone's use of the first-person plural in her poem 'Swimming' (2017):

> Knowing that we
> were not what we wanted,
>   we strayed[7]

Much like Zaffar Kunial's 'Us', 'we' doesn't necessarily refer to more than one. It expresses a desire and hope of connection, and an invitation to come along or go along with (the latter bringing with it a sense of power and control of one over the other). There's safety in numbers: we might try to think in terms of the first-person plural to try to provide security for ourselves. The line 'We pulled each other further in' suggests a mutuality in the increasingly risky swim. This mutuality is broken with the introduction of the I and you: 'I waited for you to resurface.' The I and you become disconnected. The use of the first-person plural in the final lines returns us to that idea of 'us' and 'we' being used as singular, albeit with the desire for it to refer to more than the self.

In another poem by Degna Stone, 'The River Gods' (2017), the use of the first-person plural is used to abstract from the individual: 'We gather in packs, congregate in bars.' The poem's use of the first-person plural expresses what it is to be denied an identity and be treated without differentiation: 'We fuck in alleyways, / fake orgasms for a city / that doesn't know who we are.'[8] The 'we' in the poem gestures at a group of individuals without hope, without dignity, without the care of others in virtue of that grouping together without acknowledgement of difference and uniqueness.

To return to Cavell,

> To let yourself matter is to acknowledge not merely how it is with you, and hence to acknowledge that you want the other to care, at least to care to know. It is equally to acknowledge that your expressions in fact express you, that they are yours, that you are in them. This means allowing yourself to be comprehended, something you can always deny. Not to deny it is, I would like to say, to acknowledge your body, and the body of your expressions, to be yours, you on earth, all there will ever *be* of you.(1979, p. 383)

This is precisely what is denied in the use of the first-person plural in 'The River Gods': all that's present is 'we', not I or you. There's no expression of the individual to call for care. The result is an immense feeling of loss and emptiness for 'the souls washed out with the floods', the individual I's washed out with the imposed identity of the group.

Through vocalization, the experience of connection is given through the feeling of response (responding to me/addressing me) and resonance: vocality of one that is exposed to another and exposes the other through creating space *for* the other to respond. The voice enables discussion and exchange, and promotes understanding by exposing one's perspective to others. Resonance indicates the success in such discussion and exchange, as one that has momentum to support ongoing discussion and exchange. Where resonance isn't found, the voice fails to generate action in the other, the action of responding and speaking in response. Consequently 'The River Gods' can be seen as a response to the spectator who fails to distinguish persons.

As Izenberg comments:

> it has often seemed intuitive to see poems as fostering recognition and solidarity between persons. As public objects, poems strive to make their ideas or conceptions of personhood perceptible and durable – if not always immediately legible – to others. In the scoring of the voice, or in their stretching of the word beyond or beneath the horizons of ordinary speech, they produce opportunities for readers and hearers to extend and expand their sympathies, and to identify even the most baroque utterance or repulsive sentiment as the testimony of a fellow mind. (2011, p. 2)

The recognition and solidarity the poem seeks are not internal to the work but to readers. The nature of such recognition and solidarity, according to Izenberg, is with the care and attention one would offer another person. That's not to say that the poem itself ought to be treated as expressive of personhood; rather, through the voicing of the work, the poem creates awareness of the use of language to express and mean. However, he goes on to argue, the success of a poem is very much dependent on the qualities of the reader or audience:

> As objectifications of thought or voice destined for the eyes and ears of others, poems are dependent on the capacities of their readers for attention and perception, interest and pleasure. As a result of this dependency, works of verbal art may seem to emphasize, not the autonomy or dignity of the other of whom they tell, but rather the sense in which persons *themselves* are dependent upon the perceptions and inclinations of others for survival. (2011, p. 3)

What the experience of engaging with poetry presents is awareness of our responsibility towards others in enabling self-expression and the subtleties of the mechanisms that allow aspects of the self to be made present to others. Izenberg's claim is not that we literally encounter persons through poetry; rather, it is in part the artificial nature of poetry's use of language that we are able to reflect on our responsibilities to others.

Multivocal poetics and the choral voice: Enacting community

Susan Stewart views lyric poetry as inherently multivocal. She writes:

> Sound and voice in lyric . . . take part in these common aspects of aurality and the reception of aurality. Yet lyric also is made from silence, from the pull of sound against sense, and from places where voices are at the brink of their individuality. Such voices are filled with the voices of others who have been brought to bear on the speaking or singing person. The person is the vessel of the particular meeting of these particular voices. (Stewart 2002, pp. 145–6)

This is similar to the idea that words are shared and contain traces of other voices; that is, the connections and associations made by others with those words are carried forward in their meaning when used by other members of a linguistic community. However, lyric poetry can more directly call on other voices within a poem by invoking more than an individual's contribution to meaning enrichment of particular words and phrases.

In this section, I want to focus on communities of voice and intersecting voices in poetry. There's a distinction to be drawn between the bilingual voice (a voice that shifts between languages and cultures), collaborative voice (that is the product of more than one author working on the same piece) and the multivocal or choral work (which can exist on the page as well as on the stage).

The multilingual voice

So far, I have used the idea of uniqueness of voice to suggest we each only have one voice; however, that is not necessarily the case. One's voice can evolve through time (this certainly happens on a physiological level with the deepening in register from the voice in childhood to one's voice in later years), but we also have the ability to change our voices depending on who we are seeking to connect with. More radically, those who are bilingual (or multilingual) are able to shift between and blend together culturally distinct voices. Take, for instance, the work of poets such as Daljit Nagra (who uses Punjabi words and cultural references in his poetry). Here's an extract from his poem 'This Be the Pukka Verse':

> Tromping home trumps – here come the cummerbund
> sahibs tipsy with stiff upper lips
> for burra pegs of brandy pawnee,
> pink gin and the Jaldi punkawallaaahhhh![9]

What's notable in Nagra's use of Punjabi is how the words are connected together through assonance and consonance (e.g. the 's' sound of 'sahibs tipsy', and the 'y' sound of 'brandy pawnee'). By forging such linkages in sound, English and Punjabi are presented together as a unified language of the poem, reflecting how multilingual speakers will not always translate everything into their second language (which transfers to second, third generations etc. who may be taught the Punjabi words for particular things first and absorb those words and phrases into their everyday language, thereby extending and expanding their English vocabulary to include Punjabi rather than treating them as separate languages to translate between).

Yomi Ṣode's 'Distant Daily Ijó / YNWA' (2020) blends quotes from UK grime artists Skepta, D Double E, Ghetts, Kano and Wiley, bringing them into the fold of the poem in the same way as blending Yoruba words and phrases in the poem. Through the sound of the poem, the patterning of speech as Ṣode voices the words, the blending of these quotes, Yoruba and English creates its own language, that is, the language of the poem, that makes sense within its poetic context even if one doesn't understand the words. The Yoruba could not be translated and have the same effect since it signals a multilingual and multicultural community that comes together to dance and enjoy grime music. It is important to what the poem tries to do that it creates a sense of outsider for those who do not understand Yoruba nor recognize the quotes from grime artists:

> *Mò ngbọ èyí* with deceased friends / then wake to relish timed moments with the living / so when you chant grime / but have never cut a toothpaste in half and struggled to squeeze out its remains / you are merely a fan / I will out dance that fetish / I will skank / outline its splatter of appropriation in chalk.[10]

Rather than being incidental or being overlooked, the only words to appear on the screen in Ṣode's video for the poem are the Yoruba phrases and the quotes from grime artists, ensuring that the presence of these words is made central to the experience of the poem, regardless of the audience's ability to understand and recognize.

In both cases, Nagra and Ṣode present a multilingual voice, rather than separate voices. The non-English words and phrases are necessary to the poems and presented, on the whole, without translation. What this reveals is how voice in poetry can be used not only for self-expression but to signal one's connection to others, whether that is one's family and upbringing or communities that one is currently a part.

The collaborative voice

The dominant mode of writing poetry is to write alone; however, there are increasing numbers of poets who are exploring the potentials of collaborative writing. For instance, John Kinsella has undertaken a large programme of collaborative writing by co-authoring *Synopticon* (2012, with Louis Armand), *Monument* (2013, with Louis Armand) and *The Weave: A Work in Progress* (2018, with Thurston Moore). In each, there's no identifier of who has made what contribution and is therefore presented as genuine collaboration (a shared voice between the co-authors). In contrast, in his collection *Tangling with the Epic* (2019) with Kwame Dawes, their initials mark each contribution, with Kwame Dawes' poetry appearing on one page and John Kinsella's appearing on the opposite page. The effect is to represent and document a dialogue of voices, where one influences and shapes reception of the other, rather than the collaborative voice.

For Kinsella, such a collaborative approach to writing poetry is natural since he recognizes that poetry is rarely written without some community in mind, for instance, with reference to poetry written before and the communities the poet hopes to reach with their words:

> Poets operate in communities, and their ecologies are crosshatched. They connect and divide communities that aren't even aware of their existence. A poem is a part of an ecology – it uses and maybe gives. I've always found collaboration a way of challenging the security of self-affirmation. Of recognizing the crosshatched nature of an ecology. Of creating a field of failings and inadequacies and announcing common purposes in trying to repair and redeem. Collaborative writing can be redemptive. (Gander and Kinsella 2012, p. 37)

Although I term this 'collaborative voice' we must note that the term comes with some unintended baggage: '[c]ollaboration is a word with a long political history. It defines a relationship with one's adversaries, a befriending and "working together" for mutual advantage. It's a form of opportunism. At times, necessity informs collaboration as a strategy for survival. It defines an uneasy negotiation of terms between unequal parties' (Armand and Kinsella 2012, p. 7). We might, therefore, opt for singular communal voice to capture the positive relationship between the two poets seeking to uncover a shared poetics.

Armand and Kinsella comment that their method of writing involves 're-working, overwriting, deleting, adding, rearranging, collaging – so that at no point is there more than a couple of words that remain of either author's direct writing' (Armand and Kinsella 2012, p. 16). Through their method of co-writing, a negotiation takes place as the work of the two is combined together. A shared perspective emerges from consideration of what to include and how to edit together. A language and poetics that they both have a stake in but that is not reducible to their individual perspectives.

Another example of such collaboration is Denise Duhamel and Maureen Seaton, who produced three collaborative works *Exquisite Politics* (1997), *Oyl* (2000) and *Little Novels* (2002). Reflecting on their creative process, Duhamel comments:

> The most delightful part about our collaborating is the shared creative burden. Even when we think we are stumping one another, providing lines that seem almost impossible to finish, the other can usually think of something to follow right away. We are open to mess and mayhem. We have found what we believe to be a third voice, a voice that is neither Maureen's nor mine, but rather some poetic hybrid. (2006, n/p)

From this quotation, there are hints that the two poets take themselves to have created (or let emerge) a shared perspective through the problem-solving of each other's challenges to create a hybrid voice. In her book *Voicing American Poetry*, Lesley Wheeler discusses Duhamel and Seaton's work *Oyl*; she argues that this is a demonstration of a multivocal work that transforms 'the lyric as a social rather than a private form' (2009, p. 14). She comments that their process of writing together 'does not dismantle voice as a trope, but reveals voice as inherently dissonant or haunted, even when a work lays claim to unity. Poetic voice, seemingly singular, can help to stage profound encounters' (2009, p. 14).

Such writing together is more common in the world of performance poetry, particularly in cases where the poets intend to perform a piece together. Poet Katie Ailes also discusses her experience of writing collaboratively as part of the Loud Poets collective. She writes:

> One of the unexpected lessons from writing collaboratively for me has been realising how much my own poetic voice has shifted from working in a collective with other poets. I was initially worried that in [the 'Super-Dad' poem], our voices wouldn't mix well – that it would be easy to tell which sections were written by them and which were mine. However, when we wrote together the rhythms flowed easily into each other and everything meshed together relatively smoothly. I think this is a result of hearing so much of each other's work and absorbing those cadences. (2016, n/p)

From Ailes' reflections, it seems that the process of writing collaboratively involves allowing your own voice to respond to those of others, that is, to absorb their influence in some way ('absorbing those cadences'). The poem is not successful only because of the exchange of influence over the voice but by allowing a shared perspective to emerge, where the different poets respond and reflect on one another's contribution in putting the piece together.

Multivocal poetics/Choral voice/s

Lyric poetry does not only connect through forging of connection (in meaning and sound), writing collaboratively but through invoking other voices (bringing awareness of words spoken by others, including historical usage alongside the awareness of being spoken for the first time). There are many ways of invoking other voices. Voicing is something that can be done in the singular or plural. The plural further divides between the voice of the group, which is choral and made up of the texture of layering of voices, and voice as representative of the group, which is singular but reflects what is common to the group's membership. For instance, 'speaking for' or 'on behalf of' others is to attempt to bring voices together as one, take for instance, the use of voice in political discourse where the voices of many are represented by one spokesperson. The aim is to capture a de-personalized, universal and objective voice that can best communicate the needs and desires of a particular group or collective. When one is 'speaking on behalf of', the voices of the many are subsumed into the singular, dominant voice, and consequently, the many are denied a continuing, active voice. Consider here the example of the anthems such as national anthems ('God save the King'), political anthems ('Solidarity Forever' by Ralph Chaplin) or declarations of commitment to a particular organization (the Scout's promise). In such cases the reader/speaker is not asked to bring anything to it; instead, one must give up one's individual perspective for the collective. Individuals can be excluded from voicing in virtue of not wanting to identify with the singular voice. However, on a choral conception of plural voicing, one speaks *with* others, allowing voices to speak on their own terms. Examples of such choral voicing can be found in music where multiple voices are heard as unified (even where singing in harmony or counterpoint, the voices are heard relationally).

Rather than 'speaking on behalf of' others with a singular voice, the poet may take on the role of curator of multiple communal voices by allowing the poem to be dynamic in its voicing, that is, by drawing on other voices directly in the composition through quotation (such as Şode's poem discussed earlier) and influence in particular uses of language (such as the incorporation of dialect or other languages, e.g. Nagra and Şode). However, poetry can never be a mere collage of other voices; the poet must weave these voices together and in the process re-shape, re-voice and re-stage the words from the community. 'A Common Gift' (2021) by Momtaza Mehri explores the poet's role in bringing other voices together in the poem:

Against vanity, I try to translate this philosophy of flight,
Of time's trickling pace, the race of words catching up to intentions.
Even the bearing of witness has its limits, its gated horizons.
Bare the wound's wonders. The sparrow-sized ball of delight
Buried in the chest. Is the poet a ventriloquist of the senses?
Who buries what has been unearthed?
Lives swallowed into the fold of verses. Each voice a shard
Of glass, uniquely jagged. An intricate lattice
Of particular joys & defeats.
How to give life to the stubborn beauty of difference?
Mine the depths of the ordinary. The poet tries.
Knows there is no such thing as ordinary.
Between storyteller & subject,
Boundaries disintegrate, between what is felt & what is transcribed.
Affinity is a group activity.
Attention binds the gap.
Generous exchange of details, of entangled paths, this slow dance
Of capturing the fleeting & often forgotten.
Be with each other, the poet said. The *with* is its own expanse, a looping orbit
Of familiar ties. My story is his, hers, theirs, *ours*.
Craft a rearticulation of raindrops gracing the cheek,
A tea-stained book, the blossom
Of violets, the roar of planes overhead.
You don't have to experience something to understand it.
To preserve it in the cocoon of words is to illuminate
Some essential truth. To give it another, longer life that can
Be held in the lap
Of someone else. Nesting.[11]

What is the role of the poet in relation to the voices they bring together? 'A Common Gift' works through the possibilities: bearer, translator, witness, ventriloquist, miner, burrier, storyteller, transcriber, (re)articulator, preserver and (be)holder. No one of these roles quite captures what the poet does. Rather than dwelling on the particularities of these roles, we can look to what they share: each represents a relationship between the poet and others. Rather than understanding poetry in terms of the singular voice of the poet, poetry can be seen as relational in the way it connects voices, including the poet's own. The poet's voice is not privileged for its insight – the poet does not claim to be all knowing or have some special access to truth – but for its ability to bring (both historically and geographically distinct) voices together in companionship; in other words, the poet creates resonance, synergy, mutuality and reciprocity between voices. Therefore, there's a sense in which the poem is not of or for a community but *is* community; it 'spark[s] the communities of ideas in which communities of persons live' (Hejinian 2000, p. 166).

Saul Williams opens his book *Chorus: A Literary Mixtape* (2012) with the following:

> Shut up and sit down. New Age be damned if the old do not heed the voice and concerns of the young. Here are the voices of many, woven into one. If each face is a book, here is a testament: the groundplan of a social network. Here are our fears, disbeliefs, visions, and wishes welded into words. Here is our love, our desires, sprung from the incessant chatterbox of our adolescence. Here is the voice of the un-dead and the un-compromised. Make no tradition of this. We have had enough. (2012, p. vii)

Chorus, albeit constructed from many voices, presents a possibility to inhabit a collective voice. In creating this collection, Saul Williams gathered together 100 poems by 100 poets, removed their titles and presented them together as one voice. Williams writes, 'I made an attempt to weave poems and voices together as a DJ would, noting the tempo, mood, and theme of each piece and attempting to find a smooth way of blending into the next' (Williams 2012, p. 191). Those contributing to the project consisted of well-established poets such as Taylor Mali and Patricia Smith as well as the less well known. The different voices of each poem are united through the reader's voice. But a voice that must be responsive to Williams' own editing of the poems in deciding the sequence and suggestive of connection, as well as his highlighting of particular words, phrases and lines to produce his own 'meta-poem'.

> I've bought the bloody myth
>   swallowed that sucker
> hairy legs and all
> crawled careless into bed with a fantasy
> and now I'm hoping antsy with expectation[12]

The effect of presenting these poems as singular/choral is that the use of the first and second person is grounded in the 'we', as moments where the collective fragments do allow the individual to be heard but against the backdrop of the many. This isn't an open space to allow for appropriation of the I or space for common ground (expressing the multitude) but an invitation to speak these words together, to feel connected through joint action and expression. The effect is reminiscent of the vocalizing of a religious text, where in the speaking is affirmation of or acknowledging oneself as a member of a community, in chorus.

Anita Pati's 'Bloodfruit' (2022) is a polyphonic work that was produced from a set of interviews with women who had difficult experiences related to pregnancy and childbirth, including experiences of infertility and childlessness. Pati describes her process of writing as arranging voices on the page. In conversation, she comments that she felt it was important to leave their words untouched except for shaping into the poem. On the sleeve notes for her book, it says: '*Bloodfruit* gives voice to the less heard narratives of infertility and difficult trajectories towards becoming, or not becoming, a "mother." Here the often-fraught notions of womanhood and motherhood are also shown to feed into ideas on who is able to mother.'

In conversation, Pati notes that her voice, as a mother, is also present in the text set on equal terms with the other voices. Unlike *Chorus*, Pati's sequence poem 'Bloodfruit' is not meant to be taken as a singular voice (as one voice for the many) – the inclusion of ages and other bodily references makes clear that this is a collection of voices, of different experiences that still form a connection to one another but with self-other differentiation intact. In the process, what Pati achieves is the creation of a community of those who didn't have the expected experience. The poem offers a space for sharing difference of experiences that are too often left ignored and unheard.

> Obese they keep telling me but I pump iron like the best
> of them. The NHS makes me feel like some fat, disgusting
> whale that doesn't deserve to have kids. I'm 26.
>
> I was chubby, fat cow! they said. Took me 'til 38 before I let
> go of the body hang-ups. Worried about looking fat
> if pregnant, having to go up clothes sizes.

I look back at pictures of me at 29 and think why
did you give yourself such a headache?
Yeah, body image has affected mine and X's sex,
trying to conceive.[13]

The sequence navigates between the individual experience that is tied to particular people and their bodies and the common, the overlap, the shareable/relatable. In telling personal stories, there are moments of seeking connection with others, not to overstep their experience but to find connection especially where one feels alone and marginalized.

Poetry in performance allows for other kinds of multivocal works, where texture is added by more than one voice speaking the words simultaneously and in turn. Take for instance, 'Sons' (2013) by Terisa Siagatonu and Rudy Francisco, 'When Love Arrives' (2015) by Sarah Kay and Phil Kaye, 'Sean Bell' (2011) by team Philadelphia (Hasan, Josh and Alysia) and 'Super Dad' (2016) by The Loud Poets. The convention among performance poets is that such works are collaborative and co-written and the standard is that performers will speak the lines they've written themselves but that's not to say that the lines are written independently. Instead, the two or more poets will allow their own writing and voicing of the work to be influenced by the other(s).

'Lost Voices' (2015) by Darius Simpson and Scout Bostley plays with the idea of voice, co-writing and performing together. The poem addresses racism and sexism by drawing attention to the problem of others speaking on your behalf and the moral failure of not being able to be heard. The performance involves the two performers (one White female and one Black male) swapping mics at the beginning of the piece, leaving the two performing the lines of the other (and the one 'silenced', only being able to lip sync their words).

There are moments where both voices can be heard speaking the same words; for example, 'The first' yet only one completes the line. This reinforces a sense of the words being stolen from the other. Not simply speaking on behalf of but denial of the other to speak at all. The swapping of voices also allows for a sense of connection between the experiences to come to the fore. However, what the poets are careful to express is not that these experiences are similar but to reveal structural issues both face in being heard and acknowledged. Both are subject to another speaking on their behalf who does not know their experience. It's not a simple denial of voice since both are subject to the same denial to speak and be heard. This is reinforced by the moments where their voices overlap (where they can be heard speaking simultaneously), where either could have taken up the line. The poem culminates in both voices speaking together. At this moment, the performers return to their original places and begin to voice their own lines of the poem, thereby silencing the one who was once speaking on their behalf.

The power in such multivocal works is to attempt to create connections between people and their experiences, while resisting (or in the case of 'Lost voices', revealing) the problems of speaking on behalf of others or as a singular voice. In each case, the multivocal nature of the work gestures at the possibility of a growing community, of other voices being able to enter into the space that the poem creates.

Hearing together and reading apart: Laying the foundations for community

In *Being Numerous*, Oren Izenberg recounts an experience of attempting to read poetry with another when living apart by sending poems through the mail to be read by each as a way of experiencing connection. He calls this 'reading together apart': 'by reading together apart, the collective action I sought to accomplish was precisely the capacity for "we-intentions." I wanted to be we, and feel it' (2011, p. 183), or as he puts it a little further on, to 'realize a capacity for relation to another in ourselves' (2011, p. 183). The potential connection to another is facilitated by the poem itself as an object of (potential) joint attention. Such awareness alters the reading experience by bringing to mind the possibility of a shared perspective (with the other reader who is assumed to be engaging with the same work), not merely what do I make of this but what might *we* make of this. Thinking of my encounter with the poem as potentially shared with another shifts my engagement from considering the personal, idiosyncratic associations and connections to something more generalizable or shareable.

Although Izenberg was considering a very particular episode, his comments tap into a more everyday phenomenon of reading published poetry, that is, reading poetry with awareness of its public status, as works that will be read and engaged with by others. This need not be restricted to poetry that appears in public spaces on billboards or etched into concrete benches but to all published poetry. Poetry in the public domain has a different quality to poetry one might write that remains hidden in shoeboxes under the bed (mere external documents of private expression with the intention to be used in self-reflection and witnessing of the self). In reading a public poem, we are not only considering what the poet might be doing but how this could be interpreted by multiple others and their different perspectives. Such awareness enables a loosening from the idiosyncratic to considerations of the common – in other words, what might the poem be saying to 'us.'

Consider Robert Montgomery's 'People you love' (2010): 'The people you love / become ghosts inside / of you and like this / you keep them alive.'[14] His poem was displayed at De La Warr Pavilion in Bexhill-on-Sea, lit with solar-powered LEDs. Being staged in a public space, the words don't merely encourage the reader to reflect on how this might connect to their own experiences but raise awareness of the significance that the poem expresses something common, that is, meaning that connects to many and therefore speaks to something at a more fundamental level of what it is to be human. Through his piece 'Poem for William Blake' displayed on a billboard in Bethnal Green, London (2014), Montgomery makes use of the second person in an act of protest against the Iraq war: 'Invading kings told you to take your actual land from you.'[15] The poem draws attention to the use of the second person (through repetition and the syntax, in particular, the use and placement of 'your') and, through its public status, seeks to pick out anyone reading the words, which builds a sense of collective complicity (not necessarily the one who commits a moral harm but one who allows such harms to be committed).

In applying the concept of reading together apart to performance poetry, we must consider the relationship between audience members responding to the performance and how that is experienced as 'together'. Although in the live performance of poetry one is not in quite the same position since one is aware of other bodies around them, one can still be mistaken about whether those around are attending to the same performance as them (both in the sense of whether they are attending rather than failing to attend and whether they are seeing significance in the same places). However, that does not mean that what we feel isn't experienced in terms of 'we' thoughts that are generated by the potentially erroneous belief that other audience members are also engaging with the performance on the same terms as me. As Michael Y. Bennett argues in *The Problems of Viewing Performance* (2021), watching a performance is still an individual experience despite doing this in the presence of others. Bennett highlights a distinction between public experience and shared experience, the latter of which he takes to be an impossibility. He writes:

> facts going into the play – or, rather, the facts *about*, and *circumstances of*, the individual observers and what each observer 'attends to' and what/which emotions are brought into the theatre space at any given two-hour or so span of time – are not evenly dispersed among the audience members (and even participants). Some know the play line-by-line, others know the main stage directions, some have just read it, some have just seen it, and some do not even know the play at all. Each 'spectator,' then, uses and/or has a different *lens*, or 'spectacle,' through which he or she experiences a (largely-similarly viewed) object or action. (p. 33)

Each member of the audience brings their own perspective (not just in virtue of perceptual access but also in terms of beliefs and how information is processed) that shapes the experience of the performance.

However, that doesn't mean that an audience member cannot feel in common with others. What the experience of the poem affords in its undeniable public status is relationality of language and expression as social: it does not offer connection between a speaker and addressee (or witness) but has the power to connect a group through empathetic response (without overstepping that sense of self-other differentiation). We may feel this most powerfully in performances that ask the audience to participate in audible and bodily response through which we gain awareness and acknowledgement of one another as responding jointly to the poem (even though the nature of the response is something we can still be in error about).

In Slam poetry performances, it is common for poets to encourage audience participation not only by inviting the audience to express their connection to the work through clicks of the fingers or cheers but by the poet asking the audience to directly contribute to the poem by speaking particular lines. Such examples seek to bring the poet's voice into relation with the audience's voices, exposing the connection between the singular voice of the poet-performer and the collective, chorus from the audience – audibly contrasting an I/you and we. For example, John Hegley's 'Suitcase', in which the audience are asked to say the word 'suitcase' when prompted, thereby completing Hegley's lines in places and contributing directly to the performance of the poem. The power of the connection between performer and audience is disrupted for comic effect when the audience jump in to shout 'suitcase', when Hegley reveals the word was in fact 'umbrella'. This presents a tension between there being a genuine felt connection through the audience participation and the apparent revelation of the illusion of collaboration through the assertion of authorial control.

In Toby Campion's performance of 'Notes From The Sexual Health Clinic Waiting Room', he invites the audience to 'awkwardly cough' between poems that form the sequence. This acts as an important contrast to the laughter provoked by the poems themselves. The audience not only experience the feeling of laughing together (at the same thing) but through their participation (the cough) there is a reminder among the room of a shared awkwardness and embarrassment related to the subject of the sequence of poems. The experience of laughing together helps the audience to feel connected to others in the room, but it is through the participation of the cough that such a connection is grounded in joint attention and references shared experiences outside of the live performance space. That's not to say that the poem will be successful in creating a sense of community within the room for all individuals. Anyone who lacks experience of attending a sexual health clinic will feel excluded, but importantly, those who have had the experience will be left with a sense of 'being with' or belonging with others who signalled through laughing and coughing that they share a type of experience.

What both the example of Campion's and Hegley's audience participation in performing poetry reveals is the potential for the performance space to serve as the commons – a place that is created together and accessible to a community. Such performances directly enlist the audience in the performance space, and without the audiences' contribution, the poem would fail to be performed. In contrast, the experience of (privately) reading poetry one takes to be in the public domain is to feel possibilities of connection with other potential readers. This experience triggers reflection on the connections and associations one sees in the work as offering potentials to share meaning with others.

Conclusion

Lyric poetry, whether on the page or in performance, can help to cultivate a greater 'sense of us', a sense of community by raising awareness of what it means to be a part of a community. How poetry might achieve this is twofold, either by bringing to the fore the meaning, significance and value of plural interpersonal relationships or by seeking to create or reflect community through voice in the work (e.g. presenting a multivocal piece, using a multilingual voice or through requiring the audience to participate and be heard in the performance space of the poem). This also helps us to reflect on how communities can be voiced in poetry while resisting a 'speaking on behalf of', which fails to recognize self-other differentiation.

To fully understand plural interpersonal relationships, one must appreciate both when community forms successfully and when it doesn't and to distinguish between mere hopes for connection with others and actual connection. Poetry also can help us acknowledge how we might gesture at connection, where one might experience a 'sense of us' that doesn't go beyond mere sociation – in other words, how one can be mistaken about potentials to connect with others in more meaningful ways. This also reveals the difficulty and fragility of community for it requires ongoing mutuality and reciprocity from each individual at the core of that community in developing and maintaining a shared perspective (even where the perspective itself might change, it still belongs to *them*).

In the next chapter, I will argue further for the significance of recognizing and being sensitive to self-other differentiation. I will extend this understanding of self-other differentiation to include the body and the embodied voice. Even though one might feel connected to the language of the poem, share in its connections and associations, there are important examples where the body of the performer necessarily contributes to the meaning-making of the poem. The words are experienced as being connected to their embodied voice rather than as communal. However, such embodied voice can also be significant in gesturing for connection with others who struggle to be recognized as speakers of their words.

4

Embodied voices

Introduction

The main purpose of the book has been to position poetry as an inherently social art form. The use of voice and coming together of voice in poetry forms a foundation of sociation whether on the page or in performance. The experience of being brought into relationship with another through poetic voice is significant not only for its affective power but also for its enhancement of our understanding of our relationships with one another and awareness of our coexistence with others (whether positively in terms of connections between people or negatively in terms of a lack of connection). Such a position of relationality can only be appreciated through actively seeking connection to others. Both writing and reading/hearing poetry involves a seeking of connection with others (poet to reader/audience; reader/audience to poet) and can therefore support development of understanding of the value and significance of the ways we relate to one another.

Throughout the preceding chapters, I have been careful to provide a positive account of voice in poetry, with the assumption that all voices have equal potential to be heard. Unfortunately, this is an ideal that is not reflected in society. There are many who find themselves members of unjustly marginalized groups (whether due to ableism, homophobia, racism, sexism or other factors) and consequently experience additional barriers to having their voices heard and acknowledged. Furthermore, the argument of the book is to make the case for a particular kind of contribution to the understanding of human relationships provided through engagement with works of poetry. To fail to hear voices within that context means denying individuals their epistemic contribution and therefore perpetuating harm. Consequently, it is important to be sensitive to power dynamics within society when engaging with poetry to ensure that poetry enables expression rather than hinders it. As I will argue, not only can poetry help counter oppression by enabling one to find their voice through poetry but the experience of engaging with poetry cultivates intellectual and affective virtues of listening and seeking connection that are essential to hearing the voices of others.

That unjustly marginalized people experience silencing has been much discussed in feminist philosophy. For instance, Jennifer Hornsby argues that for some, their use of language fails in doing what they intend to as a consequence of the audience failing in their willingness and ability to recognize the intention of the speaker and failing to respond appropriately to what was said. Hornsby argues, 'The silenced person is someone who literally cannot do with speech what she might have wanted to, whether because the language does not let her (ineffability) or because a certain kind of communication is not possible (inaudibility)' (Hornsby 1995, p. 138). What is needed, according to Hornsby, is reciprocity between speaker and listener:

> When there is reciprocity among people, they recognize one another's speech as it is meant to be taken: An audience who participates reciprocally does not merely understand the speaker's words but also, in taking the words as they are meant to be taken, satisfies a condition for the speaker's having done the communicative thing that she intended. (p. 134)

In other words, the speaker intends to communicate something with their words, but for communication (i.e. their *using* of language) to be successful, an audience is required to recognize what was said, understand it and respond appropriately to it (which is a consequence of understanding). As established in Chapter 2, being heard is not something that is in the control of the individual speaking; it requires a certain effort on part of the (intended) listener. The speaker needs the listener to be making some kind of effort to hear her. Consequently, to speak and be heard is relational; that is, it involves mutual recognition and reciprocity. As put by Kristie Dotson, 'to communicate we all need an audience willing and capable of hearing us' (2011, p. 238).

Although one might argue that poetry can help individuals respond to ineffability by allowing the poet to open up language and subvert everyday meaning, my concern in this book has been with the reception of and engagement with poetry on the page and in performance. Therefore, I will focus discussion on how poetry might serve to counter or mitigate inaudibility since this will show a role for poetry in cultivating virtues in readers and audiences that may help the unjustly marginalized be heard. The response to inaudibility is the relationality of poetry. Sheri Irvin argues, 'When members of a subordinated group attempt to capture their own experiences, they may feel a greater need for poetry that breaks open language in order to forge new semantic networks or to act directly on the reader to produce an experience rather than merely describing one' (Irvin 2015, p. 108). The need to 'break open language' through poetry places pressure on the reader and audience in terms of their willingness and ability to hear non-conventional uses of language. To express or communicate such experience and be heard depends on the audience/reader accepting affective completeness of the work despite not being able to settle completely the meaning of the work. All that is required for understanding is the felt grasp (that produces an experience for the audience/reader and opens up possibilities of meaning rather than being reduced to description). The poem not only facilitates expression but invites witness (in the form of mutual respect), response and ultimately connection/shareability. The poet and the reader/audience share in their mutual vulnerability that comes from the awareness of the unknown and unknowable (i.e. not knowing the other and the consequent risk of failure in successful expression and appropriate response) that results from self-other differentiation where connection and shareability are incomplete, fragile and momentary.

What I want to argue is that poetry in performance has the power to enhance the speaker/listener dynamic; it helps us to learn to listen better as members of an audience but also as readers. Crucially, through performance, we become aware of the significance of the embodiment of words in meaning-making and expression. This is not only important for aesthetic appreciation of the work but is ethically significant. In making the case for the aesthetic and moral significance of the embodied voice, I will highlight two ethical issues in the performance and reception of poetry. The first issue arises when looking at the example of the re-performance of Patricia Smith's 'Skinhead' by Taylor Mali. In the case of Mali's re-performance, there is an aesthetic failure that amounts to a moral irresponsibility (as a consequence of inaudibility). I will use this case to highlight a more general ethical issue with how audiences and readers treat works of poetry in performance and on the page. I argue that failure to recognize the role of the embodied performance in aesthetic appreciation of the work can give rise to harm. Therefore, as audiences and readers, we must be sensitive to the context provided by the embodied voice. Listening well goes beyond attending to the words to appreciating the words as performed/written by someone who is trying to use them in an act of expression.

Embodied words

What the body contributes to meaning-making is a grounding of the perspective of the poem, that is, a way of thinking and feeling (patterns of value) that is presented by the poem. As argued in Chapter 2, it is the performer's body that provides the evidence of 'sufficient subjective life such that we can justify our ascription of psychological and expressive predicates to it' (Kim and Gibson 2021, p. 98). Additionally, as highlighted by Peter Middleton, the body also signals agency and action; the words of the poem are *doing* something to/for the audience:

> These words arise out of the speaker, whose bodily presence and identity is their warrant, and whose delivery shows what it means to think and say these words and ideas, indeed, shows what it means to live them for at least the moment of their delivery. The presence of a speaker is a reminder that the words are temporarily invoked from an individual with a particular point of view, a particular body, a particular experience and history. (Middleton 2009, p. 224)

The live performance is an embodiment of perspective. To help make this clear, it is helpful to consider how the performance of poetry is different to acting. In acting, the body is used as a prop in a game of make-believe. The audience are to treat the actor on stage as a representation of some character; that is, they are to see the actor *as* that character. This aspect of seeing-as in the case of acting also impacts the sense of space and time on the stage in that the stage is to be seen as other and the sense of the events unfolding in time is to be treated within the temporal framework of the play (e.g. day can turn to night in seconds as the lights on stage are dimmed). The role of seeing-as in the theatre performance also explains the disruptive power of 'breaking the fourth wall', where actors speak directly to the audience and thereby draw attention to the artificial and fictional nature of the performance on stage. In the case of the poetry performance, the audience are not engaged in seeing-as;

instead, the performance has the quality of presentness, that is, a speaking in the now. There is no breaking of the fourth wall because there is no separation of performance space and audience. In performing a work of poetry, the words are being used in this moment to bring about some action that takes place now between the performer and the audience in front of them, within the shared space of the event.

Take for instance, Claire Collison's award-winning poetry performance 'Truth Is Beauty' (2020), which is staged as part of a life-drawing class. In her performance, she presents her poetry as intimately connected to her body, which she describes as her 'single-breasted monologue', having undergone a mastectomy as part of her treatment for breast cancer. The audience are not invited to see her body as that of some character but to attend to her real-world body in relation to the words of the poem in the present:

> Returning to the life room following a mastectomy, life modelling has had the opposite effect: despite the pressures to hide and disguise, I see the evidence that I am whole and complete. I am still a complex series of planes and surfaces, light and shade. And that's down to you. Please, draw what you see.[1]

On her website, Collison comments, 'Why are the thousands of women like me so hidden? What anxieties do we share as a society, where disguise is regarded as important as treatment? And how can women make informed treatment choices when there is so little representation of us within mainstream culture?' Her performance attempts to disrupt mainstream culture and challenge dominant views of the female body by using the performance space as a place to be heard and be seen. Collison's performance isn't to be taken as an aside to the everyday but to be put in conversation with the everyday. In the simple request 'please, draw what you see', she is asking the audience to participate directly in the performance. The performance doesn't serve merely to express an individual perspective but to create a space through attention to the body for others to share, that is, a space where the invisible is made visible and the inaudible made audible. Whether or not the words themselves are autobiographical, the body cannot fail to express its own history; in this case, the scars are the legacy of surgery.

Rather than autobiography, expectations of authenticity arise in virtue of the embodied performance and the relationality between the physical presence of the audience and the co-presence of the performer. As Katie Ailes (2021) points out, the value of authenticity in poetry presents a tension between the quality of being direct, natural, honest, confessional yet crafted, edited and performed. She argues that the achievement of feelings of authenticity is where the poetic craft is not visible to the audience. Of course, one might prioritize being natural, honest and confessional over artistry but that would result in bad poetry (and would also place emphasis on the content not the form, and thereby fail to draw aesthetic attention to the use of words). What Ailes is highlighting is a distinction between expectations of autobiography and poetry performance presenting 'what it means to live them for at least the moment of their delivery', that is, the felt quality of authenticity. The latter does not require the former. However, where the confusion arises is that both the autobiographical and authenticity make reference to the body of the performer. We may therefore take the poem to be autobiographical when in fact it does nothing more than offer the feeling of authenticity. The confessional poem may well do both. But in other kinds of performance, the body of the performer merely grounds the use of the words in the here and now, as the speaker who is doing something with the words in the performance space.

To help unpack this idea of the poet-performer 'living the words' as distinct from the autobiographical, we can turn to Paisley Livingston's discussion of what it is to author a work. He offers the following definition: an author is 'an agent who intentionally makes an utterance, where the making of an utterance is an action, an intended function of which is expression or communication' (Livingston 2005, p. 69). To put more plainly, the author is the one who is trying to say something by producing the artwork. The author doesn't have to identify with the content of the utterance but with the act of making the utterance within a particular context. This understanding of an author works well in the case of poetry since I have argued that works of lyric poetry should be treated as an event rather than an object (including many works of page poetry). A work of lyric poetry is produced by someone who is doing something (i.e. expression or communication) through this poetic use of words. In order to count as an author of a work in this sense, the poet must be successful in producing a work that expresses their intended perspective.

According to Livingston, a consequence of this view is that authors always endorse the attitudes expressed in making the utterance (which can be distinct from the content of the utterance itself e.g. in cases where such expression is insincere, misleading, or intended to be fictional): 'In making an utterance, an author acts on an expressive intention, the content of which is a schematic representation of some attitude(s) to be indicated, and of some means of so doing (such as saying or writing words having such-and-such a linguistic meaning, so that anyone who knows the language has evidence about the attitudes to be expressed)' (p. 70). The notion of 'expressive intention' is helpful in making the point that the author need not endorse the content but have the intention of expressing some attitude towards that content. The content of the expressive intention may be distinct from the content of the linguistic expression itself (the difference between what you say and what you are doing in saying that). Where the author has been successful in the production of the poem, they will have successfully expressed as intended; in other words, what is available to the audience/reader is both an appreciation of the meaning of the words and what the poet is doing in using those words.

As David Davies argues, 'the performer differs from the mere agent whose behavior is subject to evaluation in that she *intends* for her actions to be appreciated and evaluated, and thus is consciously *guided* in what she does by the expected eye or ear of an intended qualified audience' (2011, p. 6).[2] The performer intends for their words to be heard by an audience and, therefore, considers the reception of their work in designing the performance. In order to be in a position to appreciate and evaluate the work, the poetry audience must contextualize the words of the poem as embodied; as centred in and related to the body of the performer because only then is it properly grounded in their intention to communicate or express.

Trying to get clear on how the body is relevant in our engagement with poetry, we can consider cases in which the body of the poet is disconnected from the work in a re-performance or re-voicing of that work. Such cases raise a number of questions: When is it appropriate (or inappropriate) to perform the work of another? What role does the body of the performer play in the meaning-making and interpretation by the audience in the performance space? To be clear, this isn't an issue of plagiarism; examples of re-voicing works of poetry found in everyday life don't involve any claims of authorship, such as readings at weddings, funerals and school recitals. However, re-voicing may still be problematic in some cases. Poet Katie Ailes comments, 'if a man were to perform my poems "Swallow" or "Flesh," which concern issues specific to the experience of having a female body, the embodied performance would obviously contradict . . . the text of the poem, and indeed would probably come across as a cruel parody undermining the central messages of these poems' (2015, n/p). Elizabeth Harvey in *Ventroloquized Voices: Feminist Theory and English Renaissance Texts* reveals that the separation of embodied voice from text is not just a contemporary problem but reaches back to early modern texts. Harvey argues that through the persona poem, the feminine voice was represented by male authors. She argues that such 'ventriloquizations of women in the Renaissance achieved the power they did partly because so few women actually wrote and spoke, but the representations of feminine speech that were current in literary and popular accounts, as well as in ventriloquizations, fostered a vision that tended to reinforce women's silence or to marginalize their voices when they did speak or write' (1992, p. 5). Rather than giving women's voices the chance to be heard, the persona poem broke the link between the body and voice, which resulted in a mere representation of the female voice by men, thereby rendering the female voice reduced and sexualized.

Compare this idea of re-voicing with the controversy surrounding the case of the proposed Dutch translation of Amanda Gorman's 'The Hill We Climb' (2021) – that she performed at Joe Biden's presidential inauguration – by Marieke Lucas Rijneveld. Many at the time argued that Rijneveld would be doing something wrong in translating the work. The complaint centred on the thought that embodied knowledge of what it is like to be a young, Black woman is essential to the poem, and therefore, it was argued, Rijneveld, who is White and non-binary, is unable to connect with the poem and be able to translate it adequately.[3] This is quite different to the sort of thing Ailes has in mind since Rijneveld would have been engaged in the practice of *translation* and not *re-voicing* the work. Implicit in the production of a translation is that what results bears some relation to but is not a mere version of the original; there is an acknowledgement that there is a gap between the original and the translation, yet the aim is for both to have value independently of one another. The translation is secondary to the original; translation involves using a text as the basis for another in an attempt to take some of the ideas of the original into a new context. Given this understanding, there seems to be little issue in Rijneveld's translation of Gorman's poem since it in no way attempts to replace or speak for Gorman's work. However, there is a question of whether there was a point to translating Gorman's poem (which includes putting it on the page and in a different language) given its association with a major public, civic event in the United States. If it's about a particular moment in the United States and the embodied voice is important in that context, it's not clear that any translation has value but that is not an issue about re-voicing the poem that Gorman performed since Rijneveld wouldn't be altering or claiming Gorman's expressive intention but adding to it.

The need to see the use of words in poetry as connected to the body has a consequence for how we read poetry and how poetry is performed when written by those who have experienced oppression, particularly where what the poet intends to communicate relates to their embodied knowledge. Thinking about Nelson Goodman's (1976) distinction between autographic and allographic works, we are content with the idea that some works (particularly of the performing arts) can be performed many times involving different performers provided they respect the work's notation, which allows for re-interpretation to some degree and still counts as an instance of that work. In the same way, the re-performance of works of poetry is not in itself problematic. However, there are some works that are limited in their potential to be re-performed without damaging the work both aesthetically and morally.

Take for example, 'Skinhead' (2010) by Patricia Smith, which brings the relationship of the embodied performance and the meaning-making experience of hearing the poem in performance into sharp focus. This 'persona' poem gives voice to a (fictional) White supremacist. When performed by Smith herself, a relationship of tension and critique is established between the voice of the persona and the embodied voice of the poet/performer. As a Black American woman, Smith's voicing of a (fictional) White supremacist transforms the words spoken.[4] The expressive intention of the performance is to critique (by revealing tension in) the attitudes expressed by the words of the poem. Unlike in Ailes' hypothetical case, the intention here is for the embodied voice to deliberately undermine the audio text of the poem. It is in the relationality of the two voices (Smith's as performer and the poetic persona) that creates the necessary tension resulting in an anti-racist poem that seeks understanding, through embodying another's voice, how such racism can exist and flourish in American society. 'Skinhead' demands that the audience acknowledge the words of the poem, the persona represented by the words and the embodiment of those words. It becomes a problem for the audience to deal with in terms of the conflict between the voice of a White supremacist and a Black American woman.

> I'm riding the top rung of the perfect race,
> my face scraped pink and brilliant.
> I'm your baby, America, your boy,
> drunk on my own spit, I am goddamned fuckin' beautiful.
>
> And I was born
>
> and raised
>
> right here.[5]

The use of the second person emphasizes the challenge to the audience 'I'm your baby, America, your boy', which raises the question to the average American citizen, to what extent are you complicit? The use of the first person in the final words collapses the two identities, both the White supremacist persona and Patricia Smith's herself, which helps to reinforce the sentiment that the conflict present in her work is a product of the society that enables such White supremacism to flourish. What is brought to the fore is not merely racist expression but connection to the victims of such racist expression. The tension manifest in the performance is not just confined to the performance space but is situated in the context of life in the United States today. The live performance invites the audience to make the real-world connection in responding to the performance of the work as an event taking place between the poet-performer and the audience since it calls on the audience to see what is being said in the context of the harm it causes.

In his book *Artistic Creation and Ethical Criticism*, Ted Nannicelli draws a useful distinction between the attitudes and ideals expressed through a set of words and the action performed in giving voice to those words. In making his case, he gives the example of work songs. He argues,

> the ethical merit of [work] songs is partly, but not entirely, a matter of the attitudes or ideals articulated in the lyrics. . . . [By] singing the lyrics, one performs another action – in this case, protesting unjust labor conditions, or, in the case of hate speech . . . inciting violence. So, it is not just the lyrics themselves, but the action an agent performs by voicing them, that is ethically evaluable. (Nannicelli 2020, p. 162)

In performing this poem, Smith is doing more than communicating what the words of the poem mean. Through her embodied performance, she is also performing another action, namely one of critique. To fail to recognize the significance of her body in performance is to fail to see the poem as anti-racist and therefore to fail to see the performance as ethically significant.

To make the point more explicit, Susan Somers-Willett discusses what happened when Smith's poem was performed by Taylor Mali, a White male at an event to celebrate the work of Smith: 'Because Mali is visibly hailed as a white male himself, most of his audience could not readily recognize this voice as a persona and confused the supremacist's position with his own' (2012, p. 93). She comments that the performance was met with strong disapproval, including by those who recognized that the poetic persona was not his own: 'Such a reaction is evidence that Smith's embodiment of "Skinhead" is just as much a performance of her own identity as a Black woman as it is of her persona's identity and views' (2012, p. 93). Furthermore, Smith intended to do something with her words that Mali did not, which amounts to both an aesthetic and moral irresponsibility on the part of Mali. He failed to listen to her performance properly and failed to see the aesthetic significance of her body and the moral significance of the poem. Consequently, he performed a poem that was both aesthetically and morally inferior to Smith's. Although he wasn't intending to endorse the views of the persona (his intention was to celebrate Smith's work), he nonetheless failed to deliver the critical counterpoint provided by Smith's embodied voice. Simply put, in voicing the words of the poem, Mali performs a different action to Smith. Would it have been different had he contextualized his performance by saying that it should be heard in Smith's embodied voice? This would have certainly alleviated the worries of the audience but it still wouldn't be Smith's poem that he performed. Smith's performance contrasts the attitudes expressed by the words of the poem with the attitudes expressed by her embodied, contextualized performance of those words. In other words, the necessary context is given in the performance itself and doesn't require the audience to apply additional information to it. Taylor Mali's performance undermined the complex affective relationship between audio text and body text and thereby reduced both the aesthetic complexity and moral value of the poem, leaving important aspects of Smith's expressive intention inaudible.

In this example, the same work performed by different people, that is, different embodied voices, resulted in performances that do something and mean something very different from one another. The words (and gestures) are the same but voiced by different bodies with different identities. bell hooks' comment on the nature of performance seems particularly apt here: 'In one context performance can easily become an act of complicity, in the other, it can serve as critical intervention, as a rite of resistance' (1995, p. 211). Mali's performance became an act of complicity in oppression (in virtue of making aspects of Smith's expressive intention inaudible), whereas Smith's serves as critical intervention. The difference between the two performances is what they are each able to do with the words of the poem in virtue of the embodied voice, that is, the action they perform through the performance of the poem. Mali's body fails to provide any tension with the words spoken, and consequently, the action performed (albeit not intentioned) is one of endorsement of the words spoken.

Poetry is more than words. But so is theatre. As I have already suggested, the poetry performance and the theatre performance have much in common. For instance, Zamir's comments on acting also apply to poetry performance: 'a performed act transcends the incarnated character and touches the identity of the actor in a manner that evokes ethical questions' (2013, p. 354). My examples are also cases where a performance transcends the poetic persona and touches the identity of the performer in a manner that evokes ethical questions. In both cases, the body is made present in the performance.

However, there is an important distinction between the poetry performance and the theatre performance. Although, as Zamir argues, the actor can be implicated by their performance (he gives the example of a vegetarian actor consuming meat – it is not just the performed character eating meat but also the actor), the way in which the performer of a poem is implicated is different. Within the performance poetry scene, it is rare for poems to be performed by someone other than the poet. This convention leads to an expectation on part of the audience that the performer is the author of the work (as noted earlier, that does not mean that the works are necessarily autobiographical). As discussed in the introduction, Julia Novak writes,

> live poetry is characterised by the direct encounter and physical co-presence of the poet with a live audience. The poet will predominantly perform his/her own poetry and is thus cast in the double role of 'poet-performer.' The story and images of the poem are conveyed through the spoken word rather than through theatrical ostension, as focus is placed on the oral verbalisation of the poetic text. (Novak 2011, p. 68)

This expectation that the performer is the poet implies endorsement of the performance by the performer that is not present in the actor's performance. The audience, therefore, takes the performer to be using the words of the poem for self-expression, that is, with expressive intention to do something with their words. This may be straightforward with the use of the first person or may be more complex in the creation of a poetic persona that is clearly distinct from the identity of the poet-performer. Crucially, what these works have in common is that they have the following structure: the poet-performer is taken to be using the words to express some perspective, that is, a way of seeing the world, an affective-emotional response or a set of values. That does not entail that the words themselves are acts of self-expression, only that using the words is an act of self-expression. The audience, therefore, must go beyond hearing the words and interpreting their meaning in isolation from the performer and their embodied performance.

In the case of acting, there is no implied endorsement of the performance of words; the world of make-believe constructed in such a performance remains intact. In the case of the poet-performer, any aspect of fictionality is always treated relationally to the real world, which includes the body and identity of the poet-performer themselves. The actor may use real-world events and features in service of the fictional creation; the poet-performer may use the fictional to enhance real-world aspects of self. Of course, an actor may feel implicated by a role they are playing (for instance, where the ideology of a character seems to undermine their own beliefs and commitments), but this is different to the poet-performer who puts such beliefs and commitments at the fore of their performance and is central to understanding the expressive intention motivating the work.

Failure to recognize the role of voice and body in expression

The example of Mali's performance of Smith's poem may seem like a rare and peculiar case that although interesting does not have much to tell us about other cases of re-voicing poetry or the relevance of the relationship between the embodied performance and the words of the poem more generally. However, I argue that the body is not just relevant to the meaning-making experience of the poem but that failure to appreciate the relationship between embodied voice and the words of the poem (such as Taylor Mali's failure to appreciate the significance of Smith's body to performance of the work) can result in harm, which is not only relevant in performing, and evaluating a performance, but also in the act of reading. Here I will draw on the cultural appropriation debate to help make sense of this potential harm. I argue that re-voicing is not strictly an example of appropriation. Nonetheless, there is attempted appropriation at work and the harm caused by such attempted appropriation can be understood in similar terms to successful appropriation.

In 'Profound Offense and Cultural Appropriation', James Young identifies three types of cultural appropriation: (1) subject appropriation, e.g. when a work depicts members or objects of another culture; (2) content appropriation, e.g. when an artist uses aesthetic features of another culture in the production of their work; and (3) object appropriation, e.g. when a work is taken out of its cultural context. In all three kinds of cases of appropriation, what's going on is that something is taken from one cultural context and placed in another whether that's representations of people or objects, aesthetic or stylistic features, or a whole work. The re-voicing of a work of poetry might seem on the surface like it has got most in common with object appropriation. We might say that the poem is taken out of its original context and placed in a new context, and where that seems to be problematic akin to cultural appropriation is where the poem is tied to the identity of the speaker. This could well be the case in which a school adopts a poem as its motto (where the poet didn't produce the poem with this context in mind).

However, as I have been arguing throughout this book, lyric poetry is not merely a set of words in a particular form; in other words, the poem is not reducible to the word meanings plus the formal features (which would be to treat the poem as an object). Instead, the poem should be seen as an event. In discussions of appropriation, there is little focus on what sorts of things are candidates for appropriation. Not everything is a possible target for appropriation. For example, I can appropriate a phrase used by my friend to describe the passing of time but I cannot appropriate the words of a judge sentencing a criminal. I can attempt to appropriate the words of the judge, but in my version, the action performed in using those words does not carry over (the action is tied to *who* is speaking and *the context* of the utterance). Just as with the case of the words spoken by the judge, it seems that the performative context of a poem means that it is not subject to appropriation. Given how I have characterized works of lyric poetry on the page and in performance as an event (in which the poet is performing some action), it seems that many works of poetry are also not candidates for appropriation (the event of expression is not re-creatable); instead, there may still be attempted appropriation albeit necessarily unsuccessful.

Someone might attempt to appropriate a poem but the result will be that they create a different poem (because of the context sensitivity of the event of the poem in which embodied voice contributes a layering of meaning in the work). Attempted appropriation doesn't necessarily mean creating an aesthetically and morally inferior work. In cases where the poet is a marginalized speaker, failure to acknowledge the significance of their embodied voice, that is, the action performed in the writing and performing of the poem (of communication/expression) in future performances (i.e. re-voicing) and reception of the work (as reader or audience), is to perpetuate oppression and cause harm. Although I have argued that the embodied performance is always significant, failure to recognize that significance will not always amount to harm but may just amount to failure to fully appreciate the work aesthetically. The moral significance will hinge on contingent features of society and the situatedness of the speaker/poet/performer and the relative dominance and privilege of the audience/reader. Furthermore, the poetry performance offers a space for those unjustly marginalized in society to be heard and seen and acknowledged as knowers, and this is what's potentially at stake in neglect of embodied voice in appreciation of poetry.[6]

Let's return to the example of Patricia Smith's performance of 'Skinhead' and Taylor Mali's re-voicing of her work. Mali attempts to appropriate Smith's poem but fails to do that. Mali's performance does not do the same thing that Smith's does. The failure in Mali's performance is grounded in the change of context of his act of voicing the words of the poem. It also seems that there is some sort of harm caused by Mali's failure, in that he renders aspects of Smith's expressive intention inaudible.

In discussions of cultural appropriation, the moral harm is thought to be due to power in-balances in society, where a vulnerable group's culture is appropriated by a dominant/oppressive group (although I note that the intimacy account gives a different analysis).[7] By applying this idea to the context of re-voicing works of poetry, we can argue that there is a moral harm where the words of an unjustly marginalized voice is subject to attempted appropriation by a dominant voice, thereby doing harm to the individual who originally aimed to use their words to perform a particular action. By removing certain significant contextual features, one's intentions are undermined due to the privilege and dominance of the one appropriating those words.

Erich Matthes writes, 'Whether a particular case is most saliently understood as one of silencing, exploitation, misrepresentation, or offence, what ultimately makes particular instances of cultural appropriation wrongful, and thus what grounds objections to them, is the way in which they manifest and/or exacerbate inequality and marginalization' (2019, p. 1004). The problem with re-voicing or neglecting the embodied voice in the reception of poetry is that it potentially contributes to silencing of the voice of the poet by divorcing the action they intended to perform from the words of the poem, thereby denying recognition of the poet as expressing a perspective. As Matthes writes, what makes this wrongful is when such silencing serves to exacerbate inequality and marginalization.[8]

Failure to recognize the contribution of the voice and body to the poem not only potentially changes what the work can do but denies the epistemic contribution made. Attempted appropriation of a poem may therefore be an example of what Emmalon Davis calls 'epistemic appropriation'. She writes, 'The harm of epistemic appropriation . . . is twofold. First, while epistemic resources developed within the margins gain intercommunal uptake, those resources are overtly detached from the marginalized knowers responsible for their production. Call this first harm *epistemic detachment*' (Davis 2018, p. 705). Re-voicing of certain works of poetry by certain poets will cause such epistemic detachment – embodied knowledge that was intended to be expressed through the performance of the work is detached from the body of the poet-performer. Davis writes, 'When epistemic detachment occurs, the intercommunal pool is expanded to incorporate new epistemic resources (e.g., concepts, interpretations, stories, and meanings), but the participatory role of marginalized contributors in the process of knowledge production is obscured' (ibid.). Applying this to the case of poetry, we can see how detaching the words of the poem from the context of the body (and the performance of identity) and attaching to a new body and context will alter the meaning of the work, concepts evoked, interpretation as well as the action performed. Therefore, on my view, the harm is characterized in terms of not only the epistemic denial but denial of agency.

Davis characterizes the second harm as follows: 'Epistemic misdirection occurs when epistemic resources developed within, but detached from, the margins are utilized in dominant discourses in ways that disproportionately benefit the powerful. That is to say, the benefits associated with the epistemic contributions of the marginalized are misdirected toward the comparatively privileged' (ibid.). By re-voicing, damage is done to the notion of authenticity in the performance of poetry, since the body is forgotten in the appreciation and evaluation of poetry. Therefore, on my view misdirection is more than an unfair distribution of benefits; it is also a failure to pay adequate attention to the value on offer in the poem (so misdirection in the sense of putting focus in the wrong place). As argued earlier, it is the poet-performer's body that grounds the words of the poem in showing what 'it means to live them [i.e. think and feel them] for at least the moment of their delivery' (Middleton 2009, p. 224) and, consequently, the action performed through them. The body provides the reference point, that is, the coming together of thoughts and feelings; to give the work a different embodied delivery is to change the reference point for those thoughts and feelings as expressed by the words and potentially change the action performed by those words. In the case of Taylor Mali's re-voicing of Smith's poem, the work becomes lesser for having been re-performed. But this would also be the case for a work such as Clare Collison's 'Truth Is Beauty' and her desire to make visible the invisible.

As Davis argues, in such cases the harm is not a result of denying members of marginalized groups the ability to contribute knowledge but in not recognizing them as knowers and as having made *that* epistemic contribution. She writes, 'Targets of epistemic appropriation are not prevented from putting knowledge into the public domain; rather, they are prevented from being recognized as having put knowledge into the public domain. That the members of marginalized groups are never acknowledged as contributors is essential to the perpetuation of their epistemic marginalization' (2018, p. 722). Failure to have one's contribution recognized is to render one's speech disempowered for one loses the power to be seen and heard in the context of that use of language (the poet's role in communicating through their poem is significantly diminished). Davis doesn't go far enough here since in the Mali case he was not denying Smith's authorship. In his act of re-voicing her work, he denied her ability to perform a particular action with her words. In other words, in his attempted appropriation, Mali removed the agency from the author of the words, thereby separating the expressive intention from the content.

Engaging with poetry is not enough to guarantee that the voices of unjustly marginalized poets are heard. The reader and audience of poetry must develop a sensitivity and awareness of the contribution of the embodied voice to meaning-making of the work. This ought to extend beyond poetry that straightforwardly references the body to poetry written about any subject since it is the poet's embodied voice that ultimately shapes the perspective of the poem and produces the action performed by those words. Limiting another's epistemic contribution to only knowledge that directly relates to certain characteristics of their body is just as much a problem as complete denial of voice and agency in perpetuating oppression. For instance, consider the following passage from *Poverty Safari* by Darren McGarvey:

> The second I wandered off that topic people started shuffling their papers and things got awkward. It seemed my criticism was often deemed not to be constructive enough. Despite the constant talk of empowerment and giving voice to the voiceless, it was obvious many of these people were only interested in my thoughts if they were about my experience as a 'poor' person. It was assumed that people like me had very little insight on anything else. (2018, p. 104)

The epistemic and performative contribution is connected to that individual's perspective, that is, patterns of thought and feelings that configure value informed by but not limited or reduced to embodied experience. The perspective is conveyed by the embodied voice, that is, the audio text, body text and context of performance. Recognizing this complexity is why we value hearing poets read their own work.

In the context of the poetry performance, it is the failure to recognize the contribution of the body in performance that causes harm in that it denies the voice of the poet-performer as having made that contribution and may limit what the poet is able to do with their words (for the words have shifted in meaning in virtue of that separation of words and embodied voice). Furthermore, such failure may in some cases have the consequence of excluding or diminishing the role of people from marginalized groups from developing communal understanding of relationships for which we need to appreciate individual experience and how we relate to one another. To deny certain voices the ability to contribute to such development of understanding is to perpetuate oppression and ultimately weaken understanding of human life.

Re-voicing and intertextuality

So far, I have considered the moral harm that can arise from re-voicing or re-performing a work by another. However, re-voicing doesn't always result in a moral harm and can in fact be morally beneficial and enable empowerment rather than hindering it. In some cases, rather than denying another their epistemic contribution, re-voicing/re-performance allows for multiplicity of perspectives to come to the fore.

In his article 'The Ethics and Aesthetics of Intertextual Writing', Paul Haynes applies the debate on cultural appropriation to the production of literary texts that incorporate texts from other sources. His project is to chart a difference between appropriation and expropriation in aesthetic rather than merely moral terms. He argues that 'appropriation (or misappropriation) includes instances in which characteristic narratives, techniques, symbols and artefacts are taken or imitated in a way that diminishes the original sources'. In the case of appropriation, the quality of the original source is undermined in its new presentation in that the aesthetic value of the appropriated text is diminished. 'In contrast', he writes, 'expropriation includes the act of repurposing narratives, techniques, symbols and artefacts in ways designed to enhance the original or provide benefits for the common good' (2021, p. 302). In the case of expropriation, the re-presentation of a text enhances its aesthetic value.

He argues that

> intertextual writing . . . expropriate the characters of a canonical work and insert them into novel relationships so that new aspects of identity or its setting can be elaborated and extended beyond its established world. In this way, the voices repeated within the intertextual work are not those of the author of the original or the derivative work, but are intermediaries, (re)writing the literary event that opens up new possibilities for the reader. (Haynes 2021, p. 303)

The key distinction for Haynes between permissible and impermissible appropriation of this sort is whether such appropriation reduces, closes off meaning of the original work (to serve dominant standards) or whether it serves to open up new meanings, thereby adding complexity to the original work (and critiquing dominance). Haynes analysis suggests that there are two standards at work in our evaluation of appropriation, namely, the aesthetic (whether appropriation results in opening or closing off meaning) and the political (whether appropriation causes harm or results in benefits to unjustly marginalized groups) but the two don't necessarily overlap.

Found poetry is a clear example of appropriation of texts. This is not mere attempted appropriation because they are not attempts to reproduce the original in another context but a transformation of words from one context to another. Poets have used texts, including newspapers (e.g. Edwin Morgan's headline poems), public documents (e.g. *I Hope Like Heck: The Selected Poems of Sarah Palin* by Michael Solomon, which uses the emails from Alaskan senator Sarah Palin) and even literary works (e.g. Terrance Hayes 'The Golden Shovel' and John Ashbery's cento 'To a waterfowl'). The stand-up comedian Dave Gorman is well known for taking comments that appear 'below the line' of online articles and turning them into poetry, performed as part of his TV series 'Modern Life Is Goodish'. The appropriation of such texts is placed in a poetic context that draws attention to the language use and consequently highlights the absurdity in the comments (there is no denial of agency). This example highlights how the appropriation of texts does not create a new, distinct work but one that is put in conversation with the original text. In this case, the performance of the words as poetry functions as a comment on the original text. As poet Annie Dillard writes, 'By entering a found text as a poem, the poet doubles its context. The original meaning remains intact, but now it swings between two poles. The poet adds, or at any rate increases, the element of delight. This is an urban, youthful, ironic, cruising kind of poetry. It serves up whole texts, or interrupted fragments of texts' (2016, n/p).

Reginald Dwayne Betts' redacted poems in his collection *Felon* (2019) use legal texts filed by the Civil Rights Corps on behalf of those imprisoned because they cannot afford bail. In creating his poems, he uses the blackout technique to redact parts of the texts as a way of drawing attention to the human tragedy. He writes in a short note at the end of the collection: 'These poems use redaction, not as a tool to obfuscate, but as a technique that reveals tragedy, drama, and injustice of a system that makes people simply a reflection of their bank accounts' (2019, p. 91). One might be tempted to treat such a work as concrete poetry, that is, poetry which prioritizes the visual and grounded in *opsis*. However, what's at the heart of Betts' blackout poems is a subversion of the act of redaction – whereas such an act often obscures meaning and revelation of truth, his act of redaction seeks instead to highlight the ways in which the legal system fails to respond with dignity. For instance, the redaction brings to the fore the repetition of the phrase 'It is the policy', which expresses how people can become trapped in the system without being able to be heard as individuals:

> Asked / for mercy /
> The court / ordered him to serve 44 days[9]

Another way in which meaning can be enriched in performance is by giving a work a new embodied voice (and therefore context). Take for instance, *Strange Fruit*, originally a poem by Abel Meeropol (a White Jewish man). The words of the poem lead us to contemplate the depths of racism experienced in the USA in the 1930s and the lynching of Black Americans. The poem is transformed when sung by Billie Holiday in 1930s/1940s American at a time when Black Americans were suffering daily violence. The staging of her performance highlighted her body with a simple spotlight and framed by silence.[10] The emotional, affective and attitudinal features of her performance transform the words beyond expression of moral outrage.

When sung by Holiday, the meaning of the lyrics is altered; we do not simply hear the words of the song as isolated units of meaning but they are set in the context of being performed by a Black woman in the United States. Voicing the words of another is not just an act of identification ('these words represent *my* experience', where what one does is using the words of another to speak on one's behalf) but is transformative ('I am *using* these words to represent *my* experience', using the words of another to highlight difference and to contribute one's voice to concept formation and meaning-making). Such re-voicing makes a positive contribution to meaning-making activities, opening up new possibilities for the audience not available in the original work (unlike the Smith-Mali example, this doesn't deny Meeropol's expressive intention but adds to it, in a similar manner to the example of translation) and gives voice to those who have been marginalized in society. Although an example of a musical performance, this highlights important features common to poetry performances, namely the relationship between words, body/voice and staging in meaning-making.[11]

The example of Billie Holiday's re-voicing of 'Strange fruit' also brings into focus the potential value of not merely re-voicing but doing this within the performance space. The performance space can be a site to invert who is heard and who is silent, thereby serving an important role in rebalance of power and attention. The audience, for the duration of the performance, may come to appreciate what it is to listen to another and, in doing so, appreciate what it is to not be heard themselves. To put it another way, the audience becomes aware of the power of silence in how it enables a voice to be heard in the strong sense. Through the performance space, those who have been silenced in society can now be heard in a space that demands the silence of the audience (or, where the poet may call on response from the audience, this is within their control in performance).

The important environmental features of the live poetry performance go beyond the silence that comes in the moment before and after the performance (during the performance, there is a degree of silence but, as we will see, there is also space for the audience's response to be heard). This acts as a frame to the performance, which creates a heightened sense of attention and privilege in whose voice ought to be heard. The experience of watching a performance of a poem heightens awareness of silence that amplifies the voice of the poet (as it stands in contrast to the silence). In the poetry performance, every word is privileged and treated as significant in the way it punctuates this silence. Hearing the voice of the poet is relational: one encounters the voice of another – it is externally located both in the sense of being centred in the poet on the stage but also in how their voice reverberates around the room – but one always hears in relation to oneself (the location of the hearer).[12] As a consequence, the audience must resist separating the sound of the words from the speaker and actively attend to the words as centred in another.

The features of the staging of poetry and the way in which it demands the attention of the audience provide the poet with a unique position to shift focus with a shift from first-person to second-person pronouns.[13] In Smith's performance poem 'Skinhead', the first person is used for the majority of the piece but employs a powerful shift to the second person, which acts as a direct address to the spectator. As Culler notes, such a shift is from 'reflection to invocation' (2015, p. 189). In that moment, the audience might experience the feeling of being caught out if they had not listened attentively and deeply enough to the poet's embodied delivery:

The poet rich in attention and privileged by the silence of those listening (or noise should they wish to invoke it), might direct everyone's attention onto the spectator. If that spectator is not entirely comfortable or engaged, they may feel implicated or unwelcomely involved in the politics of the eyes. (Bearder 2020, p. 228)

In such a moment, the body of the speaker becomes ever present in addressing the other, for it draws attention to the affective relationality between speaker and hearer, and calls for a response from the audience. What a focus on poetry in performance can reveal is the value of the performance space in terms of offering not only a space for one to speak but also as a space to aid in the aesthetic education of learning to hear others well: not only hearing the words of the poem in a communal space in which one is aware of one's response in the context of other audience members but also the affective relationship between the words, voice and body that come together to make meaning that is not reducible to the meaning of the words.

The aesthetic experience afforded by the poetry performance demands attention to the individual personal expression because of the role of voice and body in the performance. However, there is an additional need to reflect on the situatedness of the poet-performer and other potential performers in the performance, staging and programming of performed poetry. It is only with this awareness of situatedness that we can see the distinction between appropriate appropriation and inappropriate appropriation, and ensure the positive civic function of the poetry performance remains.

Context sensitivity and page poetry

In presenting her reader-response account, Ronsenblatt writes, 'Every reading act is an event, or a transaction involving a particular reader and a particular pattern of signs, a text, and occurring at a particular time in a particular context. Instead of two fixed entities acting on one another, the reader and the text are two aspects of a dynamic situation' (Rosenblatt 1983, p. 1063). Each reading occurs within a particular context; not only does that make reference to the reader's own circumstances (their knowledge, expectations and own experiences) but also the context of the poem. Of course, page poetry presents an opportunity to read a poem ignoring its context (who the author is, when it was written and any other information available). In many cases, that will not affect appreciation of the work and won't be morally relevant. However, there are cases of page poetry in which to fail to acknowledge the context of the work is to fail to consider what the poet is doing in presenting their work and therefore denying the poet agency and acknowledgement of their epistemic contribution. Just as in the performance case, it is for the reader to consider the significance of the context of the work. Jessica Mason makes an obvious but important point: 'If readers do not make a link then it does not exist within their experience of that text and plays no role in their reading' (2019, p. 3).

Take for instance, the sequence 'Whereas' (2019) by Layli Long Soldier. Long Soldier identifies as both a US citizen and a citizen of the Oglala Lakota Nation (in virtue of her membership of the Oglala Sioux Tribe). In the introduction to the sequence, she writes, 'in this dual citizenship, I must work, I must eat, I must art, I must mother, I must friend, I must listen, I must observe, constantly I must live' (p. 57). The poems bring to the fore the difficulty of living with dual citizenship and dual identity in a world that seeks to highlight division.

She notes that the sequence itself is a response to the Congressional Resolution of Apology to Native Americans signed by Barak Obama in 2009. One of the functions of her poems is to draw attention to the event of an apology; to apologize is to perform an action. She notes that neither was the apology read aloud at the time nor was it addressed to the Native American community for no representatives of the community were invited to witness the event of the document's signing. There was an event of signing the document but there is a problem in viewing this as the event of apology; the apology itself cannot be located at a particular time, which is a necessary feature of being an event. Long Soldier's poetic sequence highlights the problem of such an apology that doesn't have the status of an event through the event-making features of a poetic use of language.

The opening of the poetic sequence could be taken as simply a personal expression of how one feels about receiving apologies:

WHEREAS when offered an apology I watch each movement the shoulders high and folding, tilt of the head both eyes down or straight through me[14]

In the event of apology, more is communicated than the words of apology. One is able to judge for sincerity, acknowledgement and accountability. The fluid grammar of her whereas statement that lacks punctuation is in contrast to the legal language structures adopted in the original text. The effect is to prioritize the affective and emotional expression, which is left out of the legal text.

Her sequence follows the same tripartite structure as the apology: whereas statements, resolution, disclaimer. In a legal document, the term 'whereas' is used to mean 'considering that' to introduce statements. For example, the text of the apology opens with 'Whereas the ancestors of today's Native Peoples inhabited the land of the present-day United States since time immemorial and for thousands of years before the arrival of people of European descent'. In contrast, Long Soldier's sequence opens with a Whereas statement that undermines the idea of an apology as legal text, and her sequence can be read as a counter to the original text.

Long Soldier's response in her 'Whereas statements' documents the ways oppression manifests for an individual: 'Whereas at four years old I read the first chapter of the Bible aloud I was not Christian',[15] which makes reference to the practice of forcing Native American children to Christian boarding schools where they were taught to conform to Euro-American culture. Here, the personal contrasts with the generalized statements in the legal document.

To fail to consider the context (given in her introduction to the sequence) would mean to fail to appreciate Long Soldier's expressive intention in writing the sequence since it is only when contextually situated with acknowledgement of her identity and the apology that the reader is able to understand the functioning of the poetic sequence as critique: it is seeking to undermine, expose and comment on the apology. This is brought into sharp focus with the inclusion of her disclaimer. The original disclaimer reads:

Nothing in this Joint Resolution—
(1) authorizes or supports any claim against the United States; or
(2) serves as a settlement of any claim against the United States.

In her book, she changes 'against the United States' to 'against Layli Long Soldier by the United States' and ends with 'here in the grassesgrassesgrasses', which functions to return us to the land and makes plain the way in which the disclaimer in the original text undermines the apology and retains the assertion of the United States as owners of the land on which citizens live.

Conclusion

The discussion in this chapter has highlighted the significance of the embodied performance of poetry both in terms of the aesthetic contribution the body makes to meaning-making in the experience of the poem but also in terms of how the body of the poet-performer draws attention to the expressive intention behind the work, that is, to what the poet is doing in using these words. In many cases, the embodied reading of poetry represents what it is to live these words, to inhabit them, even if just for the duration of the performance; the use of words is connected to the particular person speaking those words and therefore defines the relationality to the audience. As we have seen, consideration of the contribution of the body to the performance is not merely aesthetic but may be, in some cases, morally significant. Where meaning of a poetic text is reduced (and problematically so, for instance, by losing the expressive intention of critique), not only is the work reduced aesthetically but may result in a moral defect in the work.

On the other hand, where meaning of a poetic text is enhanced (by adding in further layers of complexity, for example, through the addition of voices), not only does the work become aesthetically richer, but may, potentially, have (moral and political) benefits for the performer of the work. What the examples of positive cases of re-voicing works reveal is that poetry can disrupt silencing by carving out space to be heard, placing readers/audiences in a relationship to the unknown and unknowable (by respecting self-other differentiation), and subverting power dynamics in society that underwrite their marginalization. One upshot of the view I have presented is that re-voicing some works of lyric poetry can aid reparation when poet and reader/audience are brought into relationship through the poetic work, where the reader/audience must acknowledge the poet without being able to fully grasp the words independently of the felt grasp of the performance.

The nature of poetry in performance entails a role for the audience. Words are not merely embodied but require an audience to make the connection between words, voice and body. Although the body of the poet is not present in the same way when reading a poem off the page, that doesn't mean that we are always free to engage with the poem without appreciation of contextual features (such as who the author is, when they were writing and any other information made available together with the work). Consideration of the words used with expressive intention that makes reference to the poet can enhance aesthetic appreciation of the work. Furthermore, greater awareness of the potential expressive intention of the poet in creating the work may be important for simply recognizing them as contributing knowledge and being heard, which is significant in a world in which not everyone's voice is heard equally.

5

Poetic cognitivism

Introduction

The arguments of this book support the claim that engaging with poetry is important for our understanding of different kinds of (positive and negative) relationships, such as loneliness, loss, togetherness, community and belonging, that go beyond mere conceptual grasp to require a social understanding of how people (do/don't) relate to one another and the significance of relationship. In this chapter, I argue that although enhancement of such understanding is an important cognitive gain, there is a further, more important, cognitive gain to be had from our engagement with poetry, namely, that engaging with poetry on the page or on the stage can also help to cultivate the intellectual virtue of humility.[1] I will argue that one's engagement with the perspective on offer in the poem is central to poetry's role in cultivating humility.

Lorraine Code characterizes intellectual virtues as 'a matter of orientation towards the world, towards one's knowledge-seeking self and towards other such selves as part of the world' (1987, p. 20). Intellectual humility can then be seen as part of one's perspective, that is, the ways one thinks, feels and interacts with the world in virtue of their network of beliefs, desires, values and commitments. Intellectual humility enables one to approach the world and others with a sense of the limitations in their ability to understand and have knowledge of the lives of others that one relates to. In other words, intellectual humility is to acknowledge and embrace self-other differentiation, and to consider relationality as central to the understanding of human life (rather than prioritizing one's own subjective and personal experience). Although there are many features of humility proposed in the philosophical literature,[2] I am going to focus on just those dimensions that are applicable in the poetry context. Of course, this will have the result that engaging with poetry is not sufficient for the cultivation of humility but I can still make the argument that reading poetry provides an important framework for developing some aspects of humility, which is not insignificant. What this will reveal is the link between intellectual humility and understanding relationships.

Alessandra Tanesini (2018) argues that intellectual humility consists of both modesty and self-acceptance. Modesty captures how the humble person approaches the world and others; self-acceptance captures what one does with the information one receives. Tanesini writes, 'self-acceptance is a way of caring that one has limitations because of their effects on the pursuit of various epistemic goods such as truth or understanding, rather than for their potential impact on one's reputation or one's sense of self-esteem' (Tanesini 2018, p. 405). Following this analysis, I will argue that modesty is needed in the reader and audience in order to make the effort to try to understand the perspective of the poem, rather than expecting meaning and communication via the poem to be transparent. Furthermore, it is modesty that brings to the fore self-other differentiation because one approaches the poem with the awareness that full understanding may be unavailable due to the limitations of one's perspective. The very act of engaging with a poem involves a degree of failure. Although something constructive may come from one's engagement with the poem (such as triggering awareness of language and self-reflection), it also helps one to realize the gap between their own perspective and that of the poem. Humility is a matter of not merely recognizing self-other differentiation but also *valuing* self-other differentiation and showing care for the other despite not being able to fully bridge the gap between. Self-acceptance is required in order for the reader/audience to acknowledge where the limits are in their understanding or grasp of the perspective of the poem, in other words, that their own perspective that they bring to the poem will get in the way of fully appreciating the perspective of the poem. At best, what can be achieved is a recognition of overlap or shareability between perspectives. Humility therefore requires that one appreciates both the limitations of what is available to one in understanding and what counts as success in understanding another. In the latter, I argue that poetry helps us to appreciate felt grasp where full cognitive grasp is lacking and that this can still count as understanding.

It is important to my project to demonstrate that the way in which poetry cultivates intellectual humility goes beyond what is achievable through attention to the ordinary use of language. The cognitive gain may be achievable in a number of ways, but in order to maintain a cognitivist view, I must argue that the substantive cognitive gain is a result of engagement with the poem; in other words, it is the aesthetics of the work that give rise to the epistemic gain. To illustrate, take for instance growing a plant from seed. There may be a number of ways of growing a seedling (placing in moist compost, suspending in water, using rooting powder), but those ways are only appropriately tied to the success of growing if they are the features responsible for yielding those results. I can easily misattribute my success to playing Mozart's Requiem on repeat during germination, yet it is simply the fertile compost, warmth and moisture that are responsible for providing the beneficial context required for germination. The playing of music is completely incidental (the result would be the same with or without the music). One of the complicating factors when considering the cognitive value of works of art is that they make use of the everyday, such as depiction in the case of visual art. In the case of poetry, this is simply the use of everyday language and appeal to meaning. To make the cognitivist case for poetry one needs to show that the epistemic gain is not simply in the use of words (particular sentence formation and units of linguistic meaning) but in the *poetic* use of language.

Additionally, it is important to make the case that engagement with poetry goes beyond offering mere trivial cognitive gains (e.g. merely another experience, rather than another kind of experience that delivers something unique from what is available in the everyday). My argument here is to say that what is available in the work of poetry is the experience of encountering another's perspective and attempting (yet ultimately failing) to understand it. Therefore, the epistemic value lyric poetry offers is twofold: first, it develops our understanding of the value and significance of relationships between perspectives (which depend on appreciation/acknowledgment of the ways in which we relate – or fail to relate – to one another). Second, in doing so, it cultivates the intellectual virtue of humility by attending to the limits of perspective and bringing to the fore the significance of self-other differentiation.

This isn't a claim about uniqueness as such. One can develop both understanding of relationships and intellectual humility by other means. It's also clear that we are able to use and understand interpersonal concepts without reading poetry. Instead, the claim is about the unique experience that engaging with lyric poetry provides for self-reflection on one's own perspective and therefore refinement in understanding. The epistemic benefit of engaging with works of lyric poetry is integral to the poeticity of the works.

The discussion in this chapter may well point to the value of engagement with art more generally. One might argue that perspective shows up in other art forms, such as in works of painting, photography, sculpture and installation.[3] Rather than being a problem, it is a benefit if such analysis of engagement with poetry can reveal value in other artworks beyond. By placing us in relation to others and other perspectives we may find connection through overlapping perspectives, that is, what we share as human beings but it also highlights what we don't share, that is, those moments of disconnection. This double experience of connection and disconnection asks us to consider how we relate to others, and our own place in the world in relation to theirs. Understanding the difference between our perspectives can promote greater insight into those things that bring us together, where our perspectives overlap despite our differences. To appreciate and acknowledge connection and disconnection simultaneously is the mark of intellectual humility as well as being essential to properly understanding the value and significance of human relationships.

Humility and perspective

Intellectual humility is essential to empathy. Empathy is often characterized as a form of feeling *for* and *with* another. To empathize with another, one must not only have the other as the focus of their emotion but share in their emotional response as well (what is often referred to in the literature as affective matching). John Gibson argues, 'Empathy makes possible an especially intimate and powerful form of *identification*. It underwrites our capacity . . . to feel not just *for* another but *as* another. To this extent, empathy has as its goal the overstepping, in emotion, of the space that runs between oneself and another' (2016b, p. 234). In Gibson's analysis of empathy, he highlights the power of empathy to bring two people together through shared feeling. It is not simply being in the same affective state (which could be accidental by responding to the same stimulus or as a result of emotional contagion) but being in the same affective state because of one's attention to the other and consideration of their point of view. For instance, to feel empathy for a friend who isn't successful with a job application isn't just to feel sorry for them but also to share in their feeling of disappointment because you are aware of why they are disappointed. One way of unpacking this thought is to appeal to the role of perspective and to characterize empathy as a form of perspective-taking. Feelings of empathy go beyond merely having an awareness that another is feeling a particular way towards something to considering the context of that feeling in terms of the person's wider beliefs, desires, values, etc. The idea that feelings of empathy require one to take up the perspective of the other is to explain how one's feeling of empathy is properly rooted in temporarily activated concern for the other.

Such perspective-taking is often considered as a kind of imaginative exercise (as distinct from other kinds of emotional responses such as sympathy or compassion that might involve a feeling for or with another but lack the imaginative component).[4] For instance, Olivia Bailey argues that 'empathetic emotion [is] a special category of thought-directed emotion, one that is directed at what we take to be our imaginative recreations of other people's situations' (Bailey 2022, p. 53). In other words, empathy is the product of a particular kind of cognitive and affective exercise of attempting to recreate imaginatively another's perspective. Or as Bailey puts it, empathy is 'the activity of imaginatively re-centering one's perspective' (Bailey 2022, p. 55).[5]

This emphasis on imaginative perspective-taking has provided support to those who want to argue for the cognitive value of art and literature by appealing to the value of imaginative perspective-taking for cultivating empathy.[6] Maureen Donnelly argues that 'engaging in literary fiction involves practice in making sense of actions from a point of view other than our own' (Donnelly 2019, p. 11). Likewise, Elisabeth Camp argues that what's on offer in one's engagement with literature is a form of conceptual knowledge that is acquired by 'trying on' the perspective in the work. What this means is that we are not simply stepping into a character or narrator's shoes where what we would be doing is imagining being that person and experiencing what they do: 'Trying on a perspective requires more than just imagining that a set of propositions is true, or even imagining experiencing something. Rather, it involves actually structuring one's thinking in certain ways, so that certain sorts of properties stick out as especially notable and explanatorily central in one's intuitive thinking' (Camp 2017, p. 74). What we engage with is not simply a character but a character who is represented in a particular way by the use of description, metaphor and imagery that in turn governs interpretation of a particular character's actions and responses.

According to Camp, one's engagement with a work of literature calls for the reader to enter into the perspective it embodies, leaving to one side one's own perspective. Engaging with literature on this view allows one to experience a radically different way of thinking from the habitual thinking of one's own perspective. By adopting a different perspective (even if temporarily), one experiences what is involved in valuing and thereby prioritizing different thoughts, and so on that governs connections made with other beliefs and shapes emotional response that may or may not have a bearing on one's own perspective going forwards.

Given my own view of poetry as perspectival, it might seem straightforward to argue that the cognitive value of engaging with lyric poetry is to be found in how it enables the reader/audience to try on different perspectives (distinct from their own). However, in my analysis of our engagement with poetry I have also highlighted two other key features which complicate this perspective-taking view, namely, how poetry draws our attention to relationality, which in turn helps to prioritize self-other differentiation, and that the perspectives on offer in a poem are incomplete and fragmentary (despite affective completeness). Therefore, in reading a poem we not only attempt to understand the perspective embodied by the work but we do so with awareness of the connections and disconnections with our own perspective. Rather than this being a barrier to empathy, I will argue that in fact this is a requirement for empathy. In other words, this is to reject the analysis of empathy as involving identification and overstepping, and instead to argue that self-other differentiation and awareness of the limitations of our own perspectives are at the heart of empathy. Consequently, I will argue that empathy is central to poetry in that it is experientially guiding and affective.

Self-other differentiation

Rather than being something that enables proper empathetic response to another, 'overstepping' is problematic where one might seemingly feel *for* another yet what is actually going on is a kind of identification or recognition of similarity of experience. For instance, when someone recounts their story of some tragedy, the other responds with 'I feel for you. That happened to me'.

Through identification, the object of the emotional response shifts from the other person to oneself. Such identification fails to count as empathy since it is not a genuine instance of sharing in the emotional response of the other (with temporarily activated concern for the other) but is a simple projection of the self onto the other. It is merely one's own – imagined or remembered – emotional response. To put this in other words, there is a forgetting that it is not you but the other who is in the situation. What happens in the case of empathy is an attempt to appreciate a situation from another's point of view without losing sight of this being experienced by the other. In other words, we attempt to consider what it is to experience such circumstances with a particular set of beliefs and desires that we take the other to hold (which may or may not overlap with our own).

Bailey argues that

> critically, this emotion only qualifies as empathetic if I who am experiencing it persistently understand my own emotion in a particular light. I must retain a firm awareness of two facts: first, my emotion is responsive to a situation that is not actual for me, and second, it is responsive to a situation that is actual for the other. Furthermore, I must interpret my own emotion as corresponding to at least some degree to other's original emotional response to their situation. (Bailey 2022, p. 53)

Here Bailey is specifically pushing against the idea that empathy involves identification in a strong sense; although I recognize a relationship between my feeling and the other person's (affective matching), I must also appreciate that my feeling has arisen in a different way to the other's. For them, it is in response to their actual situation; for me, it is through my imagining being in their situation (with some degree of appreciation of their perspective and concern for them). Heidi Maibom writes that empathy

> involves some comprehension that one's own feeling is not a merited response to the situation one is in oneself, but is a response better suited to the other person's situation (or possibly state of mind). At the same time, one must understand that one's emotional response is not simply irrational or inappropriate. It is appropriate *as related to the other*. (Maibom 2017, p. 2)

Amy Coplan also emphasizes the importance of self-other differentiation in her analysis of empathy: 'empathy is a complex imaginative process in which an observer simulates another person's situated psychological states while maintaining clear self-other differentiation' (2011, p. 5).

To help make clear why self-other differentiation is crucial to empathy proper, Coplan (2011) distinguishes between self-directed perspective-taking and other-directed perspective-taking. In the case of self-directed perspective-taking, I simply imagine what it would be like to be in *that* situation without regard for the other's point of view (their desires, beliefs, ways of thinking). In other words, one simply considers what it would be like for them to be in the other's shoes. Amy Coplan describes self-directed perspective-taking as a 'type of pseudo-empathy since people often mistakenly believe that it provides them with access to the other's point of view when it does not' (Coplan 2011, p. 12). She writes, 'In other-oriented perspective-taking, a person represents the other's situation from the other person's point of view and thus attempts to simulate the target individual's experiences as though she were the target individual. Thus I imagine that I am you in your situation, which is to say I attempt to simulate your experiences from your point of view' (2011, p. 10). It is important to note Coplan's use of the word 'attempt' here. I do not need to think and feel exactly as the other does but to appreciate ways in which they might differ from me (and where I might not be able to properly simulate their situation). My simulation can be more or less accurate. In the case of other-directed perspective-taking, self-other differentiation is a key part of the experience; although I am sharing (in some sense) your affective state, my feelings have arisen by my concern for you. Following this thought, Coplan argues, 'Taking up one's perspective without clear self-other differentiation can result in enmeshment or in self-oriented perspective-taking, which prevents one from successfully representing the other's experience and leads to personal distress, false consensus effects, and prediction errors' (Coplan 2011, p. 17). In such cases, one loses sight of the other who is actually experiencing whatever has caused the emotion and instead one represents it as happening to them. If this picture is correct and self-other differentiation is essential to proper empathy, then this is where we can find a role for humility.

To avoid the problem of overstepping, one must develop an attitude of humility in order to be appreciative of where one's perspective overlaps with another (through recognition of experience that enables understanding of the other's position) but also where the limits of one's own perspective lies, that is, what of the other person's perspective is unavailable to me. Through sharing a meal, for instance, there will likely be some overlap in our experience since we are attending to the same thing but how we experience it will be different in virtue of what we each individually bring to that experience. I can try to consider things from your position (perhaps you are eating with a knife and fork, whereas I am using my hands), but there will always be aspects of your experience and how you think that are unknowable to me (and ungraspable due to my own perspective and consequent way of thinking). One might be aware that their perspective has limitations, but to fully appreciate what that means, one must experience those limits.

Although Donnelly argues for perspective-taking, she is careful to draw a distinction between subjective *perspectives* and subjective *experiences*. She writes:

> I take a subjective perspective (or, point of view) to be the way the world is characterized for a particular person in his experience of it. My perspective includes common characterizations (for example, like my friend, I see my cats as furry and four-legged), characterizations that may be unique to me (for example, I see my cats as pleasing and comforting), and general beliefs about types of things (for example, I believe that all cats are sentient and deserve moral consideration). A perspective is not an experience – though the way in which things are characterized for me changes over time, my perspective is not an event that unfolds in time and space. It is more like a grid through which my experience is structured. (Donnelly 2019, p. 14)

In empathizing with another, I will try to recreate their subjective perspective; what I don't get is access to information about their subjective experience. Furthermore, my appreciation of another's subjective perspective will be an approximation which explains why attempts to empathize are not always successful. Susan Dwyer puts this more strongly:

> I cannot take up your perspective on the world. I can imagine it, I can empathise with your situation, but I can never really see and experience life as you do. My grasp of your understanding and experience of things will always be mine. We are, as it were, locked in our minds. And these barriers are as relevant to my grasp of your experience of me as they are to my grasp of your experience of eating ice-cream. (2008, p. 6)

However, that doesn't reduce our efforts to mere self-directed perspective-taking but instead highlights the limitations with other-directed perspective-taking; regardless of the limitations of our perspectives, we must seek ways of connecting with others despite this and attempting to appreciate the difference in how they think and feel. As Donnelly points out, taking up a perspective on something does not entail a complete shift in perspective but an imaginative exercise which doesn't require that I let go of my current perspective:

> Imaginative engagement in literature always involves perspective shifting. Objects and events that are not present or currently unfolding from the reader's perspective are depicted as being present or as currently unfolding. People who are not important, beloved, or desirable from the reader's perspective are depicted as being important, beloved, or desirable. (2019, p. 15)

What is needed here is for the reader to appreciate the difference between their own perspectives and those of others. In other words, appreciating that others have different perspectives and perspectival relationships gives rise to the recognition of self-other differentiation. And this doesn't involve any kind of imaginative identification or stepping into the shoes of another; in fact, it requires recognition of separation and difference. According to Donnelly, all that is required to appreciate another's perspective is to recognize things as making sense to that person.

What I am doing in empathizing is considering the limits of my own perspective, and through imagination, I am attempting to extend those boundaries by considering feeling and thinking differently (with another providing a framework in which to attempt to feel and think differently). The motivation is consistent with intellectual humility in that my focus on the limits of my own perspective is not out of concern for any gains available to me but out of concern for the other, of wanting to understand them and how they are feeling despite our differences (and my own limitations).

Humility and limitations of perspective

One problem with the talk of perspective-shifting is that this covers two types of claim: radical perspective-shifting, which takes place on a global level. If one were to radically shift perspective, then one would change every aspect of how they think and feel in an attempt to match that of the other. Modest perspective-shifting, on the other hand, takes place at a local level. To undergo modest perspective-shifting, one only needs to attempt to isolate particular beliefs, desires, values and commitments and consider what would be the result of thinking and feeling otherwise. On the modest view, the rest of one's perspective remains intact and therefore continues to contribute more widely to how one processes information, including the consideration of hypothetical beliefs, desires, values and so on. Although talk of perspective-shifting in the literature suggests a wide acceptance of modest perspective-shifting, where the activity is characterized as a form of imaginative contemplation in a more or less isolated way as opposed to a rejection of one's existing network of beliefs, values, commitments and so on it's clear that the modest view incorporates a wide range in degree of perspective-shifting.

The task is not that of self-directed perspective-taking, where one simply imagines being in a particular situation or thinking/responding in a particular way. Instead, trying on a perspective (or engaging in perspective-shifting) is empathetic. It involves both an imaginative exercise (in order to generate a representation of the other's situation) and awareness that the perspective one is engaging with is distinct from one's own (and consequently, not fully graspable). One, therefore, does not need to actually reject any existing beliefs, desires, commitments or values or change the way these relate to one another. Instead, one engages in a form of representational thinking.

In making sense of this, Derek Matravers' distinction between 'confrontations' and 'representations' is helpful: 'confrontations are situations in which action is possible. Representations are situations in which action is not possible because what is being represented to us is out of reach' (Matravers 2014, p. 47). If what we are engaging with is a kind of thinking about the other that generates a representation of them in their situation, it is clear that there is an awareness of self-other differentiation and that my representation may be more or less accurate of their actual situation. Being a representation and not a confrontation places me, the empathizer, in a different relation to the object of emotional response, one in which one is 'governed by and to some degree replicat[es] how that other experiences his or her (or its) situation. In empathizing, my sense of another's situation and of his or her concerns in that situation sets the terms for my experiential perspective' (Maibom 2017, p. 306). In other words, the exercise of empathetic engagement is the representation of another's subjective perspective that produces my experiential perspective of the other's perceived emotional response.

Further support for this imaginative-representational understanding of perspective-shifting comes from the thought that in our engagement with a work of literature, including works of poetry, we must begin from one's own perspective in order to begin the process of understanding and appreciation of the work. One's own perspective provides the initial basis of our orientation towards the perspective on offer in the poem. The perspective of the work cannot provide such a framework for the reader to adopt from the outset, since it is something that unfolds through engagement with the text. It's therefore clear that in order to engage with the work, one needs to use their own perspective in attempting to understand, appreciate and respond to the work.

However, such a view suggests some crucial limitations of perspective-shifting in virtue of it being an exercise of imaginative recreation or representation of another's point of view. As Morton argues:

> Imagination is always partial and very often inaccurate. This is evident and inescapable in non-psychological imagination. Even imagining the layout of some very familiar location, such as your own home, you will leave out many details and get many others, for example the relative proportions of different walls, wrong. Incompleteness and limited accuracy is a feature of all imagination. Another way of saying this is that we imagine representations of facts, and we humans can never imagine all of any fact and always misimagine something about it. Imagination is in this respect like belief or expectation or memory, even when its vehicle is image-like. (Morton 2017, pp. 183–4)

How we go about such perspective-shifting will be governed to some extent by how we perceive the other's situation (informed by our own perspective) and further limited by our inability to fully and accurately imagine something as complex as another mind.

Rather than perspective-shifting being characterized in terms of the new perspective adopted, it instead ought to be characterized in terms of the negotiation that takes place between reader/audience and poem. As Luca Pocci argues, engaging with works of literature involves 'a process of negotiation between reader and text, between what is important for her and what is important in it' (Pocci 2007, p. 100). This idea of negotiation between reader and text suggests differences in the perspectives of the reader and the perspective embedded in the text but yet that there is a possibility to develop a shared or sharing of perspective through the experience of engaging with the work.

In Chapter 1, I argue that the way in which we use our individual and unique embodied voices expresses (and makes available at least in some limited way) our own perspective, that is, the way in which our engagement with the world and our sense of place within it is governed by a network of commitments, concepts, that configures value (it orientates us through prioritization of what we care about). Lyric poetry makes use of voice. In the live performance, the audience is made aware that they are encountering the expression of another's perspective through attention to the embodied voice. In reading, the reader is confronted with a perspective that is uncoupled from a body; it is incomplete and fragmentary without being grounded in a particular body. The reader must give voice to the words on the page yet that does not mean the reader is free to ignore the constraints on voice that are given by the structure of the work. Instead, the reader must find a way in, a way to make the connections alive in the work through the use of their own voice. As I argued in Chapter 2, this is by no means an easy task; it is a negotiation of perspectives (reader's and poem's) in which the experience of a felt gap within that negotiation is just as much a part of the poem as the connections the reader successfully expounds in the poem. In either case, the live performance or the private reading experience, one encounters another's perspective that is not completely within reach from one's own perspective.

That's not to say that one cannot grasp a belief held by or shared with another; for example, grass is green (my belief is similar to someone else's since they are both the result of attending to the same stuff in the world) – there will be lots of overlap in our beliefs, for instance, in virtue of our being members of the same linguistic community – but how central that belief is in a system or network of thought will differ (I might not hold the belief as firmly as you do; that is, it would take less to convince me otherwise).

> The same feature may be assigned different structural roles within the same overall set of elements, which can in turn imbue that feature with different affective, evaluative, and even conceptual significances. Thus, a spatio-temporally equivalent gesture can seem threatening or merely awkward, depending on one's overall characterization of the person performing it, including especially demographic features like race and gender. (Camp 2017, p. 81)

Such a hierarchy of beliefs shapes how thinking goes on, that is, how new beliefs are incorporated into the network of beliefs, commitments, values and so on. How that belief connects to value and particular connections to other beliefs (associations, entailment etc.). This, of course, explains difference in critical reception to works of literature.

In my essay 'Linking Perspectives', I argue:

> In the case of a poem, we are engaging with something that relies on shared language and invokes shared concepts; therefore, the reader is encouraged to move beyond their idiosyncratic perspective to a more sharable perspective, a human perspective. What the poem does is give us an awareness of the different perspectives one can adopt by setting up an encounter with other perspectives presented as part of a complex whole, rather than demand we understand it as a unified whole. (Simecek 2022, p. 312)

What engagement with poetry offers is the experience of stretch or tension in one's own perspective in the attempt to understand the perspective of the work through a process of negotiation between my own perspective and ways of understanding and what I take to make sense to the other.

The claim I wish to make in relation to poetry is that in our engagement with a work of poetry, we encounter other perspectives, but these are not perspectives we can simply take up and try out but perspectives that enable us to extend our perspectival horizons through the effort of trying to understand another perspective from within our own. Total understanding of another's perspective is an impossibility given this would entail abandonment of one's existing perspective but there is value in the experience of effort in trying to grasp another perspective (albeit ultimately failing). As Collingwood writes, 'a partial and imperfect understanding is not the same thing as a complete failure to understand' (Collingwood 1958, p. 309). Cultivating humility, then, is important in enabling cognitive growth for an individual. Appreciating where the limits of our perspectives are and trying to stretch them in some small way allows the development of one's perspective (and may potentially lead to changes to that perspectival framework to accommodate the new information). Poetry is difficult but so is understanding other people. Poetry can help us to appreciate that difficulty and show ways in which we can attempt to understand others however imperfect that understanding might be.

Cultivating humility through poetry

The experience of engaging with much contemporary poetry reveals a gap between an aesthetic grasp of the work and a cognitive grasp; in other words, the poem feels complete (gives a sense of being whole) yet the reader/audience might not fully understand the poem and be able to fully resolve it. In her essay, 'Poetry and Directions for thought', Eileen John points to the difficulty and complexity of understanding and appreciating a work of poetry in terms of fully grasping what the work is doing, that is, in fully grasping its perspective. John writes:

> While the value of an experience that is only incompletely thinkable for me, or only thinkable in a kind of surrendering mode, is not straightforward – I probably have not, for instance, directly learned anything – it has what I will call a quality of growth. I have the sense that my resources have been used, even if I have not controlled how they have been used, and I have reached a different structure of associations and tendencies for further thought. (John 2013a, p. 468)

What is apparent in John's description of her experience of reading poetry is central to what it is to approach poetry with humility – there is a care expressed for the perspective of the poem and the act of self-expression that the poem represents that is not rewarded by (and even resists) cognitive grasp. She also makes the point that one is using one's own resources in engaging with the poem. This is important since it is through the challenge of applying one's own perspective to something that presents a different way of forging connections that results in the growth John makes reference to. However, the reader/audience must approach the poem with a willingness to adjust their perspective to accommodate a different 'structure of associations and tendencies for further thought'.

What the poem offers is something we can grasp affectively. As Charles Bernstein writes, 'the sound and tone and mood of the poem [can be] perceived intuitively, as one hears a song without necessarily concentrating on it or being able to say what it is about' (2011, p. 47). Where affect goes, cognition tries to follow but this is where we encounter difficulty. What we are able to do with the perspective of the poem is affectively engage with it; we have a felt grasp but not a complete cognitive grasp. I feel my way through the unfolding of the poem and feel the connections it suggests but I am left not being able to fully make sense of all the connections in the work, that is, the particular perspective from which the poem makes sense as a complex whole. The poem unfolds as an event that I, the reader/audience, am left to interpret. The promise of felt coherence of the work is resisted by not being able to fully settle the connections in thought that the poem seems to make. It is this striving to understand the thinking/perspective of the poem that results in the growth John points to. I must stretch my own way of seeing to its limit in an attempt to accommodate the poem but even then, I will not be able to achieve this fully. This is crucial for enabling growth in one's perspective – one needs to feel that it is important to try to make linkages and to try to overcome tensions and incompatibilities in thought between one's own perspective and that on offer in the poem.[7]

To illustrate let's consider Rae Armantrout's poem 'Relations' (2010) from her collection *Versed,* which presents a set of possible connections between the words 'head' and 'bring', 'bobble' and 'bauble', 'Rosy' and 'Lonely', and the concepts of 'you' and 'me', and 'time' and 'proof'. It is left to the reader to try to appreciate what might connect these words; the poem merely asserts or, perhaps, gestures at an assertion of relationship between them. Aesthetically, the words are presented in (a)symmetry forming the beginning and end of the poetic unit. The sense of relationship is heightened and developed as the single line develops into a stanza 'What will you / little chimes / bring me?' – a connection through questioning that resolves in a connection through explanation in the following stanza. The poem ends:

Bring me the friendship

between solving
and dissolving.[8]

The command of 'Bring me the friendship' sets the reader the challenge to locate an understanding of friendship between 'solving' and 'dissolving'. Approaching such a poem with humility allows the reader to treat the poem as a complex whole and as presenting a perspective that makes sense of the connection between these words and ideas. The reader approaches the text with the assumption of making sense to someone despite not being able to fully resolve this themselves. This openness results in an intellectual activity of attending to (and returning to) the words of the poem, its structure and felt quality, allowing for different possibilities of meaning and interpretation to emerge without prioritizing any one; any kind of resolution is for the reader to find through their negotiation of perspectives.

In order to cultivate humility, poetry must do two things: provide motivation to approach with humility and offer space to practice such an approach. Ordinary language use and communication do neither of these things. On one level we feel a sense of coherence when engaging with a work of poetry yet cognitively, we are unable to fully resolve the meaning of the use of language. In ordinary communication, where use of language fails to deliver meaning, either the utterance is dismissed (and ignored) or the speaker is asked to clarify. In other words, such a failure to deliver clear meaning (or bring about a specific action) is seen as a failure in the use of language. Of course, ordinary language is hugely sophisticated. For instance, one can deliberately make use of ambiguity (perhaps as a way of hedging one's bets). How we respond to such use of language in everyday communication doesn't usually generate the same kind of attention to its possibilities as we see in the poetic use of ambiguity. In poetry it becomes one of the objects of attention because we don't have the context provided by ordinary use that enables us to resolve, dismiss or request clarification regarding intention. In other words, because of our awareness that language is being used in a self-conscious way (in order to do something) and with an expressive intention that is not transparent in the work or the context it provides, how we make sense of this is left for the reader/audience to deal with. The relationship between the aesthetic and the cognitive in the work of poetry draws attention to the significance of the using of language (i.e. making central the question, what is the speaker doing in using this precise language in this way?).

In Chapter 2, I argued that the thematization of the first person in poetry cultivates awareness of self-other differentiation and in doing so reveals the limits of one's perspective. In her essay 'More than Make-Believe', Maria Jose Alcaraz Leon argues that what makes the aesthetic context distinct from the everyday is the perspective taken on the everyday in virtue of the grammar of the medium for the work of art and by making features of the everyday the focus of aesthetic attention, the audience's relationship to the everyday is transformed: 'By thematizing and exploring some of the conditions of ordinary experience through the particular grammar of each medium, the spectator becomes experientially aware of those conditions themselves and their impact or role in our broader ordinary experience' (Alcaraz Leon 2023, p. 211). In the case of poetry, that's not to say that language loses its ordinary function but that we experience a duality, that is, a twofoldness: a use of language and an awareness of the functioning of that use of language. Prinz and Mandelbaum argue:

> In poetry words are objects of attention in their own right, independent of what they express. To achieve this end, poets often avoid using words and phrases that are so familiar as to be habitual. For ordinary forms of address, listeners ignore the words (and semantically unimportant changes in word

orderings) and move straight away, as it were, to what those words express. (2015, p. 69)

As they put it, the particular attention to the use of words in poetry attempts to resist transparency of expression.

Applying the concept of twofoldness from Wollheim,[9] Prinz and Mandelbaum argue that in poetry, we are simultaneously aware of the expression (meaning of the words) and the medium of that expression. The two aspects have equal weight in our experience of the poem, and an important part of the experience of the poem is appreciation of how the two interact, that is, how the words give rise to the expression but also to gestures of meaning beyond expression, in other words, affect. My claim about poetry is different to Prinz and Mandelbaum in that the interaction of expression and medium of expression is significant in how it shapes our appreciation of the poem. For instance, it is not simply an appreciation of first-personal expression alongside awareness that the poem uses the first-person pronoun to express but an attention to and awareness of the structural aspects of language, in this case, the relationality of the first person to the second person, which is due to the present quality of the poem as unfolding in the 'now'.

One of the distinctive marks of the poetic is the attention to the aesthetics of words, that is, paying appreciative attention to the experiential dimension of words themselves, including the musicality that arises from aesthetic connection between words and patterns of speech. The lyric voice (whether performed or co-created, in the case of reading) brings a self-conscious awareness of the aurality and felt bodily experience of hearing (or perceiving) words. In reading or hearing a poem, one must engage in wilful attention to the act of communication (meaning and expression) and how the words are experienced (the aesthetic awareness of the words). As Prinz and Mandelbaum highlight, the former is common to ordinary experience of language, while the latter together with the former is specific to poetry. Here I wish to borrow an example from poet Don Patterson from his book *The Poem*. He writes:

> Take our old standby, the word 'moon'. Give it some space, some page-silence, as we do with words within a poem; stare at it for a minute
>
> > moon
>
> What kind of reading have we just made? Firstly, our reading has become an act of determined and wilful *oversignification* – of 'reading in' far more than

we would in a simple monosemic interpretation: we might start to think of all connotations and alternative senses of the word 'moon'. . . . Secondly, it's one of conscious *overattention* to the photosemantic dimension of the language, that interfusion of sound and sense which produces synaesthetic effect. That might lead us to *hear* the nasal-rounded, empty white sphere of the moon. Thirdly, it's one of unconscious, receptive *oversensitivity* to its physical properties, its acoustic mark, its music, its rhythm. Here, we feel the shape of the word 'moon' in our mouth, its envelope of nasals and its long vowel, and experience its lyric effect. (2018, pp. 167–8)

What Patterson offers here is an explanation of how poetry thematizes language, that is, how it makes language an object of oversignification, overattention and oversensitivity. From his example of the word 'moon' treated poetically, it is clear that such thematizing of language helps the reader/audience to make new connections. The poem enables a sort of creativity; it is the reader/audience who generates the connotations and associations, connections between word meaning and sound, and between the aesthetic experience of the use of words and feeling. The poetic presentation of the words merely suggests that there are such possibilities to realize in the poem. Let's take a moment to apply Patterson's treatment of 'moon' to the lyric I. Consider the following stanza from Claudia Rankine's 'What if' (2021):

> I am here. Whatever is
> being expressed, what if,
> I am here awaiting, waiting for you[10]

The effect of oversignification brings awareness of its linguistic structure, that is, its relationship to 'you'. The presence of the I on the page acts as a calling to 'you' who is able to perceive the expression of the self and translate the I to you as well as being the you of address. We also attend to the different ways in which we use the phrase 'what if', that is, the difference between asking how things could be otherwise (which suggests a feeling of hopelessness) compared to mere speculation (which in the possibilities it generates brings feelings of hopefulness). Overattention brings feelings of singularity, perhaps isolation and loneliness as it presents as a solitary mark set against the silence of the white space on the page. A feeling that is reinforced by the coupling of 'I am here awaiting' and 'waiting for you'; a pairing that should feel complete with the you presented to the I that waits but the use of 'awaiting' rather than simply 'waiting' suggests incompleteness (that the waiting will continue and be left unfulfilled), which is reinforced by the lingering 'what if' of the previous line. The effect of oversignification together with overattention may reveal an affective relationality in the form of a desire for connection (it's felt as incomplete or lacking). Oversensitivity to the words draws attention to the assertion and consequent felt presence of 'I am here'; its simplistic rhythm places weight on each monosyllabic word. The oversensitivity to the physical does not just lead to embodiment of the word but leads to our relationship as a reader of the word to the I of expression; the experience of the words is as other with awareness of self-other differentiation.

What all three ways the reader treats the words on the page does is to treat everyday language with a heightened sense of its function and use. In doing so, the use of the first person makes one more aware of the distance between their own use of 'I' to self-refer and the physical mark of the 'I' on the page, an I that doesn't seem to be attached to a body unlike one's own use of 'I', yet functions expressively (in that it centres expression). The shape of the words on the page also suggests to the reader that these words have been crafted and are, therefore, all serving some purpose in the poem; there is intention behind the work and this is something which therefore requires interpretation. Elsewhere Don Paterson writes:

> Our formal patterning most often supplies a powerful typographical advertisement. What it advertises most conspicuously is that the poem has not taken up the whole page, and considers itself somewhat important. . . . Silence – both invoked and symbolized by the white page, and specifically directed by the gaps left by lineation, stanza and poem – underwrites the status of the poem as *significant mark*. (2007, p. 62)

Paterson sees the white space on the page as doing more than just showing that it has been crafted; the shape itself has significance and the white space suggests silence, reinforcing the sense of significance of the words that are on the page. This connects poetry with other art forms such as photography and painting, where the frame guides us to consider only what falls within the frame, to focus on that particular perspective which can help us notice something we ordinarily would not. The physical shape of the poem and the visual impact of the words on the page affects the meaning, which, it can be argued, is expressed when read aloud in the form of tempo.

When considering poetry in performance, there is still a heightened sense of awareness of the *use* and *using* of language but rather than the white space triggering a different engagement with language use that is subject to overattention, oversensitivity and oversignification, the performance space itself helps to thematize the language use spoken in the context of the poem not only through the framing of the words with the silence, the pause before the poem begins and at its end but the relationship established between audience and performer and the relative privilege afforded to the latter. Rather than the voice being seen as a mere vehicle of communication as is the case in ordinary language use, on the stage the voice, in the way it punctuates the silence and presents as significant mark, is elevated in the experience of the words as contributing to the meaning-making of the use of language. The body of the performer is framed by the stage, lighting and orientation to the audience. In terms of oversignification in the performance of a poem, not only do we read more into the words themselves as Patterson describes in the case of page poetry but we acknowledge its taking place in the present, as unfolding on the stage in front of us. Overattention in the poetry performance results in the audience considering the aesthetics of the words as spoken, which includes how the words are spoken (intonation, rhythm) but also the contextual contribution of the body and texture of the voice itself (accent, emotional expression). Oversensitivity is a matter of how the words feel in the space and the affective shaping of the performance space, for instance, how the rhythm, and the pauses feel to the audience. The effect of overattention, oversensitivity and oversignification is to create a space for reflection on the use of language for self-expression, in terms of not mere information gathering (trying to grasp *what* was expressed) but how such self-expression works (where it succeeds and where it fails – the latter is just as important to our understanding of our relationships with one another as the former).

The poem, whether on the page or in performance, therefore, rewards humility for it is only in approaching the work with the awareness that it may be trying to say more than the literal meaning of the words and may fail in its attempt at self-expression that one is able to properly engage with the work.

The value of poetic humility

Humility is essential for avoiding some of the moral problems raised throughout the book, such as overstepping through identification (where another 'identifies with' or 'takes up' the words of the speaker as if it refers to them together with a failure to recognize self-other differentiation), failure to recognize the role of voice and body in meaning-making (where the listener fails to appreciate the context of expression as relevant to what was said, not only leading to denial of another's epistemic contribution as speaker but in difference in action performed by the words spoken) and the problem of speaking on behalf of others (where one voice is used to represent many and in problematic cases, results in the many not being able to be heard but replaced by a mere representation of voice). Although all are problems that occur in everyday life, it is within the context of engaging with and appreciating poetry that such problems are made plain. In each case, the moral issue arises where there is a failure to appreciate the importance of balancing attempts to reach another by understanding the words spoken and the necessary separation of persons (i.e. that some aspects of your experience and perspective are unavailable to me). In this section, I will discuss each problem in turn and explain how poetic humility, that is, the way in which poetry cultivates humility, can raise awareness of these problems and show ways to mitigate them.

Overstepping through identification

The first problem, introduced in Chapter 2, is *overstepping through identification*, where one considers the ways in which one connects with the expression of another without appreciation of self-other differentiation; in other words, one identifies with the use of words of another as if they refer to them without consideration of the difference in use and meaning between. In one's engagement with the expression of another, one only notices connections and overlap with one's own perspective and may look over or ignore those aspects that are not shared. The example I focused on in Chapter 2 was the way in which we might treat the lyric I, or use of first person in a poem. Although there is no problem in identification with certain ways of expressing something, where you might take that as a useful way of expressing something you want to say, to treat the poetic use of such expression as being nothing more than this is where the problem lies. Mere identification with the lyric I will result in a failure to appreciate the poem since identification blocks relationality and therefore the communicative function of poetic uses of language.

Why this is problematic is that there is a danger that one approaches the expression of another without humility and takes their own perspective to be more significant/important. The way in which another expresses a thought or feeling *can* be really useful to an individual, especially where they had struggled to articulate a similar thought or feeling before. I am not denying this benefit to identification. However, such take-up of another's expression can lead to a failure to appreciate one's relationship with another which is characterized by not only the ways they connect but the disconnection and difference. There is more significance to be gained by appreciating how two people connect despite their differences than to merely appreciate what they have in common only. The point I am making is that when one identifies with the expression of another and takes that expression to reflect how they think or feel personally, they must acknowledge the context of the original expression and the difference in meaning between the two uses of that expression.

Let's return to the example of Rankine's poem 'What if', which opens her collection of poems and essays *Just us*. Throughout the poem, there is a repetition of the phrase 'I am here' alongside the repeated I-statements, such as I feel, I think, I want, I smell and I've been told, which draws attention to the use of the first person and what each of these assertions has in common: the desire to say something and be heard. The poem isn't merely an example of self-expression in terms of the words themselves expressing the thoughts and feelings of the author but is expressing the difficulty in being heard and acknowledged. It brings to the surface the problem of how to make yourself visible in a world that marginalizes and suppresses. Whereas identification is singular (and is without self-other differentiation), seeking connection with self-other differentiation at the fore allows one to consider what is shared and shareable. Identification may well be the first step but sharing goes beyond mere identification because it requires one to approach the expression of another not for what it offers them but what it offers us together.

Iris Vidmar Jovanović observes that art can play an important role in helping us to 'become more sensitive to the plurality of voices that participate in our social reality, and to the hardships of reconciling individual perspectives with shared experiences' (2021, p. 81). The central point from Vidmar Jovanović is that although in some sense we can take ourselves to have a shared experience with others, that does not mean the experience is the same for each individual that shapes that experience. Empathy serves as an important mechanism for revealing the mismatch between the individual perspective and what we might share with one another. Although there is some commonality in our experience (in terms of an overlap of some sort, which is where we might recognize moments of identification), we each bring something unique that is ours and shows the value in relationality.

Failure to recognize the role of voice and body in expression

The second (related) problem is where one fails to recognize the contribution of context of the voice and body in meaning-making, instead believing that the words alone express all the content there is; in other words, there is a separation of voice from words spoken. This can occur even when an individual doesn't identify with the expression of another. There may well be appreciation of self-other differentiation, where the listener acknowledges these words as the words of another but fails to recognize the difference in use of the words as a consequence of the other's embodied voice.

As discussed in Chapter 4, poetry in performance highlights the significance of the voice and body with the words uttered, and that different speakers can perform different actions using the same words. One speaker adopting the words of another in an attempt to perform the same action may fail to in virtue of the embodied voice. The words uttered are the same and there may be some overlap in the meaning of the two performances, but the action performed may not transfer from one speaker to another. The central example discussed in Chapter 4 of Taylor Mali's attempt to reperform Patricia Smith's poem 'Skinhead' revealed how two speakers using the same words can differ in the action performed in their use of those words, which in this case resulted in Mali's version being lesser both aesthetically and morally. However, such an example highlights a more general issue with potential failures in responding to another's attempt at expression since the problem with Mali's re-voicing is not just in his performance of Smith's work but in what this shows about his appreciation of Smith's own version. By attempting to perform Smith's poem, Mali demonstrates that he didn't appreciate the way Smith's poem works as a performance, namely, that the poem is not made up of the words alone but the context provided by her embodied performance. To remove the words of the poem from that (embodied) context is to create another (albeit related) work that in this case lacks the depth aesthetically and meaning that was present in the original. The example of Layli Long Soldier's poem made clear that this is not merely an issue for poetry performed but also page poetry, where the voice of the poet provides context for their poems that shapes how we engage with and interpret the words on the page. Just as poetry readers are trained to notice the relevance of form, I argue that we must also pay attention to the voice and context of the poem. And just as with form, we must learn what is and what isn't relevant to the aesthetics of the work by considering what enhances meaning-making and results in value maximization of the work.

The value of engaging with poetry is not just in appreciating the poem but has something of more general relevance to show us about expression. Just as poetry might help us to appreciate the significance of not only what is said but how it is said by revealing how meaning can be opened up through playing with the non-standard presentation of words, we can also come to appreciate difference in actions performed through the use of words. Poetry prompts reflection on the use of words – through oversignification, overattention and oversensitivity – which can help to reveal the ways in which the voice and body contribute to meaning-making, including the illocutionary and perlocutionary dimensions of language use. This helps to attend to who is speaking and encourages a sense of care towards the other in their use of language and not valuing the words as expression in isolation (in other words, we must attend to the use of words to express together with the act of someone expressing something by them). Mali's error in his appreciation of Smith's poem is not isolated to this one case (or even to poetry) but where the listener is inattentive to the embodiment of expression. The only way to judge whether the body contributes to the work aesthetically and/or morally is to be attentive to the embodiment of the words.

Speaking on behalf of

The final problem, discussed in Chapter 3, 'speaking on behalf of', is where one fails to recognize the potential contribution of other voices, instead believing that one voice can represent or serve as a proxy for others.

Engaging with poetry on the page and (especially) on the stage helps to raise awareness of the value of individual voices. Some poems are only able to be read by the poet due to the way accent is incorporated, for instance, where the poem fits with the palate of the author. The so-called dialect poetry, in which the poet draws on regional dialect and non-standard English in their work, can be challenging to articulate for those unfamiliar with such patterns of speech. Take for instance Benjamin Zephaniah's 'She's Crying for Many' and Ian McMillan's 'The Meaning of Life'. And there are many more subtle examples where the rhythm of the poem is only achievable by one who is comfortable speaking the words and where rhymes are only achievable with a particular texture of voice (e.g. Riz Ahmed's 'Where You From' (2020), Joshua Idehen's 'My Dad Poem' (2017) and Neil Hilborn's 'OCD' (2017)). This is probably most apparent in certain works of performance poetry and particularly rap, where the flow and speed of delivery is difficult to replicate in those other than the original performer and may require a degree of imitation of voice to get close to the original performance (consider here rappers such as Chali 2na, Little Simz and Tech N9ne, whose style is closely connected to their voice. You can even find videos on YouTube of 'How to Rap like Kendrick Lamar', which suggests the difficulty in trying to replicate his voice and perform his work). What such examples of poetry highlight is the value of the unique voice; albeit subtle, there are some things that can only be said by particular voices. This is not a claim about meaning – that what is said can only be said in that voice – but a claim about the aesthetic experience that such voices give rise to. However, the aesthetic is relevant to the meaning-making experience of the work since other voices may well be unsuccessful in recreating the aesthetics of the poem and therefore lose something of its meaning-making potential afforded to the reader/audience.

Not only is there value in hearing different voices that speaking on behalf of might obscure but there is a further worry that the practice of speaking on behalf of might lead to the suppression of voices in such a way as to disempower particular individuals. Part of the problem will arise from the speaker's location and to what extent that serves to authorize or disauthorize speech. Linda Alcoff argues that 'a speaker's location (which I take here to refer to their social location, or social identity) has an epistemically significant impact on that speaker's claims and can serve either to authorize or disauthorize one's speech' (1991, p. 7). This becomes a problem when considering the relative privilege of a speaker's location to the people they are attempting to speak on behalf of. She goes on to add that 'not only is location epistemically salient, but certain privileged locations are discursively dangerous. In particular, the practice of privileged persons speaking for or on behalf of less privileged persons actually resulted (in many cases) in increasing or reinforcing oppression of the group spoken for' (Alcoff 1991, p. 7). Here the issue is that the practice of 'speaking on behalf of' raises the worry about who gets to speak in society and how it can result in only the privileged being heard. She further states that the solution cannot be simply to say that one can only speak on behalf of others when one belongs to the same group for 'what basis can we justify a decision to demarcate groups and define membership in one way rather than another? No easy solution to this problem can be found by simply restricting the practice of speaking for others to speaking for groups of which one is a member' (Alcoff 1991, p. 8).

Of course, there are situations in which a singular, representative voice is needed to speak for a group, take for instance representatives in the houses of parliament. A singular voice of an elected official will speak on behalf of their constituency and attempt to represent their interests as a group, to have their concerns and demands heard by the government (for instance, they may vote for or against a particular bill on behalf of their constituents). The work of government would stall if on every issue we sought to hear from each individual whose lives are affected by a particular decision. And so it goes for many forms of collective action; how can a group act together without being able to speak as a group? Although clearly necessary in many cases, it is a mistake to fail to recognize that speaking on behalf of is an imperfect way of hearing from a group of individuals. As Alcoff argues, 'One is still interpreting the other's situation and wishes (unless perhaps one simply reads a written text they have supplied), and so one is still creating for them a self in the presence of others' (1991, p. 10). Alcoff suggests another case where speaking on behalf of seems positive and necessary, where the speaker can raise awareness of the experiences of oppressed and marginalized groups (even if done inaccurately). The thought is that it's better to raise awareness even if by imperfect means. Furthermore, Alcoff argues that although in such cases speaking on behalf of brings about good, it still comes with dangers since any act of speaking on behalf of doesn't encourage and empower individuals to speak for themselves, which results in subtle differences in meaning contributed by those individuals to be lost or omitted from public discourse.

Not only can poetry reveal the importance of hearing the individual voice but it can also show alternatives to speaking on behalf of. In Chapter 3 we saw how polyphonic or multivocal works attempt to bring different voices together in aesthetic coherence. Such works bring different voices into relation by forging connections through the poetic structure of the work rather than blending the voices to become one. Merely having individuals speak together or in turn does not address the reasons why we might feel the need to speak on their behalf. What is needed is to show these voices as connected and allow them to speak as a community. Engaging with poetry reveals the way in which voices express perspectives that go beyond the literal meaning of the words uttered. This is important in demonstrating the value in appreciating our relationality – how we relate to one another, how and where shared perspectives emerge and why that is of value. Speaking on behalf of assumes, and therefore covers over, both ways individuals in a group connect, where there is disconnection and the value of coming together as a group, as a community.

Conclusion

By accepting that poetry has a role to play in cultivating an intellectual virtue, we can claim that it is not just a handful of works of poetry that have cognitive value. Any work that offers a perspective (through voice) and thematizes the use of language (which is what makes poetry distinctive from other art forms and ordinary uses of language) contributes to this project. The more we read, the more we become aware of our relationality to others. Repeated encounters with awareness of self-other differentiation are essential to appreciating the limits of perspective.

This may well point to the value of engagement with art more generally. By placing us in relation to others, we may find connection through overlapping perspectives, that is, what we share as human beings, but it also highlights what we don't share, those moments of disconnection. This double experience of connection and disconnection asks us to attend to how we relate to others and our own place in the world in relation to theirs. To appreciate and acknowledge connection and disconnection simultaneously is the mark of intellectual humility.

Notes

Introduction

1. For further discussion of the non-paraphrasability of poetry, see Currie and Frascaroli (2021), Feldman (2020), Kivy (2011), Lamarque (2009), Leighton (2009).
2. See Koethe (2001), Ribeiro (2009), Mark Rowe (1996), who each discuss poetry's relationship to thought and thinking.
3. Hamburger (1973) makes this point in *The Logic of Literature*; Culler (2015) makes a similar point by emphasising both the illocutionary act and the perlocutionary in understanding poetry.
4. 'A Litany for Survival' from *The Black Unicorn* by Audre Lorde, Penguin Classics, 2019. Copyright © 1978, 1997 by Audre Lorde and by permission of the Abner Stein Agency.
5. As examples of philosophers who take page poetry as the paradigm, see for instance, de Gaynesford (2011, 2017), Gibson (2016a, 2018), John (2013a), Lamarque (2009, 2015), Rowe (1996) and Walton (2015). Although Ribeiro (2015a) notes poetry's origin as an oral art form, she also offers an analysis of poetry as a written text.
6. See Gaut (2006, 2007).
7. See Rowe (1996).
8. I discuss the possibility of bringing together poetry and philosophy in my essay Linking Perspectives (Simecek 2022).
9. And to read Plato's *Symposium* is to take another (and a different kind of literary approach to Oswald's poem).
10. 'Wedding' from *The Thing in the Gap Stone Stile* by Alice Oswald. Extract printed by permission of *Faber & Faber Ltd*.
11. See Simecek (2019a) for more on the idea of poetry as event.
12. A number of poets emphasize the significance of 'hearing' in the experience of poetry such as Leighton (2009), Pinsky (1998), Stevenson (2017). See also Joan Shelley Rubin, *Songs of Ourselves: The Uses of Poetry in America* (2007). Rather than seeking commonality between the heard and the unheard, such views unfortunately exclude a large and valuable body of poetic work and are,

consequently, unnecessarily narrow in their understanding of what poetry is and how it works.

13 'Infect the World with Doves' by Philip Wilcox. Copyright ©2020 by Philip Wilcox. Reproduced by permission of the author.

14 Copyright © 2022 by Elizabeth Acevedo. First printed in Inheritance. Reprinted by permission of Creative Artists Agency.

15 Mills (2022) also uses this language of 'perspective' in relation to poetry. Following a Nietzschean perspectivism, Mills understands perspective as 'related to a subject's interpretations' (p. 118). However, on my understanding of 'perspective', the difference between people is not a matter of difference of interpretation (although this is perhaps a consequence) but a difference of orientation given by the values, beliefs, commitments that we each hold that determines what we take to be significant and where we see connection and disconnection. According to Mills, we are able to take on different perspectives, that is, different interpretations, and this is precisely what poetry offers. On my view, we are not easily able to shift perspective since to appreciate other ways of seeing would involve having to change one's network of beliefs, values and commitments.

16 See DePaul (1993) for interesting discussion of the problems of naivete (where a thinker holds a consistent but limited set of beliefs) and corruption (where a thinker only tracks what is compatible with a problematic set of beliefs, ignoring anything that is inconsistent or incompatible).

Chapter 1

1 Culler's *The Theory of the Lyric* (2015) provides a good discussion of voice in lyric poetry but does not go beyond the experience of voice in page poetry to consider ordinary discourse or performance of poetry.

2 The UK TV series *The Trip* (dir. Winterbottom 2010; 2014; 2017; 2022) is an excellent study of voice, where we see the two main characters compete for the best impression of a number of famous voices.

3 Ventriloquizing is the ability to de-centre one's voice. The uncanny feeling is the result of the de-centring: we know that it is not *really* the voice of the puppet but yet the voice appears to be centred in the puppet's body. The uncanniness is precisely the result of this deviating from our ordinary encounter with voice in everyday communication.

4 Zamir (2012) refers to this as 'vocal blocks'.

5 Dolar writes 'Only the voice implies a subjectivity which "expresses itself" and itself inhabits the means of expression' (Dolar 2006, p. 15).
6 Nancy expresses a similar view to Cavarero: 'To be listening is thus to enter into tension and to be on the lookout for a relationship to self: *not*, it should be emphasized, as relationship to "me" (the supposedly given subject), or to the "self" of the other (the speaker, the musician, also supposedly given, with his subjectivity), but to the *relationship in self*, so to speak, as it forms "a self" or a "to itself" in general, and if something like that ever does reach the end of its formation. Consequently, listening is passing over to the register of presence to self, it being understand that the "self" is precisely nothing available (substantial or subsistent) to which one can be "present," but precisely the resonance of a return' (Nancy 2007, p. 12).
7 See Vicente and Martinez Manrique (2011) and Roessler (2016) for more on inner speech.
8 Of course, there are many things we do that count as expression: action, gesture etc., but I'm only concerned with vocal expression. That might involve these other things but in addition to use of language.
9 Green defines signal as follows: 'a *signal* is any feature of an entity that conveys information (including misinformation) and that was designed for its ability to convey that information. That information might pertain to how things were, are, will be, or ought to be. The design in question might be due to the work of intelligent agents, or be the product of evolution by either artificial or natural selection. When a signal succeeds in conveying the information for which it was designed, communication takes place' (p. 49).
10 Dorit Bar-On (2010) presents a good argument for modifying Green's view by limiting self-expression to two types of showing: showing as perceptually available and showing-how. She argues that showing-that is problematic and unnecessary part of his account.
11 Green adds that expression can be both voluntary and involuntary: given my concern is just with vocal linguistic expression, this means that the affective shaping of an utterance may be the result of voluntary or involuntary gestures that still, provided no issue with sincerity, express the beliefs, emotions and experience of the speaker. Also, self-expression does not always succeed. Self-expression can be difficult. He argues that it must be the kind of thing that can be known by introspection.
12 Charles Bernstein also emphasizes the significance of the embodied voice in performance and how that relates to the reading experience: 'Any reader can perform the written text of a poem and indeed many poems need to be read

out aloud in order to make tangible the rhythm and sound patterning. But a poet's reading of her or his own work has an entirely different authority. The poet's performance, both live and recorded, poses an arresting issue for poetry, for the difference among the alphabetic, grammaphonic, and live are not so much ones of textual variance as ontological' (2011, p. 123). The embodied performance does not merely contribute an aesthetic layer to the work but defines the work itself (another voicing will amount to a different work, albeit related).

13 Copyright © Joelle Taylor (2012). Printed with permission of the author.
14 'Renegade' from 'Everything Speaks in its Own Way' (Zingaro) © Kae Tempest.
15 Copyright © Raymond Antrobus, reproduced by kind permission by David Higham Associates.
16 This term is borrowed from Rosenblatt (1983, p. 27), who argues for this kind of reader-response criticism.
17 *This Connection of Everyone with Lungs* by Juliana Spahr Copyright © 2005 by the Regents of the University of California. Reprinted by kind permission of University of California Press Books.
18 Nerys Williams comments 'Spahr in effect creates a series of encounters between bodies that replicate, unfold and disseminate into synchronous movement' (Williams 2013, p. 185).
19 Copyright © 2005 by the Regents of the University of California. Reprinted by kind permission of University of California Press Books.

Chapter 2

1 Reprinted from *Ten Poets of the New Generation*, ed. Jaren McCarthy Woolf (Bloodaxe Books, 2017) with kind permission from the publisher.
2 Of course, this has the consequence that the poem might offer the reader or audience a perspective not intended by the poet. The words may have been designed to do what the poet thought the reader/audience would do with them but the reader/audience can do more with the words.
3 See Kaplan (1989) for his distinction between pure indexicals and true demonstratives. In poetry, what Kaplan calls pure indexicals e.g. 'I', 'today', 'tomorrow' take on the character of what he calls true demonstratives where the meaning/how it refers is determined by the context of the work (the poet's intentions). Thanks to Tom Brown for pointing me towards this distinction.

4   John McDowell: 'Suppose someone says to me, "You have mud on your face". If I am to understand him, I must think an "I"-thought, thinking something to this effect: "I have mud on my face: that is what he is saying"' (1984, p. 222). See also Longworth (2013) for a helpful discussion of the shareability thesis.
5   Although, a thought containing the first person is not necessarily a case of first-person thought; e.g. 'He thinks I ate the last one'.
6   See Evans (1985).
7   See also Collingwood (1958), who also seems to suggest such an extension of the identification model: 'If what [the artist] is trying to do is to express emotions that are not his own merely, but his audience's as well, his success in doing this will be tested by his audience's reception of what he has to say. What he says will be something that his audience says through his mouth; and his satisfaction in having expressed what he feels will be at the same time, in so far as he communicates this expression to them, their satisfaction in having expressed what they feel' (p. 312). Collingwood argues that although the audience use the words of the poet ('through his mouth'), it is both the artist and the audience that express something shared, in collaboration (as Collingwood puts it).
8   The concept of 'me' is also shared with others in some sense in that we each can understand ourselves in those terms. However, the difference here is that my appeal to my 'me'-ness is necessarily exclusive, whereas the aspects of self that are properly shareable with others are inclusive and allow for overlap with others. Thanks to Tom Crowther for helping me clarify this point.
9   Copyright © Jen Hadfield. *Nigh-No-Place* (Bloodaxe Books, 2008). Reproduced with permission of Bloodaxe Books. www.bloodaxebooks.com
10 Here we might note Austin (1962) on the distinction between locution, illocution (acting through saying something e.g. by saying 'I promise' you are also making a promise) and perlocution (the effects of saying something, such as causing your addressee to expect something as a result of your promise). Austin noted that for words to have illocutionary force, one must have the right kind of authority; e.g. for one to hand down a sentence in a court of law, one must have the required qualifications to be a judge in a court of law and be recognised as such). However, Hadfield's poem reveals a different dimension to the illocutionary force of 'I promise' since it is met by desire yet lacks sufficient authority.
11 It turns out these names do denote but that is not the point of the poem and flattens what the poem does. Thinking about these names as references to real places means you're not attending to the *naming* of them, the significance that the name has and relationship between places (that goes beyond geographic

location). See https://oldweirdalbion.wordpress.com/2009/10/12/i-will-meet-you-at-pity-me-wood/ The place names are drawn from different areas of the UK (Lancashire, Staffordshire, North Yorkshire, Co. Durham, Shetland, Alberta, Canada). The poem presents these places as if they are connected yet geographically they are far from one another.

12 For more on 'We'-thoughts, see Bratman (2014), Korta (2016), Schmid (2018), Smith (2018) and Vallée (1996).

13 'Define loneliness?' from *Don't Let Me Be Lonely: An American Lyric* by Claudia Rankine published by Penguin (UK) and Graywolf Press (USA). Copyright © 2004 by Claudia Rankine. Reprinted with the permission of The Permissions Company, LLC, on behalf of Graywolf Press, graywolfpress.org and Penguin Books Ltd.

14 T. S. Elliot's *The Waste Land* also represents a work that depends on the shifting of voice, the ambiguity of who is speaking and the disorientation that provides.

15 'Life is a form of hope?' from *Don't Let Me Be Lonely: An American Lyric* by Claudia Rankine published by Penguin (UK) and Graywolf Press (USA). Copyright © 2004 by Claudia Rankine. Reprinted with the permission of The Permissions Company, LLC, on behalf of Graywolf Press, graywolfpress.org and Penguin Books Ltd.

16 From *Arrow* by Sumita Chakraborty, published by Carcanet. Copyright © Sumita Chakraborty. Reprinted by permission of Carcanet Press Ltd.

17 From *Arrow* by Sumita Chakraborty, published by Carcanet. Copyright © Sumita Chakraborty. Reprinted by permission of Carcanet Press Ltd.

18 From *Arrow* by Sumita Chakraborty, published by Carcanet. Copyright © Sumita Chakraborty. Reprinted by permission of Carcanet Press Ltd.

19 '4' taken from *Bluets* by Maggie Nelson published by Jonathan Cape. Copyright © Maggie Nelson 2009. Reprinted by permission of The Random House Group Limited.

20 '72' taken from *Bluets* by Maggie Nelson published by Jonathan Cape. Copyright © Maggie Nelson 2009. Reprinted by permission of The Random House Group Limited.

21 '92'/ '94' taken from *Bluets* by Maggie Nelson published by Jonathan Cape. Copyright © Maggie Nelson 2009. Reprinted by permission of The Random House Group Limited.

22 '177' taken from *Bluets* by Maggie Nelson published by Jonathan Cape. Copyright © Maggie Nelson 2009. Reprinted by permission of The Random House Group Limited.

Chapter 3

1. Copyright © Imtiaz Dharker. 'This Line, This Thread' from Imtiaz Dharker's *Luck Is the Hook* (Bloodaxe Books, 2018). Reproduced with permission of Bloodaxe Books. www.bloodaxebooks.com
2. Of course we don't know whether we actually share those values, concerns and commitments, but the important point is that we at least view ourselves as sharing a set of values, concerns and commitments (with others); that is, we think others who share that aspect of our identity ought to hold this set of values and concerns, and we can hold each other to account on that basis.
3. 'Glory be to the Gang, Gang, Gang' by Momtaza Mehri © Momtaza Mehri, reproduced by kind permission by David Higham Associates.
4. 'Community' in *Poor* by Caleb Femi, published by Penguin Books. Copyright © Caleb Femi 2022. Reprinted by permission of Penguin Books Ltd and the author c/o Jo Unwin Literary Agency.
5. 'Us from *Us* by Zaffar Kunial. Published by Faber & Faber. Copyright © Zaffar Kunial. Reproduced by permission of the author c/o Rogers, Coleridge & White Ltd., 20 Powis Mews, London W11 1JN.
6. 'Us from *Us* by Zaffar Kunial. Published by Faber & Faber. Copyright © Zaffar Kunial. Reproduced by permission of the author c/o Rogers, Coleridge & White Ltd., 20 Powis Mews, London W11 1JN.
7. 'Swimming' by Degna Stone. Copyright © Degna Stone. *Ten Poets of the New Generation*, ed. Jaren McCarthy Woolf (Bloodaxe Books, 2017). Reproduced with permission of the author.
8. 'The River Gods' by Degna Stone. Copyright © Degna Stone. *Ten Poets of the New Generation*, ed. Jaren McCarthy Woolf (Bloodaxe Books, 2017). Reproduced with permission of the author.
9. 'This Be the Pukka Verse' from *Tippoo Sultan's Incredible White-Man-Eating Tiger Toy-Machine!!!* by Daljit Nagra. Published by Faber & Faber Ltd. Copyright © Daljit Nagra. Reproduced with kind permission of Faber & Faber and the author, Daljit Nagra.
10. *Manorism* by Yomi Ṣode, published by Penguin Books. Copyright © Yomi Ṣode 2022. Reprinted by permission of Penguin Books Ltd.
11. 'A Common Gift' by Momtaza Mehri. © Momtaza Mehri, reproduced by kind permission by David Higham Associates.
12. From CHORUS, a Literary Mixtape by edited and arranged by Saul Williams. Copyright © Compilation copyright (c) 2012 Saul Williams. Reprinted with the permission of Gallery Books/MTV Adult Books, a division of Simon &

Schuster, Inc., and the author c/o Charlotte Gusay Literary Agency. All rights reserved.

13   From *Hiding to Nothing* by Anita Pati published by Liverpool University Press. Copyright © 2022 Anita Pati. Reproduced with permission of The Licensor through PLSclear.
14   Copyright © Robert Montgomery. Reproduced with kind permission of the artist.
15   Copyright © Robert Montgomery. Reproduced with kind permission of the artist.

Chapter 4

1   Reproduced with kind permission of Clare Collison.
2   As Davies (2011) argues, there's no requirement that there is an actual attentive audience for a work to count as a performance, only that the performer is acting with the intention that an audience responds in the way the work demands.
3   An article for *The Guardian* newspaper provides a good overview of the controversy around Rijneveld's proposed translation of Gorman's work: https://www.theguardian.com/books/2021/mar/01/amanda-gorman-white-translator-quits-marieke-lucas-rijneveld
4   Contrast this with Kanye West's use of the slogan 'White Lives Matter' on T-Shirts as part of his catwalk show during Paris Fashion week in 2022, which is often used by White supremacist groups in response to the Black Lives Matter movement. No context was given for the use of this racist slogan and therefore the expressive intention behind its use is unclear. Consequently, regardless of West's identity as a Black American, no such critique is performed as in the case of Smith's poem and audiences of West's show are left unsure of how to interpret his actions (particularly as there is no control over who wears such T-Shirts outside of such events and how they might be taken up by others). For more on this story, see: https://www.theguardian.com/music/2022/oct/04/kanye-west-white-lives-matter-t-shirt-paris-fashion-week
5   'Skinhead' by Patricia Smith. © Patricia Smith. Reproduced with permission of Patricia Smith and The Shipman Agency.
6   For more on how performance poetry enables the unjustly marginalized to be heard, see Simecek (2021).
7   For more on the intimacy account see Nguyen and Strohl (2019) and Dodd (2021).

8   Rebecca Tuvel comments that a 'benefit of [Matthes' oppression-based] account is that it makes sense of those cases of cultural appropriation that might be wrong even if cultural members 1) do dissent, but their voices are not heard due to conditions of oppression, or 2) do not dissent because their oppression is so thoroughgoing it has become internalized' (2021, p. 362).

9   'In Alabama', from *Felon: Poems* by Reginald Dwayne Betts. Copyright © 2019 by Reginald Dwayne Betts. Used by permission of W.W. Norton & Company, inc.

10 Billie Holiday recounts her experience of performing this song in her autobiography *Lady sings the blues* (2018).

11 Another example is the 2020 project led by Professor Thomas Kuhn – 'Words as Weapons' – where homeless people from Crisis Skylight read poems by Brecht to an audience at The Old Fire Station in central Oxford: https://www.torch.ox.ac.uk/article/words-as-weapons. See also Aretha Franklin's (1967) version of Otis Redding's song 'Respect', in which her re-voicing turns the song into a feminist anthem in virtue of her embodied voice and identity.

12 A similar distinction is made by Don Ihde (2007, p. 77), who argues that there is a double dimensionality of auditory field: directionality and surroundability.

13 For further discussion of the use of the second-person and first-person pronouns in poetry, see: Culler (2015) and Simecek (2019b).

14 *Whereas* by Layli Long Soldier 2019 published by Picador (Pan Macmillan) and Graywolf Press. Picador: Copyright © Layli Long Soldier 2017. Reproduced with permission of The Licensor through PLSclear. Graywolf Press: Layli Long Soldier, excerpts from 'Whereas Statements' from *Whereas*. Copyright © 2017 by Layli Long Soldier. Reprinted with the permission of The Permissions Company, LLC on behalf of Graywolf Press, Minneapolis, Minnesota, graywolfpress.org.

15 *Whereas* by Layli Long Soldier 2019 published by Picador (Pan Macmillan) and Graywolf Press. Picador: Copyright © Layli Long Soldier 2017. Reproduced with permission of The Licensor through PLSclear. Graywolf Press: Layli Long Soldier, excerpts from 'Whereas Statements' from *Whereas*. Copyright © 2017 by Layli Long Soldier. Reprinted with the permission of The Permissions Company, LLC on behalf of Graywolf Press, Minneapolis, Minnesota, graywolfpress.org.

Chapter 5

1   As John (2013b) points out, a few have defended cognitivism through appeal to intellectual virtues. She cites Matthew Kieran and Martha Nussbaum as key examples. For instance, Matthew Kieran argues that art helps to 'cultivate

understanding'. Kieran argues, 'Good art works can develop our capacities for discrimination and appreciation' (Kieran 2004, p. 138). Eileen John states, 'The claim that art develops intellectual virtues is somewhat stronger, as possessing a virtue requires a stable disposition to exercise one's capacities well, which typically involves being motivated to do so' (2013b, p. 389).

2 For instance, Tangney (2009) suggests the following characteristics of humility: accurate assessment of one's abilities and achievements, acknowledging one's limitations, intellectual openness, low self-focus, not exaggerating one's abilities and achievements, an appreciation of the value of other people and things as having important contributions to make. Roberts and Wood (2007) provide an analysis of humility in contrast to intellectual arrogance and Vanity; Whitcomb et al. (2017) characterize humility in terms of 'owning one's limitations'. See also Snow (2020) for an overview of both historic and contemporary accounts of humility. Accounts also differ in terms of whether the characteristics of humility are considered abilities, dispositions or attitudes.

3 See Brassey (2020), for instance, who discusses perspective in relation to visual art.

4 Emotional contagion may be considered a type of empathetic response where someone's emotional or affective stated is caused by another (see Hatfield, Cacioppo and Rapson 1994; Goldie 2003, pp. 189–94), but I want to focus on cases of empathy that involve a cognitive component, in particular, where the empathizer is aware that their emotional response is caused by the emotional response of the other together with motivation to understand the other's emotional response.

5 See also Goldman (2011), who argues that empathy involves considering pretend beliefs in process of simulation of another's perceived or imagined state; Goldie (2003), who argues that empathy involves 'a process or procedure in which a person *centrally imagines the narrative* (the thoughts, feelings and emotions) of another person' (195); and Coplan (2011), who also argues for a simulation account, whereby empathy involves representing another's psychological states in an attempt to replicate the other's response.

6 For example, see Keith Oatley (2012), Susan Feagin (2011) and Eileen John (2017). John argues, 'The empathizing reader is in the process of building a not merely self-oriented sense of the meaningful environment. This experiential openness can benefit the reader as an appreciator of fiction, as well as exercising capacities relevant to attunement to real others' (2017, p. 315). See also Smith (1997) and Elliott (1972), who both develop an account of how film and literature involves imaginative engagement with the emotions of another. For

instance, Elliott argues 'We experience an emotion . . . through an imaginative assumption of the expression and situation of another person (real or imaginary). . . . I do not merely recognise that the poet is expressing, for example, sadness, but actually feel this sadness' (1972, p. 147).

7 Here we can see a distinction with narrative fiction in that it seems to work hard to set up its context for the reader. Even in cases where a work of narrative fiction is deliberately disorientating (take for instance Nabakov's *Pale Fire*, where part of how the book works is to confuse the reader at the outset about what the focus of the narrative is), the author is still trying to engage the reader with the world they have created through rich descriptions, character and narrative voice; in other words, the aesthetics engage and enable cognitive grasp rather than being the feature of the experience that provides coherence in the absence of cognitive grasp. The poem may name things and bring things into relation but that's not enough to provide a clear context or world in which the reader can make sense of the work; instead, this is left as a problem for the reader to attempt to resolve. The reader of the poem has to then decide what resources to bring to the work in order to try to grasp and appreciate it.

8 'Relations' from *Versed* © 2009 by Rae Armantrout. Published by Wesleyan University Press. Used by permission.

9 See also John Gibson (2011), who applied Wollheim's idea of twofoldeness to poetic experience.

10 Claudia Rankine, excerpt from 'What if' from *Just Us: An American Conversation*. Copyright © 2020 by Claudia Rankine. Reprinted with the permission of The Permissions Company, LLC, on behalf of Graywolf Press, graywolfpress.org and Penguin.

Bibliography

Abrams, M. H. (1977). *The Mirror and the Lamp: Romantic Theory and the Critical Tradition*. Oxford: Oxford University Press.

Acevedo, Elizabeth (2015). 'Hair'. Video, 2:15. Uploaded by All Def Poetry. 23 January 2015. https://www.youtube.com/watch?v=6rtRmFpc8D8

Ailes, Katie (2015). 'Is It Ok to Perform another Slam Poets Work?' Available at: https://katieailes.com/2015/04/01/is-it-ok-to-perform-another-slam-poets-work/

Ailes, Katie (2016). 'Writing Collaborative Performance Poems'. Available at: https://katieailes.com/2016/02/16/writing-collaborative-performance-poems/

Ailes, Katie (2021). '"Speak your truth": Authenticity in UK Spoken Word Poetry'. In J. McGowan and L. English (eds), *Spoken Word in the Uk*, 142–53. Abingdon and New York: Routledge.

Alcaraz Leon, Maria Jose (2023). 'More than Make-Believe: On the Uses of Imagination in Experiencing Artworks'. In Patrik Engisch and Julia Langkau (eds), *Philosophy of Fiction, Imagination and Cognition*, 199–217. Abingdon and New York: Routledge.

Alcoff, Linda Martin (1991). 'The Problem of Speaking for Others'. *Cultural Critique* 20: 5–32.

Antrobus, Raymond (2014). 'The First Time I Wore Hearing Aids'. Video, 1:50. Uploaded by Chill Pill Shorts. 14 November 2014. https://www.youtube.com/watch?v=5G9dy8nCbuE

Aristotle (1931). *De Anima/On the Soul*. Translated by J. A. Smith. Oxford: Clarendon Press.

Armand, Louis and John Kinsella (2012). *Synopticon*. Prague: Litteraria Pragensia Press.

Armantrout, Ray (2010). *Versed*. Middletown: Wesleyan University press.

Austin, J. L. (1962). *How to Do Things with Words the William James Lectures Delivered at Harvard University in 1955*. Oxford: Oxford University Press.

Bailey, Olivia (2022). 'Empathy and the Value of Humane Understanding'. *Philosophy and Phenomenological Research* 104 (1): 50–65.

Bakhtin, Mikhail (1984/1999). *Problems of Dostoevsky's Poetics*. Edited and translated by Caryl Emerson. Minneapolis: University of Minnesota Press.

Bar-on, Dorit (2010). 'Expressing as "showing what's within": On Mitchell Green's, Self-expression OUP 2007'. *Philosophical Books* 51 (4): 212–27.

Bearder, Pete (2020). *Stage Invasion*. London: Outspoken Press.

Bennett, Michael Y. (2021). *The Problems of Viewing Performance: Epistemology and Other Minds*. Abingdon and New York: Routledge.

Bernstein, C. (2011). *Attack of the Difficult Poems: Essays and Inventions*. Chicago: University of Chicago Press.

Berry, Francis (1962). *Poetry and the Physical Voice*. New York: Oxford University Press.

Betts, Reginald Dwayne (2019). *Felon*. New York: W. W. Norton & Company Ltd.

Brassey, V. (2020). *What Makes a Painting Sad?* Thesis, King's College London.

Bratman, Michael E. (2014). *Shared Agency: A Planning Theory of Acting Together*. Oxford and New York: Oxford University Press.

Butchart, Garnet C. (2019). *Embodiment, Relation, Community: A Continental Philosophy of Communication*. Pennsylvania: Penn State University Press.

Camp, Elisabeth (2009). 'Two Varieties of Literary Imagination: Metaphor, Fiction, and Thought Experiments'. *Midwest Studies in Philosophy* 33 (1): 107–30.

Camp, Elisabeth (2017). 'Perspectives in Imaginative Engagement with Fiction'. *Philosophical Perspectives* 31 (1): 73–102.

Campion, Toby (2017). 'Notes from the Sexual Health Clinic Waiting Room'. Video, 5:04. Uploaded by Penguin Books UK. 13 July 2017. https://www.youtube.com/watch?v=QAoxCh5LW_4

Capildeo, Vahni (2019). 'Diving into What Wreck? PART II'. *PN Review* 45, Iss. 6 (July/August): 5, 80.

Cavarero, Adriana (2005). *For More than One Voice: Toward a Philosophy of Vocal Expression*. Translated by Paul Kottman. Stanford: Stanford University Press.

Cavell, Stanley (1969/2002). *Must We Mean What We Say?: A Book of Essays*. Cambridge: Cambridge University Press.

Cavell, Stanley (1979). *The Claim of Reason: Wittgenstein, Skepticism, Morality, and Tragedy*. New York and Oxford: Oxford University Press.

Chakraborty, Sumita (2019). *Arrow*. Manchester: Carcanet.

Clark, John Lee (2005). 'Melodies Unheard'. *Poetry Foundation*. Available at: https://www.poetryfoundation.org/poetrymagazine/articles/68287/melodies-unheard

Code, L. (1987). *Epistemic Responsibility*. Hanover: University Press of New England.

Collingwood, R. G. (1958). *The Principles of Art*. New York: Oxford University Press.

Collison, Clare (2020). *Truth Is Beauty*. https://www.clairecollison.com/truth-is-beauty

Connor, S. (1999). 'The Ethics of the Voice'. In D. Rainsford and T. Woods (eds), *Critical Ethics*, 220–38. Basingstoke: Palgrave Macmillan.

Cooper, Neil (2000). 'Understanding People'. *Philosophy* 75 (3): 383–400.

Coplan, A. (2011). 'Understanding Empathy: Its Features and Effects'. In Coplan Amy and Peter Goldie (eds), *Empathy: Philosophical and Psychological Perspectives*, 2–18. New York: Oxford University Press.

Crowther, Thomas (2009). 'Perceptual Activity and the Will'. In Lucy O'Brien and Matthew Soteriou (eds), *Mental Actions*, 173–91. New York: Oxford University Press.

Culler, Jonathan (2015). *The Theory of the Lyric*. Cambridge, MA: Harvard University Press.

Currie, Gregory and Jacopo Frascaroli (2021). 'Poetry and the Possibility of Paraphrase'. *The Journal of Aesthetics and Art Criticism* 79 (4): 428–39.

Davies, David (2011). *Philosophy of the Performing Arts*. Oxford: Wiley-Blackwell.

Davis, Emmalon (2018). 'On Epistemic Appropriation'. *Ethics* 128 (4): 702–27.

Dawes, Kwame and John Kinsella (2019). *Tangling with the Epic*. Leeds: Peepal Tree Press Ltd.

DePaul, Michael R. (1993). *Balance and Refinement: Beyond Coherence Methods of Moral Inquiry*. Abingdon and New York: Routledge.

Dharker, Imtiaz (2018). *Luck Is the Hook*. Hexham: Bloodaxe Books.

Dillard, Annie (2016). 'About Found Poetry'. *Found Poetry Review*. Available at: http://foundpoetryreview.com/about-found-poetry/

Dodd, Julian (2021). 'Style Appropriation, Intimacy, and Expressiveness'. *British Journal of Aesthetics* 61 (3): 373–86.

Dolar, Mladen (2006). *A Voice and Nothing More*. Cambridge, MA: The MIT Press.

Donnelly, Maureen (2019). 'The Cognitive Value of Literary Perspectives'. *Journal of Aesthetics and Art Criticism* 77 (1): 11–22.

Dotson, Kristie (2011). 'Tracking Epistemic Violence, Tracking Practices of Silencing'. *Hypatia* 26 (2): 236–57.

Duhamel, Denise and Maureen Seaton (2006). 'Poetry and Collaboration'. poets.org. https://poets.org/text/poetry-and-collaboration-denise-duhamel-maureen-seaton

Dumm, T. L. (2008). *Loneliness as a Way of Life*. Cambridge, MA: Harvard University Press.

Dwyer, Susan (2008). 'Romancing the Dane: Ethics and Observation'. In Mette Hjort (ed.), *Dekalog 1: On the Five Obstructions*, 1–14. London and New York: Wallflower press.

Elliott, R. K. (1972). 'Imagination in the Experience of Art: R. K. Elliott'. *Royal Institute of Philosophy Supplement* 6: 88–105.

Evans, Gareth (1985). 'Understanding Demonstratives'. In *Collected Papers*, 291–321. Oxford: Clarendon Press.

Fawaz, Ramzi (2019). '"An Open Mesh of Possibilities": The Necessity of Eve Sedgwick in Dark Times'. In Lauren Berlant (ed.), *Reading Sedgwick*, 6–33. Durham: Duke University Press.

Feagin, Susan L. (2011). 'Empathizing as Simulating'. In Amy Coplan and Peter Goldie (eds), *Empathy: Philosophical and Psychological Perspectives*, 149–61. New York: Oxford University Press.

Feldman, Sarah (2020). 'Symbolic Cognition in Poetic Experience: Re-representing the Paraphrase Paradox'. *British Journal of Aesthetics* 60 (3): 283–98.

Femi, Caleb (2020). *Poor*. London: Penguin Books.

Franklin, Aretha (1967). *Respect* (song). New York: Atlantic Records.

Freeland, Cynthia A. (1997). 'Art and Moral Knowledge'. *Philosophical Topics* 25 (1): 11–36.

Gander, Forrest (2018). *Be With*. New York: New Directions Books.

Gander, Forrest and John Kinsella (2012). *Redstart: An Ecological Poetics*. Iowa City: University of Iowa Press.

Gardosi, Jasmine (2021). 'Rollercoaster'. Video, 2:24. Uploaded by PBS News Hour. 2 December 2021. https://www.youtube.com/watch?v=4qY8AoAS4Ck

Gaut, Berys (2006). 'Art and Cognition'. In M. Kieran (ed.), *Contemporary Debates in Aesthetics and the Philosophy of Art*, 115–26. Oxford: Wiley-Blackwell.

Gaut, Berys (2007). *Art, Emotion and Ethics*. Oxford and New York: Oxford University Press.

de Gaynesford, Maximilian (2006). *I: The Meaning of the First Person Term*. Clarendon Press.

de Gaynesford, Maximilian (2011). 'How Not To Do Things with Words: J. L. Austin on Poetry'. *British Journal of Aesthetics* 51 (1): 31–49.

de Gaynesford, Maximilian (2017). *The Rift in the Lute: Attuning Poetry and Philosophy*. Oxford and New York: Oxford University Press.

Gibson, John (2007). *Fiction and the Weave of Life*. Oxford and New York: Oxford University Press.

Gibson, John (2009). 'Literature and Knowledge'. In Richard Eldridge (ed.), *Oxford Handbook of Philosophy and Literature*. Oxford and New York: Oxford University Press.

Gibson, John (2011). 'The Question of Poetic Meaning'. *Nonsite* 4. Available at https://nonsite.org/the-question-of-poetic-meaning/

Gibson, John (2016a). 'A Puzzle of Poetic Expression'. *The Philosophers' Magazine* 74 (3): 56–62.

Gibson, John (2016b). 'Empathy'. In N. Caroll and J. Gibson (eds), *The Routledge Companion to Philosophy of Literature*, 234–46. Abingdon and New York: Routledge.

Gibson, John (2018). 'What Makes a Poem Philosophical?' In Karen Zumhagen-Yekplé and Michael LeMahieu (eds), *Wittgenstein and Modernism*, 130–52. Chicago: University of Chicago Press.

Goldie, P. (2003). *The Emotions: A Philosophical Exploration*. Oxford and New York: Oxford University Press.

Goldman, A. (2011). 'Two Routes to Empathy: Insights from Neuroscience'. In A. Coplan and P. Goldie, *Empathy: Philosophical and Psychological Perspectives*, 31–44. Oxford and New York: Oxford University Press.

Goodman, Nelson (1976). *Languages of Art: An Approach to a Theory of Symbols*, 2nd edn. Indianapolis: Hackett Publishing Company.
Gorman, Amanda (2021). 'The Hill We Climb'. Video, 5:42. Uploaded by The Guardian. 20 January 2021. https://www.youtube.com/watch?v=CdKdyemxbew
Green, Mitchell S. (2007). *Self-Expression*. Oxford and New York: Oxford University Press.
Hadfield, Jen (2008). *Nigh-No-Place*. Hexham: Bloodaxe Books.
Von Hallberg, R. (2008). *Lyric Powers*. Chicago: University of Chicago Press.
Hamburger, Kate (1973). *The Logic of Literature*. Bloomington: Indiana University Press.
Harris, Will (2017). 'Object'. In Karen McCarthy Woolf (ed.), *Ten Poets of the New Generation*, 54. Hexham: Bloodaxe Books.
Harris, Will (2019). 'The Ethics of Perspective'. Available at: https://willjharris.com/2019/05/10/the-ethics-of-perspective/
Harvey, Elizabeth (1992). *Ventriloquized Voices: Feminist Theory and English Renaissance Texts*. Abingdon and New York: Routledge.
Hatfield, E., J. T. Cacioppo and R. L. Rapson (1994). *Emotional Contagion*. Cambridge: Cambridge University Press.
Haynes, Paul (2021). 'The Ethics and Aesthetics of Intertextual Writing: Cultural Appropriation and Minor Literature'. *British Journal of Aesthetics* 61 (3): 291–306.
Hegley, John (2018). 'Suitcase'. Video, 2:30. Uploaded by Brian Mackrell. 10 February 2019. https://www.youtube.com/watch?v=WJX3PMsON00
Hejinian, Lyn (2000). 'Materials (for Dubravka Djuric)'. In *The Language of Inquiry*, 161–76. Berkeley: University of California Press.
Helm, Bennett (2012). *Love, Friendship, and the Self: Intimacy, Identification, and the Social Nature of Persons*. Oxford and New York: Oxford University Press.
Helm, Bennett W. (2017). *Communities of Respect: Grounding Responsibility, Authority, and Dignity*. Oxford and New York: Oxford University Press.
Hilborn, Neil (2013). 'OCD'. Video, 2:51. Uploaded by Button Poetry. 22 July 2013. https://www.youtube.com/watch?v=vnKZ4pdSU-s
Hirsch, Edward (2006). 'In the Beginning Is the Relation'. Poetry Foundation. Available at: https://www.poetryfoundation.org/articles/68414/in-the-beginning-is-the-relation
Holiday, Billie (2018). *Lady Sings the Blues*. London: Penguin Classics.
Hornsby, Jennifer (1995). 'Disempowered Speech'. *Philosophical Topics* 23 (2): 127–47.
hooks, bell (1995). *Let's Get It On: The Politics of Black Performance*. Seattle: Bay Press.
Hošek, C. and P. Parker (1985). *Lyric Poetry: Beyond New Criticism*. New York: Cornell University Press.

Howe, Sarah (2017). 'Will Harris'. In Jaren McCarthy Woolf (ed.), *Ten Poets of the New Generation*, 51–3. Hexham, Northumberland: Bloodaxe Books.

Huntington, Patricia (2009). *Loneliness and Lament: A Journey to Receptivity*. Bloomington: Indiana University Press.

Ihde, Don (2007). *Listening and Voice. Phenomenologies of Sound*. New York: SUNY Press.

Irvin, Sherri (2015). 'Unreadable Poems and How they Mean'. In J. Gibson (ed.), *The Philosophy of Poetry*, 88–110. Oxford and New York: Oxford University Press.

Iser, Wolfgang (1972). 'The Reading Process: A Phenomenological Approach'. *New Literary History* 3 (2), On Interpretation: 279–99.

Iser, Wolfgang (1978). *The Act of Reading*. London: Routledge.

Izenberg, Oren (2011). *Being Numerous: Poetry and the Ground of Social Life*. Princeton: Princeton University Press.

John, Eileen (2013a). 'Poetry and Directions for Thought'. *Philosophy and Literature* 37 (2): 451–71.

John, Eileen (2013b). 'Art and Knowledge'. In Berys Nigel Gaut and Dominic Lopes (eds), *The Routledge Companion to Aesthetics*, 384–93. London: Routledge.

John, Eileen (2017). 'Empathy in Literature'. In Heidi Maibom (ed.), *Routledge Handbook to Philosophy of Empathy*, 306–16. London: Routledge.

Kaplan, David (1989). 'Demonstratives: An Essay on the Semantics, Logic, Metaphysics and Epistemology of Demonstratives and other Indexicals'. In Joseph Almog, John Perry and Howard Wettstein (eds), *Themes From Kaplan*, 481–563. New York: Oxford University Press.

Kieran, Matthew (2004). *Revealing Art*. London and New York: Routledge.

Kim, Hannah H. and John Gibson (2021). 'Lyric Self-Expression'. In Sonia Sedivy (ed.), *Art, Representation, and Make-Believe: Essays on the Philosophy of Kendall L. Walton*. New York: Routledge.

Kivy, Peter (2006). *The Performance of Reading: An Essay in the Philosophy of Literature*. Oxford: Wiley-Blackwell.

Kivy, Peter (2011). 'Paraphrasing Poetry (for Profit and Pleasure)'. *Journal of Aesthetics and Art Criticism* 69 (4): 367–77.

Koethe, John (2001). 'Thought and Poetry'. *Midwest Studies in Philosophy* 25 (1): 5–11.

Korta, Kepa (2016). 'The Meaning of Us'. *Disputatio. Philosophical Research Bulletin* 5 (6): 335–61.

Krueger, Joel (2011). 'Enacting Musical Content'. In Riccardo Manzotti (ed.), *Situated Aesthetics: Art Beyond the Skin*, 63–85. Exeter: Imprint Academic.

Kunial, Zaffar (2018). *Us*. London: Faber & Faber.

Lagaay, Alice (2011). 'Towards a (Negative) Philosophy of Voice'. In Lynne Kendrick and David Roesner (eds), *Theatre Noise: The Sound of Performance*, 57–69. Cambridge Scholars Publishing.

Lamarque, Peter (2009). 'The Elusiveness of Poetic Meaning'. *Ratio* 22 (4): 398–420.

Lamarque, Peter (2015). 'Semantic Finegrainedness and Poetic Value'. In J. Gibson (ed.), *The Philosophy of Poetry*, 18–36. Oxford and New York: Oxford University Press.

Leighton, Angela (2009). 'About About: On Poetry and Paraphrase'. *Midwest Studies in Philosophy* 33 (1): 167–76.

Livingston, Paisley (2005). *Art and Intention: A Philosophical Study*. Oxford: Clarendon.

Long Soldier, Layli (2019). *Whereas*. London: Picador.

Longworth, Guy (2013). 'IV—Sharing Thoughts about Oneself'. *Proceedings of the Aristotelian Society* 113 (1pt1): 57–81.

Lorde, Audre (1978/1997). *The Collected Poems of Audre Lorde*. New York: W.W. Norton & Company, Inc.

Maguire, Sarah (2001). *The Florist's at Midnight*. London: Jonathan Cape.

Maibom, Heidi L. (2017). 'Introduction'. In Heidi Maibom (ed.), *The Routledge Handbook of Philosophy of Empathy*, 1-9. London: Routledge.

Mason, Jessica (2019). *Intertextuality in Practice*. Amsterdam and Philadelphia: John Benjamins Publishing Company.

Matravers, Derek (2014). *Fiction and Narrative*. Oxford and New York: Oxford University Press.

Matthes, Erich (2019). 'Cultural Appropriation and Oppression'. *Philosophical Studies* 176 (4): 1003–13.

McDowell, John (1984). 'De Re Senses'. In *Meaning, Knowledge, and Reality*, 214–27. Cambridge, MA: Harvard University Press.

McGarvey, Darren (2018). *Poverty Safari*. London: Picador.

Mehri, Momtaza (2019). 'Glory Be to the Gang Gang Gang'. *Poetry*, April 2019. https://www.poetryfoundation.org/poetrymagazine/poems/149516/glory-be-to-the-gang-gang-gang

Mehri, Momtaza (2021). 'A Common Gift. In "Of Many Voices: A poetic Gift of Togetherness", K. Simecek'. *The Poetry Review* 111, no. 3 (Autumn): 92–100.

Middleton, Peter (2009). 'Poetry's Oral Stage'. In Salim Kemal and Ivan Gaskell (eds), *Performance and Authenticity in the Arts*, 215–53. Cambridge: Cambridge University Press.

Mikkonen, Jukka (2013). *The Cognitive Value of Philosophical Fiction*. London: Bloomsbury.

Mills, Philip (2022). *A Poetic Philosophy of Language: Nietzsche and Wittgenstein's Expressivism*. London: Bloomsbury.

Montgomery, Robert (2010). 'People You Love. De La Warr Pavillion'. Bexhill-on-Sea, Sussex, UK. https://www.robertmontgomery.org/recycledsunlightpoems/2grya25po4v0uts1x9p2asxcz6l3ca

Montgomery, Robert (2014). 'Poem for William Blake', Bethnal Green Billboard, London. https://www.robertmontgomery.org/gzkuqg4f7kpaoe0maqpbc9goi6bm53

Moore, A. W. (1997). *Points of View*. Oxford: Clarendon Press.

Morton, A. (2017). 'Empathy and Imagination'. In Heidi L. Maibom (ed.), *The Routledge Handbook of Philosophy of Empathy*, 180–9. London: Routledge.

Nagra, Daljit (2009). 'This Be the Pukka Verse'. *London Review of Books* 31 (23): 3.

Nancy, Jean-Luc (2007). *Listening*. New York: Fordham University Press.

Nancy, Jean-Luc (2010). 'Conloquium', *Minnesota Review* 75 (Fall): 101–8.

Nancy, Jean-Luc (2016). *The Disavowed Community*. New York: Fordham University Press.

Nannicelli, Ted (2020). *Artistic Creation and Ethical Criticism*. Oxford and New York: Oxford University Press.

Neill, Alex (2009). 'Inauthenticity, Insincerity and Poetry'. In Salim Kemal and Ivan Gaskell (eds), *Performance and Authenticity in the Arts*, 197–214. Cambridge: Cambridge University Press.

Nelson, Maggie (2009). *Bluets*. London: Jonathan Cape.

Nguyen, C. Thi and Matthew Strohl (2019). 'Cultural Appropriation and the Intimacy of Groups'. *Philosophical Studies* 176 (4): 981–1002.

Novak, J. (2011). *Live Poetry: An Integrated Approach to Poetry in Performance*. Amsterdam: Rodopi.

Oatley, K. (2012). 'The Cognitive Science of Fiction'. *WIREs Cognitive Science* 3: 425–30.

Olson, Charles (1997). 'Projective Verse'. In D. Allen and B. Friedlander (eds), *Collected Prose*, 239–49. Berkeley: University of California Press.

O'Shaughnessy, Brian (2000). *Consciousness and the World*. Oxford and New York: Oxford University Press.

Oswald, Alice (2007). *The Thing in the Gap Stone Stile*. London: Faber & Faber.

Parker, Patricia (1985). 'Introduction', in Chaviva Hosek and P. Parker (eds), *Lyric Poetry: Beyond the New Criticism*. Ithaca: Cornell University Press.

Paterson, Don (2007). 'The Lyric Principle Part 1: The Sense of Sound'. *Poetry Review* 97 (2): 56–72.

Paterson, Don (2018). *The Poem: Lyric, Sign, Metre*. London: Faber & Faber.

Pati, Anita (2022). *Hiding to Nothing*. Liverpool: Liverpool University Press.

Pinsky, Robert (1998). *The Sounds of Poetry: A Brief Guide*. New York: Farrar, Straus and Giroux.

Pinsky, Robert (2002). *Democracy, Culture and the Voice of Poetry*. Princeton: Princeton University Press.

Pocci, Luca (2007). 'The Return of the Repressed: Caring about Literature and Its Themes'. In John Gibson, Wolfgang Huemer and Luca Pocci (eds), *A Sense of the World: Essays on Fiction, Narrative, and Knowledge*. New York: Routledge.

Prinz, Jesse J. and Eric Mandelbaum (2015). 'Poetic Opacity: How to Paint Things with Words'. In J. Gibson (ed.), *The Philosophy of Poetry*, 63–87. Oxford and New York: Oxford University Press.

Rankine, Claudia (2014). *Citizen: An American Lyric*. Minneapolis: Graywolf Press.

Rankine, Claudia (2017). *Don't Let Me be Lonely: An American Lyric*. London: Penguin Books.

Rankine, Claudia (2021). 'What If'. In *Just us: An American Conversation*. London: Penguin Books.

Ribeiro, Anna Christina (2009). 'Toward a Philosophy of Poetry'. *Midwest Studies in Philosophy* 33 (2009): 61–77 (69–70).

Ribeiro, Anna Christina (2013). 'Heavenly Hurt: The Joy and Value of Sad Poetry'. In J. Levinson (ed.), *Suffering Art Gladly: The Paradox of Negative Emotions in Art*, 186–206. Basingstoke: Palgrave-Macmillan.

Ribeiro, Anna Christina (2015a). 'The Spoken and the Written: An Ontology of Poems'. In J. Gibson (ed.), *The Philosophy of Poetry*, 127–48. Oxford and New York: Oxford University Press.

Ribeiro, Anna Christina (2015b). 'Poetry'. In Noel Carroll and John Gibson (eds), *The Routledge Companion to Philosophy of Literature*, 97–106. New York: Routledge.

Richardson, Louise (2015). 'IX—Perceptual Activity and Bodily Awareness'. *Proceedings of the Aristotelian Society* 115 (2pt2): 147–65.

Roberts, R. and J. Wood (2007). *Intellectual Virtues: An Essay in Regulative Epistemology*. Oxford and New York: Oxford University Press.

Roberts, Tom and Joel Krueger (2021). 'Loneliness and the Emotional Experience of Absence'. *Southern Journal of Philosophy* 59 (2): 185–204.

Robinson, Jenefer (2005). *Deeper Than Reason: Emotion and its Role in Literature, Music, and Art*. Oxford: Clarendon Press.

Roessler, Johannes (2016). 'Thinking, Inner Speech, and Self-awareness'. *Review of Philosophy and Psychology* 7 (3): 541–57.

Rosenblatt, Louise M. (1978). *The Reader, the Text, the Poem: The Transactional Theory of the Literary Work*. Carbondale: Southern Illinois University Press.

Rosenblatt, Louise M. (1983). *Literature as Exploration*, 3rd edn. New York: MLA.

Rowe, M. W. (1996). 'Poetry and Abstraction'. *British Journal of Aesthetics* 36 (1): 1–15.

Rubin, J. S. (2007). *Songs of Ourselves: The Uses of Poetry in America*. Cambridge, MA: Belknap Press of Harvard University Press.

Scanlon, Thomas (1998). *What We Owe to Each Other*. Cambridge, MA: Belknap Press of Harvard University Press.

Schmid, Hans (2014). 'Plural Self-awareness'. *Phenomenology and the Cognitive Sciences* 13 (1): 7–24.

Schmid, Hans (2018). 'The Subject of "We intend"'. *Phenomenology and the Cognitive Sciences* 17 (2): 231–43.

Searle, John R. (2002). *Consciousness and Language*. Cambridge: Cambridge University Press.

Sedgwick, Eve Kosofsky (2003). 'Paranoid Reading and Reparative Reading, or, You're So Paranoid, You Probably Think This Essay Is about You'. In *Touching Feeling: Affect, Pedagogy, Performativity*, 123–51. Durham: Duke University Press.

Simecek, Karen (2019a). 'New Directions for the Philosophy of Poetry'. *Philosophy Compass* 14 (6): 1–11 (e12593).

Simecek, Karen (2019b). 'Cultivating Intimacy: The Use of the Second Person in Lyric Poetry'. *Philosophy and Literature* 43 (2): 501–18.

Simecek, Karen (2021). 'Listen to Me! The Moral Value of the Poetry Performance Space'. In Lucy English and Jack McGowan (eds), *Spoken Word in the UK*. Abingdon and New York: Routledge.

Simecek, Karen (2022). 'Linking Perspectives: A Role for Poetry in Philosophical Inquiry'. *Metaphilosophy* 53 (2–3): 305–18.

Simpson, Darius and Scout Bostley (2015). 'Lost Voices'. Video, 2:59. Uploaded by Button Poetry. 17 June 2015. https://www.youtube.com/watch?v=lpPASWlnZIA

Sjöholm, Cecilia (2018). 'Voicing Thought: Arendt, Poetry, and Philosophy'. In Ranjan Gosht (ed.), *Poetry and Philosophy: Continental Perspectives*, 69–83. New York: Columbia University Press.

Smith, Joel (2018). 'The First-Person Plural and Immunity to Error'. *Disputatio* 10 (49): 141–67.

Smith, Murray (1997). 'Imagining from the Inside: POV, Imagining Seeing, and Empathy'. In Richard Allen and Murray Smith (eds), *Film Theory and Philosophy*, 412–30. Oxford and New York: Oxford University Press.

Smith, Patricia (2010). 'Skinhead'. Video, 3:37. Uploaded by urbanrenewalprogram. 28 August 2010. https://www.youtube.com/watch?v=Klb5TniRGao.

Snow, Nancy (2020). 'Theories of Humility'. In Mark Alfano, Michael P. Lynch and Alessandra Tanesini (eds), *The Routledge Handbook of Philosophy of Humility*, 9–25. London: Routledge.

Sode, Yomi (2020). 'Distant Daily Ijó / YNWA'. Video, 6:19. Uploaded by Yomi Sode. 4 December 2020. https://youtu.be/ZNO6-Q2L7Hg

Somers-Willett, Susan (2012). *The Cultural Politics of Slam Poetry: Race, Identity and the Performance of Popular Verse in America*. Ann Arbor: University of Michigan Press.

Spahr, Juliana (2005). *This Connection of Everyone with Lungs*. Berkeley: University of California Press.

Stecker, R. (2001). 'Expressiveness and Expression in Music and Poetry'. *Journal of Aesthetics and Art Criticism* 59 (1): 85–96.

Stevenson, Anne (2017). *About Poems and How Poems Are Not About*. Hexham: Bloodaxe Books.

Stewart, Susan (2002). *Poetry and the Fate of the Senses*. London: Chicago University Press.

Stone, Degna (2017a). 'Swimming'. In Jaren McCarthy Woolf (ed.), *Ten Poets of the New Generation*, 90. Hexham: Bloodaxe Books.

Stone, Degna (2017b). 'The River Gods'. In Jaren McCarthy Woolf (ed.), *Ten Poets of the New Generation*, 95. Hexham: Bloodaxe Books.

Tanesini, Alessandra (2018). 'Intellectual Humility as Attitude'. *Philosophy and Phenomenological Research* 96 (2): 399–420.

Tangney, J. P. (2009). 'Humility'. In S. J. Lopez and C. R. Snyder (eds), *Oxford Handbook of Positive Psychology*. Oxford and New York: Oxford University Press.

Taylor, Joelle (2012). 'The Last Poet Standing: A Poem for Young People'. Video, 5:28. Uploaded by The Poetry Society. 9 February 2012. https://www.youtube.com/watch?v=GasEftVfyLI

Tempset, Kae (2013). 'Renegade'. Video, 5:03. Uploaded by RosieBee. 7 June 2013. https://youtu.be/0NRYLzWovtk

Thomson-Jones, Katherine (2005). 'Inseparable Insight: Reconciling Cognitivism and Formalism in Aesthetics'. *Journal of Aesthetics and Art Criticism* 63 (4): 375–84.

Turner, Stephen (2019). 'Verstehen Naturalized'. *Philosophy of the Social Sciences* 49 (4): 243–64.

Tuvel, Rebecca (2021). 'Putting the Appropriator Back in Cultural Appropriation'. *British Journal of Aesthetics* 61 (3): 353–72.

Vallée, Richard (1996). 'Who Are We?' *Canadian Journal of Philosophy* 26 (2): 211–30.

Vendler, Helen (1995). *The Given and the Made: Strategies of Poetic Redefinition*. Cambridge, MA: Harvard University Press.

Vendler, Helen (2005). *Invisible Listeners: Lyric Intimacy in Herbert, Whitman, and Ashbery*. Princeton: Princeton University Press.

Vicente, Agustin and Fernando Martinez Manrique (2011). 'Inner Speech: Nature and Functions'. *Philosophy Compass* 6 (3): 209–19.

Vidmar Jovanović, Iris (2021). 'Fiction, Philosophy, and Television: The Case of Law and Order: Special Victims Unit'. *Journal of Aesthetics and Art Criticism* 79 (1): 76–87.

Vincent, Bridget (2013). 'In Focus: Poetry, Context, Meaning'. *Philosophy and Literature* 37 (1): 53–71.

Walton, K. (2015). 'Thoughtwriting – In Poetry and Music'. In *In Other Shoes: Music, Metaphor, Empathy, Existence*, 54–74. Oxford and New York: Oxford University Press.

Wheeler, Lesley (2009). *Voicing American Poetry: Sound and Performance from the 1920s to the Present*. New York: Cornell University Press.

Whitcomb, Dennis, Heather Battaly, Jason Baehr and Daniel Howard-Snyder (2017). 'Intellectual Humility: Owning Our Limitations'. *Philosophy and Phenomenological Research* 94 (3): 509–39.

Wilcox, Phil (2020). 'Infect the World with Doves'. Video 4:26. Uploaded by Phil Wilcox. 29 October 2020. https://www.youtube.com/watch?v=bULZduEKg3s

Williams, Bernard (2000). 'Philosophy as a Humanistic Discipline'. *Philosophy* 75 (4): 477–96.

Williams, Nerys (2013). 'Lyric Encounters with Other Places: Juliana Spahr's this Connection of Everyone with Lungs and Robert Minhinnick's "An Isotope Dreaming"'. In Ian Davidson and Zoë Skoulding (eds), *Placing Poetry*, 183–99. Leiden: Brill.

Williams, Saul (2012). *Chorus: A Literary Mixtape*. New York: Gallery Books.

Winterbottom, Micheal (dir.) (2010). *The Trip*. BabyCow Productions, BBC, Revolution Films.

Winterbottom, Micheal (dir.) (2014). *The Trip to Italy*. BBC and Revolution Films.

Winterbottom, Micheal (dir.) (2017). *The Trip to Spain*. Revolution Films.

Winterbottom, Micheal (dir.) (2022). *The Trip to Greece*. Revolution Films.

Wordsworth, W. (1802). 'Preface' to the *Lyrical Ballads, with Pastoral and Other Poems*. London: Longman and O. Rees.

Young, James O. (2005). 'Profound Offense and Cultural Appropriation'. *Journal of Aesthetics and Art Criticism* 63 (2): 135–46.

Zamir, Tzachi (2012). 'Listening to Actors'. *Theatre Topics* 22 (2): 115–25.

Zamir, Tzachi (2013). 'Unethical Acts'. *Philosophical Quarterly* 63 (251): 353–73.

Zamir, Tzachi (2015). 'The Inner Paradise'. In J. Gibson (ed.), *The Philosophy of Poetry*, 127–48. Oxford and New York: Oxford University Press.

Index

accent   31, 41, 165–6
Acevedo, Elizabeth
   'Hair'   18
acknowledgement   28, 61–2, 64, 72–3, 80–1, 95–7, 136–7
address   1–2, 12, 19, 30, 45–8, 56, 68–9, 75–8, 134–5, 157–9
affect   12, 21, 32, 35–6, 64–5, 74
ambiguity   56–8, 75, 157
Antrobus, Raymond
   'The First Time I Wore Hearing Aids'   42–3
appropriation   106, 126–35
   attempted   127–30
   cultural   126–8
   epistemic appropriation   128–9
   expropriation   131–2
   oppression account   128
Armantrout, Rae
   'Relations'   156
audience   10, 12–13, 16–19, 38–41, 43–4, 77, 109–12, 114–18
   audience participation   111–12
authenticity   19, 39–40, 129
   cf. autobiographical   117–18

belonging   88–9, 93
Betts, Reginald Dwayne
   Felon   132–3
body. *See also under* voice/vocal/vocalisation
   aesthetics of   18–19, 133–5, 161
   ethics of   125–31, 162, 164–5
   language and meaning   38–41, 116–25, 138
   text   10, 38, 121–3, 130

call for response   30–1, 39
Chakraborty, Sumita
   'Dear, Beloved'   76–8
co-creation   44–51

cognitive value (of art, poetry), cognitivism   3–8, 143–5
collaboration   100–3. *See also* voice/vocal/vocalisation
Collison, Claire
   'Truth is Beauty'   117
communication
   ordinary language   12–13, 156–7, 161
   self-expression   30–6, 38–43, 60–2, 72–4, 125, 161–3
community. *See also* voice/vocal/vocalisation
   definition   87–8
   enacting community   98–108, 111
   features of   84–7
   language   91–3, 153
   oral poetry   8–10
   poetry about community   88–9, 93–4
conversation (as community building)   94–5
Culler, Jonathan   1, 10–13

deaf poetics   12–13
   braille poetry   13
   sign language poetry   12
Dharker, Imitaz
   'This Line, This Thread'   83–4

embodied voice. *See under* voice/vocal/vocalisation
empathy
   humility   154–8
   identification   144, 146–7
   perspective-shifting   150–3
   perspective-taking   145–6, 149–50
   and self-other differentiation   146–8
expressiveness/expression (vocal expression)
   co-creating expression   44–51
   expression theory of lyric poetry   13–15
   expressive intention   119–25, 138–9

expressive subject   15, 55–6
    self-expression theory   33–6
    and thought   35–6
    witnessing self-expression   38–44
expropriation. *See under* appropriation

Femi, Caleb
    'Community'   91
fiction   2, 22, 40, 125
first-person plural (we)   72, 83, 86–7, 90,
    93–4, 96–7, 106
found poetry   132–3

Gardosi, Jasmine
    'Rollercoaster'   3
group   84–7, 95–7
    speaking for a group   167–8

Hadfield, Jen
    'Nigh-No-Place'   66–67
Harris, Will
    'Object'   56–7
hearing   26, 43–5, 51, 69–70, 135
    and attention   70–1
    being heard   30–1, 39, 58, 68–71,
        75–6, 78, 106–8, 113–15,
        117–39, 167
    cf. listening   69–70
    failure to hear   75, 78
    hearing together   109–11
    overhearing   69
    and voice   29–30, 35, 44–5, 95
humility   22, 141–2. *See also under*
    empathy; perspective/perspectival;
    self-other differentiation
    poetic humility   155–7, 161–8

identification   59–61, 64–5, 133
    and empathy   144–6, 162–4
identity poem   17–18
inaudibility   114–15, 123–7
individual voice. *See under* voice/vocal/
    vocalisation
intellectual humility. *See under*
    humility
intentions/intentionality   80. *See also*
    expressiveness/expression
    (vocal expression)
    and voice   30, 39, 43
interpersonality   15–17

interpersonal relationships   72–4,
    83–6, 94, 112
intertextuality   131–3

Kinsella, John   100–1
Kunial, Zaffar
    'Us'   93–4

language
    ordinary language   143, 157, 161, 168
    and poetry   2, 17, 37, 98, 136, 143
    use of   2, 12, 15–16, 93–5, 114, 161
listening   51–2, 68–71, 75–8, 114–16
literary criticism   2, 19, 26, 45–6
live poetry. *See* performance,
    performance poetry
loneliness   71–6
Long Soldier, Layli
    'Whereas'   136–7
Lorde, Audre
    'A Litany For Survival'   2
loss   76–8
love   6–7
lyric I, first person. *See also under*
    lyric poetry
    identification model   60–3
    relational model   13–16, 63–8
lyric poetry. *See also* expressiveness/
    expression (vocal expression);
    voice/vocal/vocalisation
    aesthetic use of language   158–61
    context sensitivity   135–7
    and the first person (use of)   56–8
    musicality of   10–12, 158
    object *vs.* event   1–2, 10–12, 16,
        40–1, 118, 127
    and perspective   14–16, 20, 57, 66,
        68, 146, 155
    and presentness (quality of)   1–2,
        22, 80, 117
    and relationality   13–16, 63–8, 71–4,
        81, 110, 115–17, 146, 162–4
    as social art form   16–17, 92–3
    and thought   58
    value of   143–4

Mehri, Momtaza
    'A Common Gift'   103–4
    'Glory be to the Gang Gang Gang'
        88–9

Montgomery, Robert
   'People You Love'   109
   'Poem for William Blake'   109
multivocal poetry. *See* voice/vocal/vocalisation
musicality of poetry (sounds, sounding). *See under* lyric poetry

Nagra, Daljit
   'This be the pukka verse'   99
Nancy, Jean Luc   87
   being-in-common   90
   being-with   90–2, 111
narrative   2, 4, 22
Nelson, Maggie
   Bluets   78–9
New criticism   19, 45

oral poetry   8–9
Oswald, Alice
   'Wedding'   7

page poetry   3, 9–11, 16, 37–8, 44–6, 68–9, 135–7, 158–60
paraphrase   1
Pati, Anita
   'Bloodfruit'   106–7
performance
   cf. oral poetry   8–9
   nature of   80, 95, 115, 116, 119, 124–5
   performance poetry   9–11, 16–19, 38–44, 102–3, 107–8, 110–11, 116–25, 130, 134–5, 153, 161, 164–6
   space   16, 40–4, 111–12, 117, 134–5
   viewing together   109–11
   and voice   37–44, 107–8, 123, 127–30, 133–4, 153, 164–5
persona poem   120–2. *See also* Smith, Patricia
perspective/perspectival   20. *See also under* lyric poetry; voice/vocal/vocalisation
   and the body   116–17, 130, 153
   and expression   33–5, 38–43, 53, 57–63, 125, 128
   and humility   21–2, 141–4, 154
   shared perspective   7, 17, 79, 85–7, 93, 101–3, 142, 154, 168
   and thought   21

perspective shifting. *See* empathy
philosophical poem   5–6
poetic address   68–9
poetic humility. *See under* humility
presentness (quality of). *See* lyric poetry

Rankine, Claudia
   Citizen   63
   Don't Let Me Be Lonely   74–6
   Just Us   159
reader response theory   46–8, 135
reading   44–51
   reading together   108–9
recordings of poems, audio-recording   44, 51–2
relationality   16, 32, 48, 52–3, 56–8, 84, 89–91, 94, 113, 141, 160, 168. *See also* lyric poetry
   and voice   55, 64–5, 135, 138, 158
Ribeiro, Anna Christina   8, 45, 59, 62

second person (you)   56, 61, 71–2, 74, 80, 106, 109, 122, 134, 158
Sedgwick, Eve Kosofsky   64–5, 68
self-expression. *See under* expression
self-other differentiation. *See also* empathy
   and humility   141–3
   interpersonal relationships   90, 94–6
   in poetry   62, 66, 68, 71, 79–80, 106, 138, 157
sense of us   84–5
shared/sharing/shareability. *See also* perspective/perspectival
   and poetry   19, 48–50, 108, 111
   relationship   64–5, 75–6, 79–81, 87–90, 94, 107, 115, 117, 144, 163
   shareability of first person thought   61–5
   shared experience   7, 110–11, 163–4, 168
   shared feeling   144–5
   shared language   15–17, 31–3, 48–9, 78–9, 91–3, 154
silence/silent   2, 29–30, 43, 49, 134–5, 160–1
   silenced   114, 120, 134
Slam poetry   18, 110–11
Smith, Patricia
   'Skinhead'   121–4

Şode, Yomi
 'Distant Daily Ijo/YNWA'   99–100
Spahr, Juliana
 This Connection of Everyone with Lungs   49–50
speaking
 with another   28, 95
 for another/on behalf of   61, 63, 120–1, 166–7
Stone, Degna
 'The River Gods'   96–7
 'Swimming'   96

Taylor, Joelle
 'The Last Poet Standing'   38–9
Tempest, Kae
 'Renegade'   41–2
translation   120–1

understanding   72–3

value
 instrumental/intrinsic distinction   4–5
voice/vocal/vocalisation
 collaborative voice   100–3
 collective voice   103–8
 communities of voice   31, 99
 embodied voice   27–36, 40–3, 51, 65, 115–16, 121–4, 127–31, 164–5
 individual voice   28–30, 165–7
 multilingual voice   99–100
 multivocal poetics   103–8
 and perspective   25–6, 33, 51, 97
 and poetry   25, 37–8, 44–5, 48, 53, 98, 103–8, 153
 and thought   32–4, 58
 uniqueness of voice   26–9
 ventriloquizing   120
 vocal expression   32–5

Walton, Kendall   58–60
we. *See* first person first-person plural (we)
Wilcox, Philip
 'Infect the world with Doves'   15
Williams, Saul
 Chorus   105–6

you-thoughts/I-thoughts   61, 72

www.ingramcontent.com/pod-product-compliance
Lightning Source LLC
Chambersburg PA
CBHW052119300426
44116CB00010B/1722